Foreign Temporary Workers in America

Foreign Temporary Workers in America

POLICIES THAT BENEFIT THE U.S. ECONOMY

EDITED BY

B. Lindsay Lowell

Q

QUORUM BOOKS
Westport, Connecticut • London

Library of Congress Cataloging-in-Publication Data

Foreign temporary workers in America : policies that benefit the U.S.
   economy / edited by B. Lindsay Lowell.
    p. cm.
   Includes bibliographical references and index.
   ISBN 1–56720–227–6 (alk. paper)
    1. Alien labor—Government policy—United States. 2. United
States—Economic policy—1993– I. Lowell, B. Lindsay, 1955– .
HD8081.A5F67   1999
331.6'2'0973—dc21   98–18500

British Library Cataloguing in Publication Data is available.

Library of Congress Catalog Card Number: 98–18500
ISBN: 1–56720–227–6

First published in 1999

Quorum Books, 88 Post Road West, Westport, CT 06881
An imprint of Greenwood Publishing Group, Inc.

Printed in the United States of America

The paper used in this book complies with the
Permanent Paper Standard issued by the National
Information Standards Organization (Z39.48–1984).

10 9 8 7 6 5 4 3 2 1

Contents

Preface

Temporary migrants to the United States, known legally as nonimmigrants, have grown in number and importance over the 1980s and 1990s. Scholars and policymakers working in the immigration arena have long appreciated the complexity of the different categories of permanent admissions, but only now are they turning their attention to the oftentimes linked temporary system with its rather different complexities.

In this volume, leading scholars examine the nonimmigrant system's major visa categories for temporary workers and foreign students. The introductory chapter by B. Lindsay Lowell summarizes the authors' observations and recommendations on a range of topics, from the overall system of nonimmigrant admissions to the effects of specific visa categories on U.S. businesses and workers, as well as our universities and students.

The authors' contributions were solicited by the U.S. Commission on Immigration Reform in an attempt to get the most up-to-date information on a topic that was otherwise little studied. The Commission was mandated by Congress in the Immigration Act of 1990 and delivered its final report in September of 1997, which included recommendations on nonimmigrants as discussed in the final chapter of this volume. Together, the chapters here comprise one of the first collections of scholarly studies on the topic, and they offer considerable scope and a solid point of departure for policymakers and others interested in the nonimmigrant system.

Foreign Temporary Workers in America

Chapter 1

Temporary Visas for Work, Study, and Cultural Exchange: Introduction and Summary

B. LINDSAY LOWELL

There always have been those who come to the United States for short stays—to work and conduct business, to study, or to visit and sightsee. No single definition best describes this type of international migrant; they have come to be known for what they are not. With a few notable exceptions (e.g., holders of H-1B and L visas), they are not intending, or not permitted under the terms of their visas, to reside permanently in the United States with the full range of rights granted to "immigrants." Legally they are, therefore, not immigrants, they are "nonimmigrants" whose legal rights and responsibilities are limited to certain activities and whose stay is of limited duration.

The numbers of those on nonimmigrant visas (NIVs) coming to the United States are substantial and, unlike permanent admissions that only now are reaching peak historical levels, they have been growing throughout the century. During the first decade after the turn of the century (1901–1910), 770,000 nonimmigrants were admitted to the United States and that figure grew to more than 7 million in the decade following World War II (see Table 1.1).

Two things are immediately apparent from these data: the rate of growth has been phenomenal, with more than a doubling across each of the last three decades, and it looks safe to forecast more than a doubling for the 1990s. The greatest share of the NIVs are issued to tourists, counted as temporary visitors for pleasure, who over the past decade have made up nearly three-quarters of all admissions by the Immigration and Naturalization Service (INS)—17 million out of a

Table 1.1
Nonimmigrant Admissions to the United States, 1951–1994

Year	Total	Tourists
1951–1960	7,113,023	4,005,028
1961–1970	24,107,224	15,473,400
1971–1980	64,314,041	45,369,373
1981–1990	123,140,403	91,469,272
1991–1994	83,159,275	65,232,217

Source: special tabulations from the Statistics Office of the U.S. Immigration and Naturalization Service.

total 22 million in fiscal year 1994 alone.[1] As of fiscal year 1994, the remaining approximately 5 million admissions comprise just more than 3 million temporary visitors for business and less than 2 million assorted other categories of admission, of which 764,000 include those addressed by the authors in this volume.

Thirteen authors describe here a core of temporary visas that authorize specific activities, namely the right to attend U.S. institutions of education, to work or conduct business, or to undertake study or work that comports with exchange agreements with foreign countries. These visa categories are among those with the greatest degree of rights and, with the exception of temporary visitors for business or pleasure, they are the most numerous. They also have not been subject to research by academics and have not received much systematic evaluation by policymakers. The articles in this volume address the lack of systematic study and set forth the policy implications of the available research.

COUNTING TEMPORARY MIGRANTS

Two broad types of visa classes—(1) workers and (2) students and exchange visitors—are most central to today's concerns and are predominantly discussed in this volume (U.S. INS 1996a).

Workers. The sole purpose of these categories of admission is to grant legal authorization to work in the United States. H-1B workers are professionals and highly-skilled individuals in specialty occupations. They are sponsored by employers who must attest that they will fulfill a number of wage and working conditions designed to protect U.S. workers. The visa for agricultural workers (H-2A), although numbers are small, is a constant source of debate. It requires a sponsoring employer and the job must be "certified" beforehand by the U.S. Department of Labor (DOL) as meeting a number of wage and working conditions designed to protect U.S. workers. H-2B visas for temporary nonagricultural workers (limited to 66,000 annually—although only 16,000 were issued in FY 1994) also require labor certification. D visas for foreign crewman require employer attestation unlike E visas for treaty traders and investors that require no labor market test. L visas are for intracompany transferees, workers who are employed by international organizations based in the United States.

The Immigration Act of 1990 created a number of new work visa categories: O visas for aliens with extraordinary ability in sciences, arts, education, business, or athletics, and those assisting in their athletic or artistic performances; P visas for internationally recognized entertainers and athletes, artists or entertainers on an exchange program or under a culturally-unique program; Q visas for participants in international cultural exchange programs; and R visas for religious workers. Additional workers, such as researchers, scholars, au pairs, and camp counselors, enter under the J visa (see below).

Students and Exchange Visitors. Both the foreign student (F) and cultural exchange visitor (J) visas are intended primarily to promote both formal education and learning by experience, and both permit limited work authorization. In the case of the foreign student (F), work is generally restricted to campus with one year of off-campus practical training allowed. These visas are issued only to students who are attending INS-accepted institutions. In the case of exchange visitors (J), whose visa may partly be governed by international agreements, some may only study, while others engage in significant work activity during their stay. The M visa is used for vocational students, who are prohibited from any employment except for postcompletion of studies and practical training.

The Number of Temporary Immigrants

Table 1.2 shows three ways of counting nonimmigrants in the fiscal year 1994. The differing methods of measuring these populations dem-

Table 1.2
Counting Nonimmigrants: FY 1994

Class of Admission	Admissions (Entries)	Visa Issuances	Person-Year (Average) Populations
All classes*	22,118,706	5,610,953	1,444,319
Foreign government officials (& families) (A)	105,299	67,190	30,997
Temporary visitors	20,318,933	4,428,011	107,027
For business (B1)	3,164,099	216,825	86,235
For pleasure (B2)	17,154,834	4,211,186	810,067
Transit aliens (C)	330,936	177,815	4,520
Treaty traders and investors (& families) (E)	141,030	30,931	54,657
Students (F1, M1)	390,001	219,941	245,319
Students' spouses/children (F2, M2)	33,720	20,955	27,876

Representatives (& families) to international organizations (G)	74,722	26,525	22,773
Temporary workers and trainees	185,988	104,143	48,815
Specialty occupations (H-1B)	105,899	42,843	31,092
Performing services unavailable (H2)	28,872	25,842	8,562
Agricultural workers (H-2A)	13,185	7,721	3,328
Unskilled workers (H-2B)	15,687	10,400	5,234
Workers with extraordinary ability (O1, O2)	6,484	3,625	2,131
Internationally recognized athletes or entertainers (P1, P2, P3)	28,055	19,938	1,822
Exchange & religious workers (Q1, R1)	7,497	4,372	2,516
Spouses/children of temporary workers and trainees (H4, O3, P4, R2)	43,207	30,584	16,943
Exchange visitors (J1)	216,610	166,639	89,651
Spouses/children of exchange visitors (J2)	42,561	32,151	29,035
Intracompany transferees (L1)	89,189	22,666	20,765
Spouses/children of transferees (L2)	56,048	26,450	24,207

*Categories may not equal total because of omitted categories (e.g., fiancees of U.S. citizens, overlapping Canadian Free Trade Agreement professionals, unknown, NATO officials and professionals, and foreign media).

Sources: Admissions (U.S. INS 1996b); Visa Issuances (U.S. DOS 1996); Person-Year Populations (U.S. INS 1996a).

onstrate both notable administrative differences between the collecting agencies, as well as the lack of a single comprehensive measure or set of measures that count nonimmigrants and their implied year-round population in the United States.

INS Admission Numbers. The first column shows the most commonly cited INS figures on admissions, which are not counts of individuals but, rather, counts of the total number of *entries*. Thus, an individual with a business visa will be counted separately each time he or she enters the United States. The number of admissions counted is consistent with the INS role in screening persons at entry into the United States and tallying each individual (entry) inspected. Clearly, admission numbers overstate the number of individuals actually involved. The count of NIV admissions or entries is, instead, the result of an administrative process.

State Issuance Numbers. The Department of State (DOS) counts its issuances of visas to individuals abroad, consistent with its role as the foreign representative of the United States. Individuals apply for their visa through U.S. embassies, and when the application is approved by the appropriate agency, DOS issues the visa for admission into the United States. But if INS admission data clearly overcount the true number of individuals who travel with a nonimmigrant visa, DOS issuance figures do not include persons from countries with whom treaties permit that the visa is "waived." Nor do all persons issued a visa necessarily use it to enter the United States in the year it was issued. Nor do the issuance figures reflect individuals who change from one visa to another within the United States (more on this below).

Person-Year Population. The person-year or "average" population reflects just the portion of a year that all NIV individuals spend in the United States. It reflects more accurately, for example, the full-time contribution of certain NIV categories to U.S. businesses: if there are 100 workers with an average stay of one-half year, they contribute only 50 person-years' worth of labor in that year. Because of the available means of measuring the person-year population, the figures will be somewhat low as they do not reflect some NIV individuals who stay more than an entire year.[2]

The table shows that INS "admissions" are significantly greater than visa "issuances," 22 million versus 5 million in FY 1994. And because the average length of stay of nonimmigrants is short, as should be expected, the person-year population is only 1.4 million. No one figure is "better" in the sense that it is more correct, instead each is useful to describe the INS or DOS administrative burden or, in the person-year figure, one gets a sense of the average "year-round" equivalent.[3] Unfortunately, counting the nonimmigrant population has even further complexity.

CHANGE OF STATUS ACROSS NONIMMIGRANT AND PERMANENT VISAS

Nonimmigrants do not always remain in the visa category under which they first entered the country. For example, a foreign student (F) may become a specialty worker (H-1B) and later adjust to permanent status.

Unfortunately, there is no reliable data readily available on the numbers of nonimmigrant changes across NIV statuses, such as the F to H-1B example above. In lieu of such figures we can only crudely estimate about how many Fs end up as H-1Bs and, ultimately, in a permanent status. One possible source of information is INS records on change of status made within the United States that suggests that perhaps as much as two-fifths of those changing status to H-1B in FY 1994 previously held a nonimmigrant visa.[4] In any given labor market that portion may be much greater depending upon the job possibilities (see chapter 5 of this volume).

Data on adjustments to legal residency allow us to gauge the portion of NIV holders who transition onward to permanent status. In Chapter 3, David North estimates that cultural exchange visitors (J) and foreign students (F) have low rates of direct adjustment, with an estimated one-sixth of Fs adjusting to permanent resident status.[5] Both the intracompany transferees (L) and skilled workers (H-1B) have substantially higher adjustment rates—a little more than one-fifth of transferees and possibly as many as four-tenths of H-1B workers adjust to permanent resident status. These relative rates are what might be expected. Students may have low adjustment rates because once their training is finished, their purpose for staying is finished as well. And as the number of students is substantially greater than that of specialty workers, it is not possible for a high proportion of students to adjust into the numerically-limited employment categories.

By contrast, specialty workers (H-1B) and intracompany transferees (L) are exempt from provisions precluding issuance of NIVs to those who intend to reside permanently in the United States. Some of these workers enter with temporary work visas to bridge the period needed to obtain permanent immigrant visas. In other cases, employers choose to retain temporary workers, to capitalize on skills learned in the United States.

It is also interesting to note the permanent categories into which nonimmigrants adjust.[6] Although nonimmigrants adjust into all permanent resident statuses, as of FY 1994 foreign students (F) were most likely to adjust into the following permanent visa categories: exempt spouse (47 percent) and skilled employment-based preference (EB-3) (44 percent). In contrast, about one-half of both specialty workers (H-1B) and exchange visitors (J) adjust through the skilled employment-based preference, while intracompany transferees (L) adjust into the United States primarily as priority employment-based workers (EB1) (81 percent). Perhaps it is no surprise that one-third of the H-1B adjusters report science or engineering occupations, while 90 percent of intracompany transferees (L) report executive or administrative occupations at adjustment. On the other hand, neither foreign students (F) nor exchange visitors (J) fall clearly into any occupational grouping. Several chapters in this volume assess this process of moving from one status into another.

Changing Status Not a Problem. Charles Keely makes the case that the process of changing status and adjusting to permanent residency is a natural consequence of the U.S. admissions' system and the global economy. He believes the process is not detrimental and is, in fact, a favorable phenomenon. Papademetriou and North recommend that the adjustment process be recognized, and since they regard adjusters as presumable successes who have gained valuable experience in the United States, they, too, view the process in a favorable light.

These authors recommend some type of dual-track temporary visa that acknowledges the process of adjustment to permanent residency status. The details of how such a visa would be granted and its terms are not spelled out, however. If a special visa were not created, the decision to grant permanent residency to an individual might somehow take into account their experience as a nonimmigrant.[7] And if there remains a concern about the ease of shifting status, North recommends that a sizable fee be assessed against the employer who petitions for a permanent visa.

Length of Stay. Despite the overall positive aspects of this process of change, several authors recognize potential abuses by individuals whose initial intent in obtaining an NIV is to remain permanently. They imply that reducing the length of stay permitted on an NIV would reduce such abuse. Such shortening of the time frame for action would be consonant with the purpose of a temporary stay, would acknowledge that some NIV stays with renewal options, etc., are too lengthy, and would lessen the possibility of individuals acclimating to the United States and drifting from one status to another. Both Papademetriou and Gregory DeFreitas recommend that the stay permitted on working visas (H-1B) be reduced, to three and two years, respectively, with no possibility of renewal without return to the home country. Barry Chiswick and North recommend that to keep individuals from endlessly pursuing education (often as a screen for unauthorized employment), student visas (F) be closely monitored with regular evaluations of academic progress.

Return Requirements. Another way in which to deal with the changing status phenomenon might be to require that at the end of their temporary stay NIV holders return to their country of origin for some period of time. Only after that return requirement was finished could the individual reapply for a U.S. visa. This is a requirement for some cultural exchange visitors (J) and could be applied to other NIVs as well. North, for example, recommends an option that would impose a two-year return on foreign students. Keely, while not advocating a return requirement for foreign students, makes a clear distinction between foreign students who pursue higher education with independent financing and those who receive funding from their home government, international organizations, or scholarship programs intent on aiding international development by education. If return requirements are put into place, he argues compellingly that return should be required only of students whose education is intended to benefit their nation of origin. DeFreitas would require working H-1B visa holders to leave the United States for one year after their temporary stay ended.

TEMPORARY WORKERS IN A POSTINDUSTRIAL ECONOMY

Both Demetrios Papademetriou and Charles Keely present the big picture of the role of temporary foreign workers in a postindustrial economy. Global firms and fast-evolving, knowledge-based products demand a very different perspective than yesterday's. Today's knowledge industries must be fast moving and their product, unlike that of yesterday's industries, does not become more expensive to produce as raw materials are used up—a process that takes time. By extension, today's knowledge industries cannot treat all workers as essentially interchangeable; training takes time and may never fully compensate for a foreigner's specialized experience in a desired foreign market. Contemporary knowledge industries face steep, up-front development costs that are recouped by volume (and ever cheaper) sales, and the race for market share goes to those who get their product out first. Getting the right worker with specific qualifications for short-term needs can be very important in these competitive marketplaces. Examples abound in pharmaceuticals, electronics, or computer software development, but the pace of the marketplace often is replicated in traditional industries like automobile manufacturing that market state-of-the-art autos on short cycles and produce just-in-time.

Positive Role of Foreign Workers. Against this backdrop, some believe restrictions on high-skilled temporary workers could well have adverse effects on the U.S. economy and its resident workforce. Keely argues that the genesis of those advocating severe restrictions is rooted not only in a profound misunderstanding of the reality of post-industrial economies but in the evolution of nonimmigrant policy and procedures. He traces NIV history from a passive admissions policy: employment-based immigrants entered unless the Secretary of Labor took steps to prevent entry based on a complaint or large level of petitioning by a single employer. However, after the Immigration Act of 1965, a more active process was introduced that Keely says:

. . . institutionalized anxiety about the impact of immigration on the labor force. Dimensions of the economy were pitted against one another in an adversarial way, as if labor force development is a zero sum game.

The legal profession and adversarial procedures have become integral parts of the admissions system for both permanent applicants and non-immigrants, and Keely believes "it is virtually naive to suggest that it could be otherwise." However, the heritage of this adversarial mentality often is based on the assumption that the labor force is static like a fixed pie. Keely argues the restrictive and bureaucratic procedures that result from this heritage can run against the needs of a modern economy for flexibility, timeliness, and access to a global labor force. Most of the authors would concur that an emphasis on facilitating employers' *genuine* needs is in the national interest and can make the United States more globally competitive to the benefit of U.S. workers.

Areas of Concern. Nevertheless, these chapters raise areas of concern, especially with the number of H-1B workers involved and the special features of their employment that may contribute to some adverse impacts. As David North argues:

. . . when there are concentrations of alien workers in a given labor market . . . there are likely to be problems of labor market distortion—lower than normal wages, higher than normal unemployment. These problems are likely to be aggravated when the workers involved have few rights or few perceived rights (such as the H-2A farm workers and the newly-arrived Indian programmers).

Where North argues that the long-term impact of the student and cultural exchange categories are "bland or scattered," he classifies the skilled worker as having an impact "of some concern." His concern is bolstered by "plenty of noise" in certain occupational sectors; North pays particular attention to the fields of science and engineering that are believed to already have an oversupply of workers (North 1995; see also Anderson 1996).

Gregory DeFreitas also articulates concerns about the number of foreign workers now in high-skilled U.S. occupations and argues that all—permanent and temporary—skill-based admissions be closely regulated. Although many economists argue that immigrants should be selected on the basis of their skills, they seem implicitly to assume either that highly-skilled workers are not adversely impacted by increases in immigration or that any impacts are small and quickly responded to by U.S. professionals without broader ramifications. There are, however, a few studies that do find the possibility for direct competition between foreign and U.S. professionals, especially among permanent residents, and DeFreitas notes that:

. . . in an era of widespread corporate downsizing, claims of skilled labor short-ages have raised growing suspicions. Unlike the early 1980s, the majority of permanent layoffs now are occurring among college-educated employees. The share of job losses accounted for by those earning at least $50,000 has doubled since the eighties.

If wage depression does occur among skilled workers it might be associated with lowered demand and less opportunity for upward mobility of low-skilled U.S. workers. And there may be further complications in relying on skilled foreign labor that are raised by use of H-1B workers.

DeFreitas argues that the current Labor Condition Application [LCA] does not adequately protect the U.S. worker from being replaced by an H-1B; nor does the LCA hold the ultimate employer responsible for the attested wage rates and working conditions of the H-1B worker. This can encourage the growth of job shops with the attendant potential for misuse of the H-1B program. Further, DeFreitas believes the program itself can sew the seeds for increasing outsourced jobs abroad because the H-1B worker, once trained in the United States and familiarized with corporate needs, becomes an ideal jobber when he or she returns home. He argues that "what is needed now is more, not less, limitation on and monitoring of skill-based temporary immigration programs." These themes surface not only from DeFreitas's close observation of the labor market and the limited number of official documents and media coverage that deal with foreign workers, but also in two field studies reported on in this volume: both were conducted on the H-1B labor force in 1994–1995, two years after the implementation of the Immigration Act of 1990, and in globally competitive industries undergoing downsizing and restructuring.

Houston Field Study. Jacqueline Hagan and Susana McCollom undertook a study of H-1Bs employed in about 30 computer programming and research organizations in the Houston metropolitan area. Their research found circumstances consistent with the nature of spot shortages that occur in fast-changing, globally-responsive businesses, at least in the case of the highly-specialized skills required in Houston's research sector:

Given what looks like a robust labor market in Houston for computer analysts and programmers, and for high level researchers in faculty positions, we were initially at a loss to explain what we encountered in the field: unemployed and underemployed computer programmers and analysts and an increasingly tight labor market for faculty positions.

Yet, employers reported a need for H-1B workers because they were unable to find U.S. workers. A spot shortage appeared to be indicated in the case of positions at university or private research settings which have gone "unfilled for months or years" because a very specific set of skills, say in robotics development, is sought. In such instances the H-1B workers, some of whom were research assistants in such settings, provided a valuable resource for the United States with seemingly little adverse impact on U.S. workers.

On the other hand, the computer programming field has developed an outsourcing strategy that involves job shops that take on the production work of larger software development firms, pointing to potentially adverse outcomes in the H-1B program. These shops permit the larger firms to get production work done as needed without employing year-round employees. Unfortunately, the authors suggest, the incentives for job shops to be competitive in lower-end programming work can lead to adverse outcomes for the H-1B worker and for similarly-skilled U.S. workers. In the case Hagan and McCollom elaborate on, H-1B workers were recruited abroad and, once in the United States, were paid less and placed in poorer working conditions than similar U.S. workers in the same organization. And the skills they needed were not necessarily those for which the employer advertised. This research suggests systematic violation of the employers' H-1B attestation that could place H-1Bs in unfair competition with U.S. workers with the requisite education, of whom there are many in the Houston area.

San Francisco Field Study. In field work on high-tech workers, Michael Smith asks, "Who is the employer?" and "What is the problem?" His study gathered qualitative data through open-ended interviews with "all parties involved in the recruitment, employment, and regulation of foreign nonimmigrant skilled workers" (i.e., employers, workers, and various representative groups). Most of the H-1Bs had master's degrees and most of these foreign workers had received that degree in the United States while on an F-1 student visa (one estimate is as many as 70 percent). Employers reported that because technologies change so rapidly, they must hire applicants who already possess the specialized skills the employers require.

Several computer consulting firms studied had changed their use of visas in response to the tightening of wage compliance and stricter B-1 enforcement. The consultants reported that the longer duration of stay permitted by the H-1B visas is reducing the number of workers who return to their home country and increasing those who stay permanently. Oddly, these consultants were critical of the client firms that hired them for not investing in the training of an available labor pool of U.S. workers displaced by the corporate downsizing of recent years. For their part, U.S. workers believed that the Immigration Act of 1990 encouraged the expansion of foreign-run consulting firms that now underbid U.S. consulting firms. All parties agreed that H-1Bs received lower wages in consulting firms than their U.S. counterparts. While industrial restructuring and, more particularly, corporate downsizing are the major forces behind poorer working conditions for laid-off workers, both appear here to be reinforced by the related growth of subcontracted work. When job shops are used as middlemen to provide low-cost production programmers to client firms—private or public—the potential for abuse and displacement may well increase.

At the same time, U.S. workers in Smith's study argued that the just-in-time skills employers claim they require are not, in fact, consonant with the prevailing practice to train and the time taken to familiarize oneself with a new client firm. For their part, professional and union associations reported three problem areas in the H-1B visa: the ultimate employer is masked; the workers have little security and thus tend not to complain about depressed wages; and the prevailing wage calculation produces low average wages.

In contrast, the study found that H-1B workers in biotechnology firms presented a different picture. Here Ph.D.'s recruited internationally (in a search process that might take as long as six months) were hired as project managers and postdoctoral researchers. Findings here do not indicate wage depression or job displacement. In the university teaching and research settings, H-1Bs tended to be hired as faculty or postdoctoral researchers. But while faculty hires required a substantial investment in hiring the very best, postdoctoral student positions were more plentiful and appeared more likely to misuse the H-1B visa. As some argue, such findings suggest that foreign postdoctoral students dominate these positions while many U.S. graduates, deterred by the low wages, look for work in the private sector.

Comments on the Current System

Having identified both strengths and weaknesses of the current system for admitting foreign workers, the authors present a range of recommendations to address problems in the current system. For the most part their recommendations focus on the H-1B.

DeFreitas recommends greater control and more protections, measures that go even further than those advocated by DOL (Reich 1995). He would restrict working visa applications to DOL-determined shortage occupations, require an application fee, reduce the permitted stay to two years, with a minimum one-year probation from applying for permanent residency following the stay,[8] apply additional employer attestations that protect U.S. workers (provisions against layoffs, lockouts, strike, and demonstration of "substantial and continuous efforts to fill the jobs for which they currently desire foreign workers"), and apply H-1B regulations to all work sites where H-1Bs are working. His recommendations would apply to all working visas.

All the authors concur in the spirit of the latter recommendation aimed at keeping the ultimate employer, not the middle-man, responsible. As Smith says:

Regulatory and enforcement mechanisms should focus on the "real employer," i.e., the clients of contract workers, including holding them accountable for paying prevailing wages to nonimmigrant workers.

Both Smith and Hagan and McCollum call for increased DOL workplace monitoring efforts, targeted especially on so-called job shops, and particularly on prevailing wages. Otherwise, perhaps because their field work found the most blatant visa violations only in the out-contracting sector, they do not advocate reforms as extensive as those DeFreitas proposes.

Smith and Hagan and McCollum also found substantial frustration among college and university employers with the H-1B visa conditions and with the unrealistic prevailing wage determination in their sector. Because of the importance of this sector, Hagan recommends the "cre-

ation of a special H category for research universities and institutes."
While Smith concurs that an "H-1C" visa should be created, he also
found some evidence that foreign postdoctoral students sometimes
compete with natives, creating a "potential for general wage depression
[and] abusive working conditions." Therefore, he recommends that the
university visa be restricted to "full-time, tenure-track, teaching and
research occupations." The resources freed up from close monitoring
of these truly select workers he would allocate toward the postdoctoral
researchers.

North recommends two possible roads to reform: making a moderate
number of changes in the existing system; or substantially reworking
the entire administrative and visa system. At the least, he argues for a
mandatory return ticket for all temporary visa holders, elimination of
employer petitions for groups of H workers, the elimination of the H-
2 visa, and the introduction of labor standards into the exchange (J)
visa (or better yet, moving J-workers into the H worker visa).

Reconfiguration of the NIV System. North's more substantial reform
proposals involve reconfiguration of the visa categories, revised screening methods that would facilitate the process with due attention to protections, and reform of the governmental administrative apparatus to
manage the entire system more efficiently and effectively. North believes several basic principles should underlie a substantially reformed
temporary visa system: the number of visa categories, as well as the
number of government agencies involved, should be limited. Instead of
eight student and working visas, he recommends four visa types: for
students; for temporary workers; for intra-company transferees; and for
H-type workers on a track for permanent residency, a transitional visa.
Like Papademetriou, he believes enforcement efforts should be at least
partly funded by user fees, should be more efficient, and should target
certain countries or employers with far more scrutiny. To ensure that
individuals leave, he calls for a required, lifetime, round-trip ticket for
all temporary visas.

Although Papademetriou finds that the current visa categories satisfy
"one or more of [the basic] requirements" for a temporary worker
system, he also recommends a substantial reconfiguration of the selection and management systems. The restructuring he considers would
move most administrative functions into the INS and couple a rigorous,
though simple, points test of foreign workers with a more stringent
employer attestation and enforcement regime. The points test he out-

lines would be applied to potential workers, including H-1Bs, to select those least likely to compete with low-skilled Americans and those whose skills and productivity are most likely to promote U.S. economic interests. Employer selection would be constrained to this pool and they would be required to file an attestation. Bypassing the cumbersome and time-consuming aspects of a certification system (in the case of H-2A and H-2Bs) could well facilitate employers' access to workers (who meet the minimum points test). An attestation requirement likewise could facilitate the process and serve as an enforcement tool for what should be (for his recommended system to work best) a renewed emphasis on the enforcement of the conditions agreed upon for the work authorization.

Temporary Workers in Agriculture: Are More Needed?

Predictably, in agriculture the role of middlemen and its potential for adverse consequences surfaces again with the H-2A visa. Philip Martin covers the economics of labor in the agricultural industry, describing its historical reliance on cheap, foreign labor. It is a story, however, that differs from the others in this volume.

There have been calls for an expanded and simplified H-2A program in agriculture, partly by some who want to rationalize the exchange of labor between Mexico and the United States. However, those most interested in the expanded/simplified version of a new guestworker visa are the growers of crops that are harvested by hand. Much of the foreign labor upon which growers of fruits and vegetables rely is unauthorized. There are extremely few legal nonimmigrant (H-2A) visas in use by growers who dislike the paperwork, the number of labor protections and requirements, and the federal control of that program.

There is, of course, a long and complex history of the demand for seasonal agricultural labor and the employment of authorized and unauthorized workers throughout the southwest. California agriculture, in particular, has played a special role in most of the twentieth-century debates involving Mexican immigration. The controversial *bracero* program brought more than 4.5 million Mexican workers to U.S. farms—more than one-half to California alone—between 1942 and 1964. California farmers were among those employers who most strongly argued that the price of their support for the employer sanctions provisions of the Immigration Reform and Control Act of 1986 (IRCA) was an assurance of continued access to legal Mexican workers. Congress established the Replenishment Agricultural Worker (RAW) program that would authorize the entry of workers in the event that they were needed. If IRCA proved to be successful, it could conceivably cut off the ready supply of unauthorized workers and the Departments of Labor and Agriculture were charged with determining if a shortage of seasonal workers developed. North reports that no shortage was found during the life of the program and no RAW work authorizations were given.

When Operation Gatekeeper along the Mexican border was launched in 1994, and again when Congress moved toward tightening restrictions against illegal immigrants in 1995, California farmers sought to secure legal guestworkers. Martin notes that the debate frequently is framed by contrasting extremes—farmers assert that there are likely to be labor shortages, farm worker advocates argue that 10 to 30 percent of farmworkers are unemployed even during peak seasonal demand and there is no need to bring in more workers. Congress has considered, and may well consider again, establishing an agricultural guestworker program that is either an altogether new visa or a simplification of the existing H-2A program.

Has stepped-up border and interior enforcement actually reduced the availability of legal seasonal laborers? Californian growers Martin surveyed in the fall of 1995 virtually all report an ample supply of farm workers. He argues there should be visible labor market responses, such as rising wages or increased applications for H-2A workers, before such programs should be considered seriously. Yet more than 90 percent of the responding farm employers reported no trouble finding sufficient seasonal farm workers in 1995; the handful of employers who reported shortages generally did nothing concrete to obtain additional workers, such as raise wages, ask the state employment service for workers, or apply for certification to bring foreign workers into the United States under the existing H-2A program. Martin finds that the evidence and the survey data support the U.S. Commission on Immigration Reform's unanimous position (U.S. CIR 1995) that no new guestworker program is needed at this time for California agriculture.[9]

Opinions on the H-2A visa tend to be strongly held. Indeed, North, who would abolish the program in its entirety, states, "This program simply transfers funds from American farm workers to agri-business; it is small but a disgrace."

On the other hand, Papademetriou does not find an agricultural worker program in and of itself objectionable. He proposes that:

... serious thought be given to replacing this category with a program that focuses on enhancing employment opportunities for U.S. agricultural workers, while acknowledging the unique nature of that labor market, its binational (primarily Mexican) composition, and the historical (and future) reliance of that sector on a foreign workforce.

His proposals for reform of the H-2A are still in development. However, it is possible to speculate about a range of options—for example, levying a user fee for a U.S. workers' fund; testing the labor market for shortages as DeFreitas suggests; and, both to facilitate growers access and enhance monitoring, bringing into the process multiple actors, such as employers, the Mexican government, and a greater INS and DOL enforcement presence.

Martin argues pragmatically that the current program may be better than some of the alternatives being considered. He concludes that:

... the H-2A program may ... not be perfect, but it does look better than the alternatives ... and I find it hard to believe that, given the history of controversy surrounding employment of foreign workers in U.S. agriculture, the United States will in the late 1990s introduce an attestation program for alien farm workers.

Recall that the H-2A application requires a vigorous up-front DOL screening and must meet each of several wage and U.S. worker protection requirements: the details of the visa application must be certified prior to entry into the United States. Simplification of the H-2A program could involve changing the certification to an attestation that is not vigorously screened up front and comes into play only if there is a visa violation reported after the worker begins. If Congress did introduce an attestation program, Martin would recommend levying a sizable user fee to be invested in a workers' training fund. Indeed, he argues for serious consideration to the development of additional safeguards if an attestation-like program were introduced.

FOREIGN STUDENTS

As Barry Chiswick notes, "The United States is a magnet for foreign nationals seeking university level and advanced (graduate) level training.'' Chiswick presents a profile of foreign students based on administrative data and an annual survey of universities. He argues that the flow of new students has not increased significantly since the 1960s, but the stock of students has risen due to longer stays.

Several authors in this volume offer reasons why foreign students are a benefit to the U.S. university system. Keely argues that the number of foreign students can be taken as evidence that U.S. colleges and universities are a successful service export industry with significant global ramifications:

The American college and university system is a valuable service export that has downstream spinoffs as alumni/ae of U.S. schools move into responsible positions in the private and public sectors of their societies.

Barry Chiswick notes that the United States most likely will remain a magnet for foreign students, especially in the sciences. Still, foreign students' share of the total student body is very small and he believes that there should not be a lot of handwringing over its possible adverse effects, most certainly not among undergraduates. While foreign students are only a small portion of the general student body (a little more than 3 percent in 1995) Chiswick reports that nearly one-half of all foreign students are in U.S. graduate programs where they make up more than 9 percent of the entire graduate student body in all disciplines.

The U.S. reputation for graduate training is well known and many foreign students come here to pursue degrees in science and engineering (S&E). Chiswick points out that not only is the United States at the forefront of research in the scientific disciplines but the jargon of mathematics and science are both universal and often written in English (while the humanities require knowledge that is highly specific to a culture or national setting). Beyond these commonplace observations, however, foreign graduate students are an integral part of the teaching and economic functions of the modern university: they learn by teaching and doing research; they provide a critical tutorial function; and they constitute a needed supply of research assistants. With a relative shortage of native-born seeking advanced study in science, he notes that foreign students step in and help keep instructional costs low and maintain the preeminence of U.S. university-based research.

Jagdish Bhagwati and Milind Rao specifically address the foreign

Ph.D. graduate in the sciences and engineering disciplines where they are concentrated. These numbers have increased since the 1950s until, as of 1990, about one-third of all U.S. university-awarded S&E Ph.D.'s went to foreign students. The authors argue that enrollment and graduation data support the notion that the increase in foreign graduate students results from the greater number of high-quality universities globally and the lure of flagship U.S. universities whose very leadership relies on government-funded S&E education. For example, the pool of S&E undergraduates has grown enormously in many Asian countries and the level of research and training at the best foreign colleges has come to be highly regarded. India graduates 25,000 bachelor-level engineers each year, of whom only 2,000 graduate from the elite Indian Institute of Technology (IIT). Yet the authors report that eight-tenths of the Ph.D.'s awarded to Indians in the United States went to these elite IIT graduates. They note that "other nations' 'brain drain' is our 'brain gain.' "

Also, the large proportion of foreign S&E students can be explained by the combination of the availability (pool) of highly qualified students, the choice of a field of study, and the funding structure of advanced education in the United States. They observe that whereas only 1 percent of the entering class in the professions and 20 percent of those pursing a Ph.D. in the humanities and education receives university funding, 70 percent of all S&E students report the university as their primary source of funding. And fully 81 percent of foreign Ph.D. students, most with limited rights to work in the United States and often with few personal resources, are in S&E programs.

Indeed, large differences in the availability of university funding by discipline may explain part of the apparent advantage foreign students have over U.S citizens in terms of securing university funding. Bhagwati and Rao note that more than one-half of African American Ph.D.'s in particular are concentrated in education, a field in the humanities with low levels of university funding, which heavily affects statistics on African Americans.[10] Frank Morris in this volume argues, nevertheless, that even in education 12 percent of African Americans report being *primarily* funded by the university as compared to 28 percent of foreign doctorates. He and North share a concern that native and minority graduate students are not financed as readily as foreign students. Otherwise, North reiterates his belief that the general impact of foreign students on natives and minorities in graduate schools—or in the labor market—is small. The specific areas of impact and the appropriate policy response both deserve more study.

There is evidence that U.S. universities prefer minority doctoral applicants over foreign applicants (North 1995:49), and other trends make it difficult to assert direct and substantial minority displacement in graduate schools. Bhagwati and Rao note that the pool of African American students with S&E bachelor degrees declined slightly over the 1980s, although 14 percent of African Americans opt for S&E degrees (where the proportion relying primarily on university funding is the same as that of other students). Yet interestingly, while the total number of Ph.D.'s awarded to African Americans continued a two-decades-long decline, Bhagwati and Rao report that total S&E Ph.D.'s awarded to African Americans increased through 1990. Because the number of *all* natives in S&E Ph.D. programs has remained constant for roughly two decades, some observers conclude that the lack of more native S&E Ph.D.'s of any race or ethnicity is due mostly to the available pool of resident S&E students coming up through the ranks (NSF 1996:2–15).[11]

Clearly, there is some agreement between several of the authors and none strongly argues for a ceiling on foreign students. Bhagwati and Rao conclude that foreign S&E graduates are a boon and that their availability may actually expand S&E capacity. Nevertheless, it is acknowledged that the potential for abuse of the student visa exists. Chiswick recommends that carefully-crafted administrative procedures be put into place and given a chance to curb abuse of the foreign student visa, particularly by those who fail to pursue their academic studies. The specific administrative procedures he recommends would require that an appropriate college or university representative regularly certify that its foreign students are making satisfactory progress toward their intended degree. North, in turn, suggests strengthening oversight of the educational institutions that petition for the right to admit nonimmigrant students. To strengthen the principle of temporary stay, both North and Chiswick consider requiring return conditions, calling for a prepaid return airline ticket for each applicant. Chiswick also recommends barring the issuance of any visa to persons who violated the conditions of a previous visa.

North and Morris share a concern for the possibility that foreign students may create some adverse effects for some U.S. residents in certain fields of graduate study. Morris's argument points to a long chain of causal events, starting with a decline in direct federal grants in the 1970s to today's university-controlled distribution of research and teaching assistant positions. The major problem he argues is that colleges and universities are now providing direct funding to foreign students that could be spent instead on minority, and particularly African American, students. He advocates that an "American incentive computation" be made in every state or federal contract with a university that supports doctoral students: points would be given based upon the proportionate representation of minority students. North speculates about the balance of U.S. government monies spent on foreign student education and, likewise, considers regulation on funding. He suggests a ceiling on the proportion of foreign graduate students funded by federal research grants.

CONCLUSIONS

On balance, these chapters argue that the nonimmigrant system meets a wide variety of goals that are in the national interest. At the same time, they raise serious questions about specific visa categories and some of the regulatory mechanisms that govern an individual's temporary stay. Readers who go carefully through each chapter will find a wealth of information not covered in this introduction and summary. Those steeped in the complexity of the system may wish for more detailed attention to some mechanisms, things as nuanced as how and where employers advertise for residents before applying for a nonimmigrant worker. However, these chapters add to our understanding of the overall effects of the nonimmigrant visa system and provide guidance regarding policies to strengthen its operation.

NOTES

1. Tourists represent a considerable boon to the U.S. economy. In 1995, an estimated 43.5 million in-bound visitors, a figure that includes tourists for pleasure plus cross-border visitors from Mexico and Canada, spent $76 billion on travel to and in the United States. International tourism provides a net trade surplus of $18 billion (dollars international visitors spend here less dollars U.S. visitors spend outside of the United States) (communication with the Department of Commerce, U.S. Travel and Tourism Administration).

2. The INS calculations for the person-year population is based upon comparing departure data with earlier entry records. Because not all individuals

depart in a given year, especially those with longer durations of stay, such as students or family members, the average stay figure will be too low. Hence, the "true person-year" population is some unknown amount greater than the one shown.

3. Which "number" of temporary NIVs would one compare to the number of legal permanent immigrants admitted to the U.S. in a given year? INS data on legal permanent residents counts individuals and, hence, cannot be directly compared to NIV admissions data. DOS visa issuance data more nearly counts individuals like the permanent admissions' data published by the INS, but issuances overstate the year-round involvement of temporary NIVs in the U.S. economy. Also, the INS (1996b:178) estimates that as of 1992, about half of the 3.4 million illegal population were persons illegally overstaying the period of their nonimmigrant visas.

4. In FY 1995, there were more than 26,000 changes of status to H-1B, out of a possible 65,000 H-1B approvals. Most were from the foreign student NIV (F) (Special tabulations of INS district offices made available to the Commission).

5. A crude, lower-bound estimate places about one-fifth of foreign students moving both from F directly *and* indirectly through H-1B to any permanent status (calculated from North's F and H adjustments to LPR status; and 1995 INS Service Center data [F to H] over DOS of F issuances five years previously [F to H status change]).

6. Special tabulations by the Commission of only principal visa holders from the INS FY 1994 permanent admissions public use data.

7. North implies that if a point system was created to screen applicants, additional points could be granted for relevant experience.

8. This recommendation is intended to reduce the waiting period for permanent residency applications and to reduce employer dependency.

9. If there were to be labor shortages that put upward pressure on farm wages, Martin argues, consumers would likely see little increase in the costs of fruits and vegetables as wages make up a minute fraction of retail prices. In the short-run, higher wages might attract more year-round and more productive labor. Over the longer term, he believes growers could even reduce the demand for labor with capital investments in new technologies and engineered crops and possibly reduce retail prices.

10. In 1993, 9 percent of all Ph.D.'s granted in education were received by African-Americans, more than four times the percentage of African American S&E Ph.D. recipients, and more than double the percentage (4.2) of all African American Ph.D.'s (Thurgood & Clarke 1995:23).

11. The total number of bachelor degrees awarded in the natural sciences actually declined through the 1980s; increased and then fell off in mathematics, computer sciences, and engineering; and only the social and behavioral sciences

have showed an increase in bachelor degrees since the late 1980s (NSF 1996:2–15). Bhagwati and Rao also note that many S&E undergraduates may choose employment or pursue careers in more lucrative professions.

REFERENCES

Anderson, S. 1996. *Employment-Based Immigration and High Technology: Issues and Recommendations.* Washington, DC: Empower America.

National Science Foundation (NSF). 1996. *Science & Engineering Indicators 1996.* Washington, DC: U.S. Government Printing Office (NSB 96–21).

North, D. 1995. *Soothing the Establishment: The Impact of Foreign-Born Scientists and Engineers on America.* Lanham, MD, New York, and London: University Press of America, Inc.

Reich, R. B. 1995. Statement of Secretary of Labor Robert B. Reich before the Subcommittee on Immigration of the Senate Judiciary Committee. September 28.

Thurgood, D. H., and Clarke, J. E. 1995. *Summary Report 1993: Doctorate Recipients from United States Universities.* Washington, DC: National Academy Press.

U.S. Commission on Immigration Reform (CIR). 1995. *Legal Immigration: Setting Priorities.* Washington, DC: U.S. Government Printing Office.

U.S. Department of State (DOS). 1996. *Report of the Visa Office, 1994.* Washington, DC: DOS, Bureau of Consular Affairs.

U.S. Immigration and Naturalization Service (INS). 1996a. *Duration of Stay of Nonimmigrants Departing the United States.* Washington, DC: INS Office of Policy and Planning, Statistics Branch.

———. 1996b. *Statistical Yearbook of the Immigration and Naturalization Service, 1994.* Washington, DC: U.S. Government Printing Office.

Part I

System Overview

Chapter 2

Skilled Temporary Workers in the Global Economy: Creating a Balanced and Forward-Looking Selection Process

DEMETRIOS G. PAPADEMETRIOU

Twentieth-century America, no less than the America of earlier times, has benefited greatly from the presence of foreign workers. Even in the 1950s, when fewer immigrants entered the United States than in any decade since, the U.S. economy may have been far less self-sufficient in terms of both talent and brawn than is generally acknowledged. For example, in addition to the talent brought in through the family and modestly sized employment categories, as well as that decade's refugee inflows, there were the large-scale "immigration" of Puerto Ricans and the even larger *bracero* program for U.S. agriculture, which admitted between 300,000 and 400,000 Mexican workers a year throughout the 1950s. *Braceros*, who were classified within the immigration system as temporary workers or nonimmigrants, provided a nonresident labor force for an industry that had faced wartime shortages. Although the *bracero* program was ended in the mid 1960s, other programs for temporary workers have continued to supplement the flow of permanent residents, contributing to the robustness of a complex U.S. economy that spans the gamut of capital, knowledge, and technological content— from advanced computer technology to agricultural production.

Today, the reality of full international economic interdependence is an inescapable fact. The figures are nothing less than astounding. U.S. exports grew from about $27.5 billion in 1965 to more than $700 billion in 1994. Imports during the same period registered similar growth, from about $22 billion to more than $800 billion (Council of Economic Advisors 1995:274–75). The total value of international economic transactions (imports plus exports) grew from a little more than 8 percent of the gross domestic product (GDP) to more than 22 percent of GDP. By 1991, total international sales by U.S. multinationals (from exports, direct investments, or joint ventures) were responsible for an estimated $1.2 trillion, accounting for nearly 30 percent of corporate revenue (Ellis 1994:62–63). Even more telling, U.S.-owned firms now are competing with foreign-owned firms, not only abroad, but also in the United States. It has thus become as difficult and, in many respects, much less useful to distinguish "American" from "foreign" firms as it is to separate "domestic" from "foreign" markets for one's products.[1] Further, a firm's productivity and competitiveness depend increasingly on its products' knowledge content, on the innovativeness of its processes, on "first-to-market" corporate strategies and on the ability to develop and exploit global connections by what Moss Kanter (1995:153) calls "managing the intersections" at the "crossroads of cultures." The constant need for specific expertise means that firms must be able to obtain some of the necessary talent easily from outside the United States—in effect, adopting a "just-in-time" approach to the composition of the work force. There is no argument among economists regarding the job-multiplying effects associated with the employment of such highly endowed professionals; thus, U.S. business should have access to the best qualified individuals for key job openings. Hiring talented foreigners *at market wages* is also in the long-term interest of U.S. workers.

Yet, attracting immigrants with the higher-level skills that our economy needs now, and from which it can benefit well into the future, is an option that should be pursued as just one part of a broad competitiveness strategy. The United States simultaneously must diligently pursue policies designed to enhance the education and training of U.S. workers while avoiding interfering too much—through undisciplined immigration policies or other initiatives—with the market's propensity to adjust to tighter supplies of highly qualified workers. These are the parameters within which we should expect our corporate citizens to make decisions about whom they propose that we admit, through what process, and whether the person should be admitted permanently or temporarily—the former typically in response to longer-term and perhaps structural needs, the latter typically in response to shorter-term needs in areas of ongoing adjustments (Papademetriou & Lowell 1991). If the recruitment and admission principles and the accompanying mechanism are well thought out, they will have self-regulating parameters that will reduce access to immigrants in times of low demand for labor while expanding access in times of high demand.

Without a flexible and well-managed economic immigration selection mechanism, many of our most competitive firms with vast global operations may reconsider their investments in additional capacity *in the United States*. Firms whose products are primarily knowledge-based, such as software developers, can choose to expand anywhere the main intangible asset they need (knowledge workers) is in ample supply. Immigration policy—no less than policies to improve the quality of our human resources, maintain an excellent infrastructure, and provide a business-friendly regulatory environment—must thus support, rather than undermine, efforts to convince firms that they *can* remain and expand their operations in the United States and still be competitive in the global marketplace.

The Immigration Act of 1990 already has acknowledged the existence of a class of "global citizens" who are essential assets to successful economic entities in today's constantly changing world. It more than doubled the number of economic stream immigrants; it encouraged and simplified the immigration of exceptionally qualified people; and it responded to the requirements of the global economy through extensive changes to the U.S. nonimmigrant system (Yale-Loehr 1991; Papademetriou & Yale-Loehr 1996). However, it passed without a focused discussion about the human capital characteristics that will be needed from the workers of the future. We must engage in that discussion now and think through more systematically the foundations—both in the permanent and temporary admissions systems—on which the economic immigration stream should rest in the context of global economic changes *and their implications for U.S. firms and U.S. workers.* The essential, and not yet answered, question is how to promote U.S. competitive interests by facilitating access to key foreign-born personnel without unnecessary procedures while simultaneously not undermining the broader social policy goal of advancing the interests of U.S. workers overall.

REFORMING THE SYSTEM: REVISED CRITERIA AND PRESELECTION

The selection of most economic stream immigrants and nonimmigrants must shift away from the shortage-based, case-by-case certification system of the past forty years. Nonimmigrants who are allowed

to work (H, B2, D, O, P, E, F, J) should be admitted to the United
States to:

- Fill a specific labor need, generally for a temporary period;
- Discharge our international obligations under a variety of trade, investment, and cultural exchange regimes;
- Facilitate international commerce and trade; or
- Enhance the cultural and artistic life of the United States.

To varying degrees, the current nonimmigrant visa categories already satisfy one or more of those requirements. In some instances, the present system also incorporates job and wage protection mechanisms that tend to focus on the unskilled and semiskilled workers who have dominated employment-based admissions throughout most of that system's life. In the future, however, the rationale—and appropriate selection procedures—for choosing among possible entrants should focus squarely on their capacity for contributing to a technologically sophisticated and global economy.

Certain administrative and programmatic guidelines also are necessary to help the United States select economic nonimmigrants efficiently and should be part of any new immigration system. The selection process should be efficient, timely, fair, and transparent for all parties. Enforcement, including postentry enforcement, should become a credible deterrent against fraud and abuse. The selection system constantly should be reviewed and adjusted to make sure that it continues to serve the country's changing economic and labor market needs. (Thus, priority should be given to the collection and reporting of accurate data critical to monitoring and evaluating the impact of any new selection system.) Finally, the functions of the various federal agencies that, in one way or the other, play a direct or indirect role in the admissions process should be reconfigured.

Further, the current work-permitting nonimmigrant categories should be divided into two subsets: those for which substantial changes are proposed; and those that require fewer adjustments. The first subset focuses on the H visas—visas available to U.S. employers for positions for which U.S. workers are generally presumed to be unavailable. (See this volume's introduction for a discussion of the various H visas as well as, more generally, the entire "nonimmigrant" system.) The second subset (B2, D, E, F, J, O, P) incorporates visas for workers whose *primary* purpose should be generally other than to work within the United States with a U.S.-based employer (B2, D, E, F, J).

PRESELECTING (H) FOREIGN WORKERS

The H nonimmigrant visa category is the main temporary foreign worker category in the Immigration and Nationality Act (INA). With some notable exceptions, the United States had for many decades prohibited the temporary employment of foreign workers. That ban was lifted in the 1952 Act, which authorized the Attorney General to admit temporary workers to "alleviate labor shortages." In FY 1994, 143,492 H nonimmigrant workers (plus an additional 40,490 spouses and children) were admitted. The size and significance of the H category hence requires the careful consideration of appropriate models for selecting the foreign workers who receive that visa.

Currently, the U.S. selects some H workers on a case-by-case basis on a decades-old understanding of the U.S. economy and the role that foreign workers play in relieving labor shortages. Many European countries use similar case-by-case methods. That concept is strikingly at odds with today's competitive realities, where firms choose workers (U.S. or foreign) because of small differences in qualifications (both in quality and, especially, in the specificity of skills). Firms generally believe that such differences can, in turn, lead to substantial differences in their ability to compete without any loss in momentum.

There are other selection methods. For instance, one can select immigrants on the basis of certain analytically derived "shortage" occupations (demand test); or one can select them on the basis of their ability to meet a set of skill and adaptability requirements (supply test).

Most of the discussion that follows has evolved primarily out of proposals for revamping the selection system for permanent immigrants and particularly the selection formula for what my colleague Stephen Yale-Loehr and I call the "second tier" economic or permanent immigrants (1996:144). Our proposed system would have three tiers:

First Tier/The Truly Outstanding. The top tier of our new economic immigrant visa system would be similar to the current Employment Based [EB-1] immigrant visa category for "priority workers." Foreign nationals with extraordinary ability enhance the economic strength of the United States and should be admitted with a minimum set of procedures.

Second Tier/Professionals Who Meet Certain Selection Criteria. Qualifying for the second tier would require a job offer; the worker considered should have at least three years' work experience and the sponsoring employer would have to make certain attestations. Individuals also would need to qualify under a selection formula, outlined below, that awards value points for certain human capital attributes.

Third Tier/Investors. Investors enhance the economic well-being of the United States through their capital investments and should continue to be admitted, although under an amended set of requirements that focuses more directly on the visa's intent.

As this chapter focuses on nonimmigrant categories, there is no detailed discussion of the proposed changes in the permanent system—except for those for the second tier. That tier's threshold requirements and calculable point total for desirable traits also is the basis for selecting workers for the H nonimmigrant categories. The proper question to ask in this regard is how to devise a system that facilitates the selection of foreign workers best suited to contribute to the U.S. economy without harming U.S. worker interests.

U.S. INDIVIDUAL WORKER LABOR MARKET TESTS

The United States uses a variety of systems for screening foreign workers admitted for work. I discuss primarily two of these systems: labor certification (an individual worker test that emphasizes preentry screening) and attestation (a test that emphasizes postentry enforcement). Although the former is more stringent, both are intended to safeguard U.S. worker interests.

Preentry Tests: Labor Certification

One way to select foreign workers is to test individual applicants against a particular job opening at a particular place and point in time. Following the 1965 immigration amendments to the INA, granting an employment-based immigrant visa is prohibited unless the immigrant's prospective employer first obtains a certification from the Department of Labor (DOL) that there are no U.S. workers who are able, willing, qualified, and available to perform the work and that the immigrant's admission will not adversely affect similarly-situated U.S. workers. The United States uses variants of this model for its H-2A and H-2B temporary labor certification systems.

Assessments of the certification system consistently have found that the system is excruciatingly complicated (Papademetriou & Yale-Loehr 1996:104). The conclusions of a twenty-seven-year-old assessment of the permanent labor certification system by David North (1971) still are applicable: labor certification had "absolutely no impact on the macro labor market" and affected the work force "only marginally" because it governed the admission of so few and because there were no controls over the worker after he or she arrived in the United States. Only about 59 percent of the labor certifications granted at the time were actually used, and about 45 percent of the labor certifications approved were issued simply to legalize foreign workers who were already in the United States (North 1971:iii). North concluded that, while the labor certification program was "an interesting (if limited) experiment in social engineering," an alternative approach was needed (1971:172).

The Prevailing Wage Issue. Then and now the most-often-heard technical critiques focus on determining an occupation's prevailing wage for certification purposes and on the effectiveness of testing the labor market for appropriate U.S. job applicants. Determining the prevailing wage is not easy. For labor certification purposes DOL uses the arithmetic mean wage, usually derived from small, nonrandom samples (U.S. DOL 1995a). Moreover, State Employment Security Administrations (SESAs) differ dramatically in the care with which they conduct their prevailing wage surveys. Some states use more sophisticated survey techniques and may allow for fine gradations within occupations (and as a result recognize more bases for wage differentials) than others. As a rule, the statistical validity of SESA surveys varies from totally invalid to valid with strong reservations.

The problem has grown more acute since 1990, when Congress imposed a prevailing wage requirement as part of the H-1B attestation process. Currently, the SESAs receive more than 60,000 requests annually for prevailing wage determinations and must conduct more than 10,000 surveys annually, at a cost of nearly $20 million to DOL (U.S. DOL 1995a). In 1992, DOL created a prevailing wage advisory panel to review existing methods and procedures. The panel made 29 recommendations for improving the determination of prevailing wages, including focusing on skill levels rather than years of experience to determine where an individual fits within an occupational range, using the median wage rather than the weighted arithmetic mean in certain wage surveys, and allowing employers to use fringe benefits in certain circumstances as part of the overall wage. Despite these recommendations, DOL made no significant changes.

Instead, DOL issued a long memorandum trying to clarify various prevailing wage issues (U.S. DOL 1995c), some of which serves only to aggravate the problems. For example, the new memo instructs SESAs to acknowledge just two skill levels for any particular occupation: entry and experienced (U.S. DOL 1995c). While this makes determinations easier, it does not accord with business reality, in which employers may set a variety of skill levels within an occupation depending on professional accomplishments, length of experience, responsibilities involved in the job, and other individual and contextual factors.[2] The new DOL memo causes additional problems by instructing SESAs to ignore distinctions between public and private and academic or nonacademic firms, although nonprofit entities typically pay less than private companies do, often in return for making the individual more competitive for future jobs.

The Job Description Issue. Most labor certification-type applications require the employer to post and/or advertise a job opening for a specified amount of time. Many resulting job descriptions are obviously designed to fit the foreign worker. Anyone skimming the classified ads in a large metropolitan newspaper quickly can distinguish a regular help wanted ad from a labor certification ad: the former typically is short and to the point; the latter are much longer because they must track the exact language of the detailed job description filed by the employer on the labor certification application. Labor certification ads, moreover, instruct interested applicants to contact their local SESA, not the employer whose name cannot even be mentioned.

The process often pits clever employers and immigration lawyers against DOL's restrictive recruiting requirements. For example, if a newspaper ad is required, employers may try to place the ad on days when fewer people are likely to read the help wanted ads. Because all U.S. applicants must be considered, an employer intent on hiring a preselected foreign national seeks to minimize the number of U.S. applicants—just the opposite of normal recruiting practice.[3]

Thousands of U.S. workers a year are nonetheless referred to advertised job openings, but few are hired. The complexity and increasing irrelevance of labor certification regulations thus regularly transform the certification process into a cat-and-mouse game. In the final analysis, SESA and DOL regulators can never be as familiar with an employer's business or industry as the employer, and they have many cases to decide with relatively few resources.

Thus, everyone is a loser in this process. The government loses, in that it is forced to play by and defend a process that is resource-intense and perverse in both execution and outcome and that offers ample grounds for cynicism among those who participate in and observe it. Many U.S. applicants see themselves as pawns in this process, and virtually all SESA and DOL officials acknowledge that the labor certification system does not protect U.S. workers. The system is vulnerable to those who would "play" it; thus, some employers might use the system to bring in their relatives, while others might—and some do—pass on the costs of the certification process to their foreign-born employees through lower wages which, in turn, adversely affects the wages of U.S. workers. The current system, especially if it is applied more stringently,[4] as some advocate, arguably could hamper the efforts of some U.S. firms to become fully competitive in the global economy and might even harm our country's long-term economic interests *without simultaneously offering substantial additional benefits to U.S. workers*. This well may be the most telling critique of labor certification and the most compelling argument for its replacement.

Postentry Tests: Attestation

Aware of many labor certification shortcomings, the U.S. Congress created a new method for protecting some U.S. workers while facilitating employer access to certain nonimmigrant foreign workers: attestation. Attestation is a simpler mechanism that reduces up-front barriers to the entry of needed foreign workers, but still attempts to protect U.S. workers through postentry enforcement of terms and conditions of employment. The first attestation system was enacted as part of the Immigration Nursing Relief Act of 1989, which expired in 1995. Under this system, a health care facility had to attest to six criteria before it could hire an H-1A foreign registered nurse. Three more attestation systems for nonimmigrants were created in the Immigration Act of

1990: one for crewmembers in the D visa category; another for foreign students in the F visa category; and a third for specialty occupation workers in the H-1B category.[5]

Attestation, at least as presently practiced, also has a number of shortcomings. Some of these are similar to those in the labor certification process. For example, determining the appropriate prevailing wage can be quite difficult for both the employer and DOL. Further, some documentation requirements of an attestation are quite burdensome. For example, an H-1B employer's documentation must include information about all other employees in the same job in question, from the date the H-1B labor condition application was filed throughout the period of employment. An employer also must specify the basis on by which he or she calculated the actual H-1B wage. Attestations also have the potential for becoming pawns in instances of troubled labor relations if worker representatives choose to interfere systematically with management's access to foreign workers by frivolously challenging attestations.

Nonetheless, attestation has several positive attributes. If conceived and implemented well, attestation can balance the need to safeguard and advance the interests of U.S. workers while offering most employers timely and predictable access to needed foreign workers. Attestation also meets an important *public process test* by giving potentially affected parties an opportunity to know about and challenge the matters to which an employer attests. A properly conceived and executed postentry test can be among the mechanisms most responsive to changing conditions in labor markets, while requiring the least amount of hands-on engagement by the U.S. government in an area where both data and procedures are the weakest. It can also be an inducement to cooperative labor relations in instances where workers' representatives and management work together to obtain the best worker available for a job opening.

Labor Market Information Model

An alternative way to select foreign workers for job needs/openings is to use generalized labor market information (LMI). Unlike the individual worker evaluation model, this method focuses on making judgments about labor shortage and surplus occupations on the basis of general labor market information gathered primarily from national level data. Employers would be allowed to bring in foreign workers freely for occupations that are determined to have a labor shortage. In theory, an LMI method has several advantages over labor certification, particularly in terms of costs and responsiveness.

However, the disadvantages of an LMI approach strongly outweigh its potential advantages. The use of LMI to categorize occupations appears more "scientific" and "rigorous" than it really is. First, it creates an illusion of objectivity while, in fact, it relies to a very substantial degree on subjective judgments. Second, the data on which a LMI approach would rely were developed for other purposes and do not measure the precise concepts needed. Third, most occupational shortages are relatively brief in duration and all shortages are dynamic; some of the data used to identify shortages simply may be picking up indications that the market is adjusting. Fourth, even if the U.S. government could identify occupational shortages appropriately and in a timely manner, it could not ensure the timely admission of immigrants with those skills. Finally, the fundamental weakness of a LMI approach is that national data tend to "average out" and, thus, routinely mask often-substantial regional and local variations.[6]

Point System Model

A point system model of economic stream immigration, at least as practiced by Canada and Australia—the other two major "countries of immigration"—differs from both the individual worker job evaluation model and the labor market information concept. Unlike the former, a point system does not focus on matching a specific immigrant with a specific job offer in a case-by-case process. Unlike the latter, a point system neither directs nor necessarily limits immigrants to working in predetermined labor shortage occupations. Instead, the point system evaluates and selects immigrants based on certain human capital characteristics deemed to advance the host country's interests.

A point system theoretically has several advantages over either an individual-worker job evaluation or a LMI model. A point system can inspire confidence as a policy instrument that applies universal and ostensibly objective selection criteria; hence, it is less susceptible to criticisms associated with the case-by-case system's gamesmanship between employers and bureaucrats. Further, a point system's appearance of impartiality may discourage most of those who otherwise might have been apt to challenge it, while its technical complexity and apparent responsiveness to long-term labor market needs is reassuring to many who worry about possibly adverse effects on domestic workers. Finally, depending on the attributes the point system emphasizes, the model may reassure members of the receiving society that economic stream immigrants are selected on the basis of criteria that place high priority on the country's global competitiveness. This makes the system more politically defensible than any of the alternatives discussed above.

Can a point system work in the United States? The answer is a qualified "yes, *but only if the concept is adapted to the idiosyncrasies of the U.S. economy, philosophy, and labor market realities."* On the one hand, despite inevitable variations that stem from location and history, the origins, scale, and composition of most immigration to Canada and Australia has not looked all that different from ours. On the other hand, a point system would require special discipline to be effective in the United States.

Our system of government is different enough from the Canadian or Australian ones to affect a key feature of a point system, its flexibility. The appeal of a point system is that it can respond quickly to shifting priorities and the Canadian and Australian parliamentary systems are well suited to make these changes. At the minister's direction, the immigration ministry professionals come up with a plan to adjust the point categories and their relative weights, and Cabinet approval can be obtained quickly. In many instances, the changes can be accomplished administratively, under broad grants of authority delegated by the relevant statute. By contrast, the U.S. system is deliberately designed to work more slowly. On immigration, most of the input comes from the legislative (and even judicial) branches, as well as from affected constituencies. Under a point system, Congress would have to be willing to delegate many of the details to the executive branch, and the executive branch would have to take on significant responsibility for managing such a system.[7]

PRESELECTION AND H NONIMMIGRANTS

Despite these cautionary notes, the advantages of adopting a point-like system in the United States are clear and compelling in the case of H nonimmigrant workers. Such a system would shift the focus from an almost exclusive emphasis on shortages to enhancing the United

States economic posture. Properly conceived and implemented, a point-like system would allow the U.S. government to do what it can be fairly good at, particularly when it does so in cooperation with the private sector, rather than forcing it to do what it is least good at, i.e., performing burdensome and ultimately unsatisfactory case-by-case and similar preentry evaluations.

Employer Sponsors and Flexible Limits. Under our proposed reforms, employers would continue to make all selection decisions,[8] but they would have to select from a pool of individuals who can pass a threshold of requirements, including a points test.

Employers also would be required to attest to certain recruitment, wage, and employment conditions. Numerical limitations would be imposed, since from a political perspective, Congress and the American people would not tolerate even the theoretical possibility of open-ended immigration however robust the safeguards or well-administered the system. For that reason, Congress should set initial caps for the H-1 and H-2B categories but allow a year's ceiling to be based on the previous year's actual usage plus an increment of, say, 10 percent. This would offer greater flexibility than a hard cap, which would require legislation to amend. This method would also allow employers adequate access to foreign workers if the economy suddenly improves or if they encounter a true shortage of talented U.S. workers in an emerging growth area and need more foreign workers with highly-specific skills.

Selection Criteria for a Point Test. In addition to employer sponsorship and attestations, there should be prior requirements that employers and prospective immigrants must meet if they wish to enter the immigration sweepstakes. Employers must select from a pool of possible nonimmigrant workers who must have personal characteristics that are essential to making a sustained and substantial contribution to the United States:

- An *educational background* that has instilled both specific knowledge or technical skills *and* a facility for abstract thinking;

- An *age* that permits one to make a substantial contribution to the economy immediately;

- The *language* ability and communications skills necessary to interact effectively with colleagues and customers; and

• A demonstrated *commitment to improving* one's own human capital endowments.

Numerical weights can be assigned for each of these preselection criteria, with different thresholds set for different visa classes—although it makes little sense to legislate fixed weights or criteria.[9] Congress moves too slowly to enact detailed changes on immigration and, just as we want the economic immigrants we choose to be able to adapt, so too we need flexibility in our selection system. Hence, immigration officials should be given authority to change both the criteria for preselection and the number of points needed to qualify as economic conditions change. Flexibility is essential for the success of a modern immigration system and Congress's need to stay engaged can be discharged by requiring that proposed changes be vetted in advance with the two subcommittees charged with oversight responsibilities. If actual usage increases by the maximum percentage one year, to help control the growth in foreign workers in the following year, administrators could investigate the causes for such an increase and might choose to raise the pass mark needed to qualify for a given nonimmigrant visa category.

Attestation requirements. Employers would have to attest that they would comply with the four conditions that they do now for H-1B purposes, as well as a new recruitment condition.[10] First, the employer still would have to offer the higher of either (1) the actual wage the employer pays to other individuals similarly employed with similar qualifications or (2) the "prevailing wage" for that position. The current reliance on SESA prevailing wage determinations should be abandoned in favor of developing prevailing wage and total compensation package information from reliable industry-specific sources.[11] Second, employers would have to attest that there is no strike or lockout at the place of employment. Third, employers would have to attest that they have given their employees notice of the filing of the attestation. Fourth, employers would have to attest that the process through which the foreign worker was selected is the employer's and the industry's customary way of making hiring decisions for this kind of position.[12] Significantly, contracting with "job shops" that supply a predominantly foreign work force would not be considered a customary recruitment practice.

International Commitments. These recommendations for the H-1 category are fundamentally consistent with U.S. international commitments in this area. As part of the General Agreement on Trade in Services (GATS), the United States agreed to freeze the essence of the current H-1B program but created room for three possible changes in the future: (1) reducing the maximum length of the visa from six to three years; (2) instituting a provision that would prohibit employers from laying off U.S. workers and then using H-1B workers in the same occupation; and (3) requiring employers to take significant steps to recruit and retain U.S. workers. These proposals are consistent with the first two of these provisions. Further, the proposed recruitment attestation requirement is consistent with the spirit of the third element.[13]

Dual Track H-1. Historically and practically we know that permanent immigrants in the economic stream typically adjust in a manner that turns the holders of many temporary visas into *"pre*immigrants.'' In many instances, employers hire them for specific needs, but also to determine whether they are suitable for permanent employment. This occurs primarily in the current H-1B nonimmigrant visa category. We propose that, at any time after the first year and before the three-year period ends, an H-1 employee could petition for an immigrant visa, putting employers on notice that they will not be able to employ a foreign worker for long periods unless the worker can ultimately qualify for such a visa. Such prospective immigrants should be assigned their own nonimmigrant visa (NIV) category and be selected from a pool of individuals with characteristics that will enhance their long-term contributions to the economic strength of the United States, facilitate international business and trade, and generally promote U.S. interests and priorities.

H-2B Visa Category. The H-2B visa would be restructured along the lines of the H-1 and should be refashioned to be more than just a catchall category, but rather a category that focuses on truly temporary jobs. Following thorough assessment, subcategories of the current H-2B category that are primarily cultural in nature, such as camp counselors, should be incorporated into a revised and appropriately reconfigured J category, etc. It is here that the *second strand* of the H-1 workers—those who employment would be truly *temporary*—would be expected gradually to find a home. In reconfiguring this category, a variation of the double-temporary standard now in existence (i.e., both the foreign worker and the job are temporary) should be maintained, as should be the maximum number of two one-year renewals.

By developing incentives and disincentives for the long-term employment of many H-2B workers, the proposition can be tested that there are some occupations in which some of the labor demand might be satisfied by training U.S. workers. This would be particularly relevant and appropriate for many low-skilled occupations—ranging from household workers to specialty chefs—where a person's personal characteristics, such as language, ethnicity, familiarity with an "ethnic" cuisine, etc., is presumably valued by the employer. It may be found that, in most cases, one could no longer show that "shortages" exist in these occupations.

H-2A Visa Category. This visa category allows employers temporarily to employ agricultural workers following a test of the labor market and strictly regulated attempts to hire a U.S. worker. Serious thought should be given to replacing this category with a program that focuses on enhancing employment opportunities for U.S. agricultural workers, while acknowledging the unique nature of that labor market, its binational (primarily Mexican) composition, and the historical (and future) reliance of that sector on a foreign workforce.

CHANGES ON OTHER WORKING VISAS

The discussion below proposes modest changes to several other NIV categories to make each of these visas comport with the priorities outlined above. Unlike the H visa, where the primary purpose is U.S.-based employment, other nonimmigrant working visas have other primary purposes. Failure to mention an existing category means that no changes are proposed.

B Visa Category. No changes are necessary in the B-2 tourist visa category. This category facilitates international tourism. In 1994, more than 16 million foreign tourists visited the United States, generating an estimated $60 billion in revenues (U.S. Bureau of the Census 1994: 264). The B-1 temporary business category also is generally fine in concept, as it facilitates international commerce and trade. However, concerns about certain types of abuses—improper use of the B-1 in lieu of the H-1B visa[14]—must be taken seriously and addressed through clearer regulations and more active enforcement, not by severely restricting or eliminating the category.

Extreme care in changing the B-1 visa is particularly necessary because of the reciprocal nature of international trade. If the United States eliminates or severely curtails access to this category, other countries may retaliate and impose similar bans on U.S. workers wishing to enter and conduct similar activities in those other countries. Our trade commitments have bound this use of the B-1. For this reason, radical changes to this visa would require difficult renegotiations and, if undertaken unilaterally, could lead to trade-related sanctions against the United States.

D Visa Category. It is unclear whether this category for foreign crewmen needs any changes. Very few attestations for longshore workers under the D category have been filed since the attestation requirement took effect after the 1990 Act. As a result, DOL and the Department of State (DOS) should prepare a report on the implementation of the D attestation process that should contain a cost/benefit analysis of the current regulations and assess whether such an interventionist regulatory regime is necessary—especially considering the small number of people it affects. One possible change might be to negotiate more balanced reciprocal arrangements with key shipping countries, rather than continuing to impose burdensome requirements on a wide universe of countries.

E Visa Category. The category of treaty traders and investors is essential to international commerce and trade and, insofar as we have institutionalized that visa's regulations in our international commitments, our ability to change the E visa is severely limited. Pending proposals for new regulations by INS and DOS are nonetheless worth testing. Among them are heightened scrutiny of E visa employees with "specialized" qualifications who are "essential" to the company. More specific issues, such as whether or not the employer can find qualified U.S. workers, and issues regarding E visa interchanges with the L visa category for certain multinational executives, managers, and employees possessing specialized knowledge, might be handled better in negotiations with other countries to achieve full reciprocity. As with the D visa, multilateral regulatory changes in many of these visa categories generally are preferable to unilateral attempts at closer regulation.

F Visa Category. Foreign students should continue to be allowed to work off-campus if the work is related to their academic studies. INS also should consider extending practical training options for foreign students in F-1 and J-1 status so that employers still would be able to hire qualified foreign nationals on a short-term basis. However, there is at least the potential for adverse effects on U.S. workers from the unregulated employment of F-1 students.[15] For that reason, we propose requiring employers of F-1 students to file a wage attestation similar to the one proposed for second tier immigrants and several "H" nonimmigrants. Work authorization for "economic hardship" also should be maintained, although INS should tighten its oversight of such grants.[16]

The pilot off-campus work program should be eliminated because it allows foreign students to engage in general labor unrelated to any verifiable unmet labor need. The F-1 attestation process has not worked; very few employers use it and, in many instances, schools can issue work authorization for their students through other available means. This recommendation is consistent with the recommendations of DOL and INS as expressed in their 1994 joint report to Congress evaluating the program.

J Visa Category. This visa for various types of exchange visitors should be retained because of the very nature of international cultural exchange, education, and training. Other nonimmigrant visa categories that contain a cultural component, such as the H-2B and Q visa categories, should, however, be incorporated into a revised, expanded, and more stringently administered J category. In keeping with the purposes of the J visa, work authorization should be truly incidental to the primary cultural exchange, educational, or training purposes. To serve U.S. worker interests better, any work authorization for J-1 visitors should require compensation at full market rates. However, if J-1 sponsors pay part of the J-1's wage, this should be factored into any determination of the total compensation package.

One of the J-1 visa programs—the au pair program—does not comport with the spirit and aims of the J visa category. Despite the U.S. Information Agency's (USIA) recent attempts to control abuses in this program and make it more culturally focused, most U.S. families who use the program view it *first* as a work program and *only then* as cultural exchange. This is one of the main reasons why USIA has been stating publicly for many years that it does not feel comfortable administering the au pair program. A radical restructuring of the regulations is required so that the au pair program serves the same purpose it does in many other countries: providing a mutually valuable cultural exchange for au pairs and the families with whom they live.

Further, the administration of the revised and expanded J program should be transferred from USIA to INS, the agency with the broadest mandate and expertise in this area. INS already has experience administering visa applications of this type, such as in the current H-2B and Q categories. It could administer J programs without significant additional expenditures, especially since much of the current J program is run by responsible officers at sponsoring organizations. The transfer should be at least revenue-neutral and, in all likelihood, could save a modest amount of money. Additionally, INS would have the enforcement oversight capability now lacking in the USIA-administered program. Thus, the recommended transfer also would move the U.S. toward *the consolidation of all functions in the immigration agency*, an objective that undergirds the comprehensive rethinking of the country's immigration function that the Papademetriou and Yale-Loehr study (1996) envisions.

REORGANIZATION OF IMMIGRATION MANAGEMENT

At present, immigration functions are scattered not only between INS and DOL, but also among the DOS's Office of Population, Refugees and Migration, the Department of Health and Human Services's Office of Refugee Resettlement, the Department of Education, and USIA. Almost all of these functions could be performed more efficiently and economically by a larger, reengineered, and more independent INS. Such a change is essential to a revamped way of managing our immigration system.

The immigration function at the federal level should be reorganized as follows.

The Immigration and Naturalization Service. Congress should give INS an independent status that accords with its size and responsibilities, consolidating most immigration functions in the agency. To make this proposal work effectively, INS needs to develop a specialized corps of adjudicators, to be posted overseas, whose sole responsibility would be to handle economic stream immigrant and nonimmigrant visa applications. This corps of INS visa adjudicators gradually would absorb most of the functions now performed by the DOS's Bureau of Consular Affairs. Having this specialized corps also would help speed adjudication of all petitions at INS regional service centers, which is critical to avoid delays.

The Department of Labor. The labor certification and related functions now performed by DOL's Employment and Training Administration (ETA) would no longer exist. Its enforcement mission should be upgraded and the Secretary of Labor should continue to play a role in the administration's deliberations on immigration policy.

The Department of State. A streamlined Consular Affairs Bureau would continue to perform its core diplomatic-related functions, such as passport issuances and citizen services. The Bureau of Population, Refugees and Migration (PRM) would continue to discharge its specialized mandate, but its refugee resettlement functions, together with the resettlement functions now residing within the Department of Health and Human Services, should be folded into INS.

Such changes are truly daunting. They require careful thinking as to allocation of specific responsibilities, personnel, and resources. They also require comparable changes in the legislative function—a function that now is divided among too many congressional committees and subcommittees. Therefore, an independent study group, which should include representatives from affected parties, should be convened to examine and report on this difficult reorganization issue.

Data Collection and Evaluation. Regardless of any changes in the administration of immigration, there must be a commitment to better data collection and critical program evaluation. Few weaknesses of our current system are more frustrating to analysts, policymakers, and the public than the various immigration agencies' inability to answer many questions regarding the characteristics, behavior, and needs of their client base with any degree of confidence or reliability. It is inconceivable that a country for which immigration constitutes such an extraordinary component of economic, social, cultural, and political change would continue to tolerate legislating in the dark. Congress must make it clear *in legislation* that it values such information and analysis, that it expects the relevant agencies to attain these goals, and that it will monitor their progress.

Compliance Enforcement. A credible enforcement regime is absolutely necessary to deter fraud and deny immigration benefits to those who do not qualify. To put its limited resources to best use, DOL should be given explicit authority to target "high-risk" employers, i.e., those with high fraud and severe exploitation practices. One way to focus investigations would be to check an employer's W-2 statements, submitted with H-1 attestations, against the required wage on the attestation form. Permitting anonymous complaints also would make sure that employers do not retaliate against whistleblowers. To promote efficiency and pay for compliance efforts, INS should develop a fee structure that reflects the agency's true costs both for doing a much better job *and for supporting DOL's enforcement apparatus*. At present, INS charges only minimal fees for helping U.S. businesses to obtain foreign workers, and DOL charges none at all. Congress should establish a funding mechanism that uses dedicated parts of the application fees for audits, investigations, and enforcement.[17]

Better Cooperation between Business and Government. An honest and open dialogue between business and government on immigration-related labor regulations is badly needed. DOL and INS should focus their regulations and enforcement sharply on targeting egregious conduct, allowing the majority of compliant businesses to make personnel decisions without having to contend with disruptive and, ultimately counterproductive, regulations. Business must, in return, help DOL and INS to obtain the appropriate legislative and regulatory tools for carrying out a renewed enforcement agenda.

For their part, the immigration agencies must seek the assistance of business in better understanding each industry's customary hiring practices, in identifying business practices that are out of the ordinary and may thus require additional scrutiny, and in devising ways to perform their responsibilities more effectively. Such negotiated rule-making would accord with President Clinton's guidelines which call on "all regulators to . . . create grass-roots partnerships with the people who are subject to [their] regulations and to negotiate rather than dictate wherever possible" (OFR 1995).

The Problem with Job Shops. One way to start a business-government dialogue might be by focusing on the implications of recent corporate trends toward flexible staffing, particularly in high-technology sectors. In the name of efficiency, many corporations are moving away from maintaining large, permanent workforces and toward acquiring the services of technically skilled workers *as and when needed*. It is now quite obvious that a large share of the most egregious violations of both letter and spirit of regulations governing temporary work-related admissions is committed by labor contractors, sometimes called "job shops," who offer flexibility to employers by recruiting and importing foreign workers. Job shops sometimes undercut prevailing wages, create oppressive employment contract terms, and refuse to invest in recruiting and training U.S. workers. Industry must recognize its responsibility to work with government to develop ways to curb such predatory practices, while DOL and INS must acknowledge reality and the benefits that flexible staffing provides.

Protections for U.S. Workers. Any programmatic revisions must minimize employer incentive and ability to exploit foreign workers by paying them less than comparably situated U.S. workers. Therefore, a number of protections must be built into the system that ensure fairness for foreign workers and a level playing field for U.S. workers. Employers should have to attest that they are paying foreign workers prevailing wages that *include* the value of all the benefits received by their U.S. workers (bonuses, health insurance, vacation, etc.). In addition to strengthening wage attestation requirements, we propose limiting the stay of temporary workers to three years, rather than the six years that are permitted under the present system, and strengthening their ability to bargain with employers by allowing them to change jobs after the first year if they are offered higher wages by another employer.

CONCLUSIONS

Although the current system's basic architecture is fundamentally sound, policy analysts and others have come to realize that certain components of the immigration system may no longer serve broader U.S. interests well—or, for that matter, the interests of many of those who participate in it. Specifically, reform must emphasize: (1) the right mix of incentives and disincentives for businesses to play by the rules yet succeed in international competition; (2) a more realistic, and ultimately more effective, understanding of what constitutes U.S. worker "protection" in the context of immigration and how best to advance it; (3) a new habit of cooperation between regulators and the regulated that could serve as a "partnership" model for other contentious policy areas; and (4) a new resolve to identify, isolate, and punish corporate citizens who habitually violate U.S. immigration laws.

The proposals made here would help to limit entry of all but the most talented—or truly needed—foreign workers. The threshold for the points test and related requirements virtually would eliminate the entry of low-skilled immigrants and temporary workers who are most likely to compete with qualified U.S. workers for entry-level jobs. More stringent requirements also should be considered for making sure that temporary workers who come in under certain parts of the H visa actually leave the country when their visas expire; such workers should also be denied readmission for at least a year. Further, employers should be required to recruit according to industry standards, something they are not now required to do for temporary workers; in particular, contracting with "job shops" that supply a predominantly foreign work force should not be considered a "customary recruitment practice" for purposes of wage attestation. Taken together, these requirements would create very significant new protections for U.S. workers.

Ultimately, the proposed scheme should be seen as a framework for a more thoughtful and forward-looking approach to selecting permanent and nonpermanent economic stream immigrants. Although some criteria for guiding selection—and priorities and numerical values for them—are suggested here, the more important objective is to generate a dialogue about a more appropriate way of looking at our country's needs and priorities for the future and the place that economic stream immigration should play in promoting those interests. As these proposals become vetted, specific details may require reconsideration. The end result of such a dialogue should be a more transparent and robust selection system that is flexible, has adequate self-regulating and enforcement features, is consistent with what our economy "values" and rewards, and is thus fully consonant with our country's long-term interests.

NOTES

This chapter is based directly on my work with Stephen Yale-Loehr (Papademetriou & Yale-Loehr 1996)

1. The "American corporation" has become less and less "American" as companies move operations overseas and foreign capital pours into the United States. Between 1980 and 1992, U.S. overseas investments more than doubled, from $215 billion to $487 billion. At the same time, however, foreign investment in the United States more than quintupled, from $83 billion to $420 billion (U.S. Bureau of the Census 1994:808, 811).

2. For example, a computer software company may have five different levels of computer programmers and pay each level a different wage. For immigration purposes, however, SESAs are supposed to calculate just two prevailing wages: entry-level and experienced.

3. Additional protections are equally likely to fail. For example, the employer cannot reject U.S. applicants unless their resumes clearly show that they fail to meet the *minimum* requirements for the job. Even if the resume is ambiguous, the employer must nonetheless interview the applicant, either in person or by phone. Further, the employer must contact a qualified applicant promptly after referral by the local SESA or face possible denial of the labor certification application. Finally, employers can reject U.S. applicants only for "objective" job-related reasons, not for subjective criteria, such as apparent lack of motivation or a person's seeming disinterest in the job.

4. Proponents of the status quo claim that the current system has some advantages. The very cumbersomeness of the process, for instance, probably discourages frivolous applications. However, frivolous applications should be weeded out through clear rules and effective, targeted enforcement, not by making the whole system so bureaucratic that it deters both meritorious and frivolous applications. DOL recently has begun a reengineering effort to streamline procedures, save money, improve effectiveness, and serve its customers better (U.S. DOL 1995b).

5. The H-1A attestation process arguably was the most complex and intrusive of the four systems because it required an employer to take "significant steps" to recruit and retain U.S. nurses. None of the others places an affirmative obligation on employers to try to reduce their use of foreign workers.

6. In practical terms, the geographic concentration of immigrants probably means that only a few local area lists of shortages would be used frequently. Legally, however, it might be necessary to develop comparable lists for all localities. Moreover, such a nationwide list would be quickly outdated, resource-intensive to update, and still would not prevent employers from claiming that, despite the LMI evidence, they could not obtain a worker for a specific need. Such a claim would return the entire process to its case-by-case determination roots.

7. A point-like system places a great burden on the immigration agency. Done properly, it requires the creation of a data collection, analysis, and evaluation mechanism that allows policymakers to determine whether the chosen categories are the right measures of economic growth and personal success and whether the categories are weighted properly. Further, the immigration agency would have to develop a more appropriate administrative infrastructure and a more open and cooperative institutional culture.

8. Not all companies need to be eligible to prequalify for the second tier attestation requirement, even if they have excellent recruitment, compensation, and employment policies. For example, Congress might consider withholding the prequalification benefit from firms: (1) that file more than a certain number of immigrant visa petitions per year; (2) whose foreign national workforce

exceeds a certain percentage of the total workforce in the company; or (3) that have been found in violation of any immigration law within a specified period.

9. It is up to Congress to engage in a dialogue about the number of points for each factor and the minimum number of qualifying points. Keep in mind that no selection system can accommodate all situations; hence, prospective employers of foreign nationals in certain occupations who are just one or two points shy of the pass mark might be permitted to submit evidence why the individuals nevertheless should be allowed entry. Alternatively, INS might have access to a variation of the current "national interest waiver" test for exceptional cases.

10. Employers would have two ways to satisfy the proposed attestation requirements: prequalification or case-by-case.

11. Currently, H-1B employers also must attest that the working conditions for an H-1B worker will not adversely affect the working conditions of other workers similarly employed. This requirement should be deleted as most of its provisions would be covered under the "total compensation package" concept and because it has not proven to be a meaningful protection.

12. To understand the industries they regulate better, we propose that INS and DOL, as a matter of course, include organized discussions with panels of human resources personnel from various industries in *all* of their training sessions and meetings on customary hiring regulations.

13. These modifications theoretically could conflict with GATS. A computer programmer with a bachelor's degree who speaks only a little English currently can obtain an H-1B visa easily; however, under the proposed selection criteria he/she might not. If not, his or her country could claim nationality discrimination. The proposed criteria, however, filter an applicant's *personal* characteristics and do not violate the equal treatment principles of our multilateral obligations.

14. This particular use of the B-1 visa should be reconceptualized and better formulated to (1) accommodate the constantly changing nature of international business and (2) provide for the sound discretion of properly trained visa-issuing officials in deciding whether the proposed activity is consonant with the visa's intent.

15. Any problem with "oversupply" of foreign nationals in graduate science and engineering programs should be dealt with by the government and the private sector encouraging more Americans to enter those fields (1) by getting young people excited about sciences when they are in elementary and secondary schools and (2) by making more public funds available for fellowships and traineeships so that more Americans can pursue advanced studies.

16. A report by Casals and Associates (1994) of the off-campus work program found that, while on average only about 10 to 20 percent of F-1 foreign

students obtain work authorization based on economic necessity, almost 75 percent of F-1 foreign students at one college worked off-campus under the economic necessity exemption. Such a statistic raises fundamental issues about possible abuse of the exemption and suggests that the "primary purpose" for which some of these students came to the U.S. may have been employment, rather than education.

17. However, INS should not try to make employers pay more than their fair share by creating numerous "indirect expenses" that the agency claims support adjudication of economic stream petitions. Criticism already exists concerning the current examinations fee account. Congress also should assist INS in making sure that fees from economic stream petitions go immediately to the examinations division at INS—without going through the normally lengthy budget planning or preprogramming procedures.

REFERENCES

Casals and Associates. 1994. *Evaluation of Pilot Foreign Student Employment Program*. A report for the Division of Immigration Policy & Research, Bureau of International Labor Affairs, U.S. Department of Labor (March). Washington, DC.

Council of Economic Advisors. 1995. *Economic Report of the President*. Washington, DC: U.S. Government Printing Office.

Ellis, J. E. 1994. Industry Outlook: Introduction: Why Overseas? 'Cause That's Where the Sales Are. *Business Week* 10 (January):62–63.

Moss Kanter, R. 1995. Thriving Locally in the Global Economy. *Harvard Business Review* (September–October):151–60.

North, D. S. 1971. *Alien Workers: A Study of the Labor Certification Program*. Report prepared for the U.S. Department of Labor under Contract No, 81–11–71–08 (August). Washington, DC.

Office of the Federal Register (OFR), National Archives and Records Administration. 1995. *Weekly Compilation of Presidential Documents*. February 21:178–82. Washington, DC: U.S. Government Printing Office.

Papademetriou, D. G., and Lowell, B. L. 1991. Immigration Reform and the Skill Shortage Issue. *Labor Law Journal* 42:8 (August):520–27.

Papademetriou, D. G., and Yale-Loehr, S. 1996. *Balancing Interest: Rethinking U.S. Selection of Skilled Immigrants*. Washington, DC: Carnegie Endowment for International Peace.

U.S. Bureau of the Census. 1994. *Statistical Abstracts of the United States: 1994*. 114th Edition (September). Washington, DC: U.S. Government Printing Office.

U.S. Department of Labor (DOL). 1995a. General Administration Letter No. 4–95, Interim Prevailing Wage Policy for Nonagricultural Immigration

Programs (May 18), reported on and reproduced in *Interpreter Releases* Vol. 72, No. 24 (June 26):848–855.

———. 1995b. *Reengineering of Permanent Labor Certification Program; Solicitation of Comments.* Notice; request for comments from the Employment and Training Administration (July 17), reported on and reproduced in *Interpreter Releases* Vol. 72, No. 28 (July 24):993.

———. 1995c. *Analysis of the Kansas City Star Article Regarding Foreign Labor Programs (Article dated July 16, 1995).* Memorandum to the Secretary of Labor from the Employment & Training Administration (July 19). Washington, DC.

Yale-Loehr, S. 1991. *Understanding the Immigration Act of 1990.* Washington, DC: Federal Publications, Inc.

Chapter 3

Some Thoughts on Nonimmigrant Student and Worker Programs

DAVID S. NORTH

BACKGROUND

For the purposes of this chapter I focus attention on the following classes of nonimmigrants: F,H,J,L, and, to some extent, M. These are, respectively, the classes for: academic students (F), most temporary workers (the various H subclasses),[1] exchange visitors (the Js, which includes people doing many things, including studying and working), intracompany transferees (L), and the small class of vocational students (M).[2]

To complicate matters, "temporary" is not very temporary in many of these programs; for example, a foreign worker with an H visa can use it to work in the United States for as many as six years. Further, many nonimmigrants move through two or more of the nonimmigrant visa categories noted above while in the United States, providing opportunities to spin out nonimmigrant status to as much as a dozen years. A final complication: a not insignificant fraction of those admitted to the United States as nonimmigrants adjust their status to that of permanent resident alien (PRA) or immigrants, but they do not necessarily do so from the nonimmigrant status that brought them to the United States in the first place.

Before discussing policy matters it may be helpful to summarize the numbers involved in these programs, the overlapping natures of the programs, and the agencies managing them.

The Numbers: The Big Picture. Table 3.1 presents two sets of numbers over the last ten years, showing admissions in the four broad classes of interest and adjustments from these statuses to that of PRA. (In the table, as in many of the data sets of the Immigration and Naturalization Service [INS], the relatively tiny M program is merged into the much larger F program.)

At first glance at the table reveals two things: (1) most numbers have grown over time; and (2) the number of adjustments is a small fraction of the admissions. Both of these concepts are correct, but the nuances are interesting as well.[3]

A closer look at the table reveals that adjustments for Hs, Js, and Ls soared in 1992; this was the first year that the 1990 Immigration Act was in full effect, and it granted adjustments to people in the backlogs for the employment-related immigration visas. Similarly, the numbers of Fs adjusting in 1993 peaked as a result of the post–Tiananmen Square Chinese Students Act, which permitted such students to secure PRA status.

The Numbers in More Detail. While Table 3.1 shows the long-term trends in these programs generally, it lumps several subcategories tosgether. These were the FY 1993 admissions in each of the subclasses of interest:

Admissions	Classes of Interest
257,430	F-1 academic students
33,379	F-2 their spouses/children
6,437	H-1A nurses (category terminated 9/30/95)
93,069	H-1B specialty occupations (usually professionals)
16,257	H-2A farm workers
15,038	H-2B other blue collar workers (mostly)
3,135	H-3 industrial trainees
37,893	H-4 the spouses/children of H aliens
197,545	J-1 exchange visitors
42,911	J-2 their spouses/children
82,781	L-1 intracompany transferees
49,642	L-2 their spouses/children
4,382	M-1 vocational students
557	M-2 their spouses/children
676,074	Subtotal, primary beneficiaries
164,382	Subtotal, their spouses/children
840,456	**Total FY 1993 admissions in these classes**

Table 3.1

Admissions of Selected Classes of Nonimmigrants and Adjustments to Permanent Resident Alien (PRA) from Those Classes (FYs 1985–1994—Numbers Rounded to Hundreds)

Fiscal Year	Admissions of Classes of Nonimmigrants				Adjustments from those Classes to PRA Status			
	F & M	H	J	L	F & M	H	J	L
1985	315,500	87,000	141,800	106,900	22,600	8,000	2,100	6,300
1986	288,400	99,100	163,000	108,000	21,000	9,200	2,000	6,200
1987	288,600	113,500	183,000	108,800	19,600	9,100	1,900	5,400
1988	337,900	133,100	202,900	101,700	20,400	10,100	2,100	5,200
1989	362,800	162,500	214,600	100,700	21,900	11,000	2,800	3,900
1990	355,200	168,300	214,600	102,600	25,100	14,600	2,800	3,900
1991	*366,100	195,200	224,200	112,900	20,900	14,900	2,600	2,900
1992	*393,000	203,100	231,900	120,800	23,600	34,700	6,200	10,900
1993	*394,800	205,100	240,500	132,400	37,900	38,900	10,300	9,400
1994	427,700	260,100	259,200	154,200	29,600	30,300	7,300	8,600

Visa Classes: F = Academic students and M = Vocational students. The former class outnumbers the latter by about 60 to 1 and INS merges the two classes in some of its statistics. H = Several classes of temporary workers, some highly skilled, some not. J = Exchange visitors, usually professionals. L = Intracompany transferees are managers and professionals previously employed overseas by multinational firms.

Note: All statistics above include accompanying family members.

Source: Most data are taken from *Statistical Yearbook of the Immigration and Naturalization Service;* admissions data from table 39 (1993) and predecessor tables and adjustment data from table 10 (1993) and its predecessors. All 1994 data and the totals with asterisks (corrected data on F and M admissions) were provided by the INS Statistics Division by telephone and fax.

Clearly people in some of these classes bring along more family members than others; presumably this relates to such factors as age of the prime beneficiary (one acquires more family members the further one is beyond one's twentieth birthday), expected length of stay in the United States, and level of prosperity. (For example, F students are young, and H-2A farm workers, who do not usually bring family members to the United States when cutting sugar cane or harvesting apples, are nonprosperous.)

The ratio of dependents to principals, as a result of such factors, is quite different for the five visa classes. The ratios among the nonimmigrant admissions were as follows in 1993:

Dependents per Prime Beneficiary	Nonimmigrant Class
.13	F
.28	H
.22	J
.60	L
.13	M
.24	all five classes

Overlapping Classes. It is useful to note the overlapping nature of these five visa classes. With the exception of the intracompany transferees (L), none of the full visa classes consists of only workers, and none consists only of students who do not work in the economy. A hierarchy, from full-time workers towards full-time students, looks like this:

Work only	L-1 intracompany transferees
	H-1A nurses (category terminated 9/30/95)
	H-1B specialty occupations
	H-2A farm workers
	H-2B other blue collar workers (mostly)
An uneven mix of work & study	J-1 exchange visitors
	H-3 industrial trainees
Study + some part-time & vacation work[4]	F-1 university students
	M-1 vocational students

In addition there are the family categories, F-2, H-4, J-2, L-2, and M-2. Some of these family members (spouses and children) may work (e.g., J-2) and some may not (e.g., F-2.)

There are often situations in which an alien could be admitted in one of two or more of the five classes of interest, usually depending on the decision of the U.S. institution involved. For example, a dean of a graduate school grumbled to me about a decision by the Department of Labor (DOL) raising the salaries of some postdocs hired as H-1Bs. He said that, if the salary were raised too much, he would simply bring in the desired worker under his university's J-1 programs.[5] While there are some mild labor standards in most H programs, there are none in the J-1 program.

Agencies Controlling the Programs. One final item of general background: What agencies play roles in the control of these programs? Thumbnail sketches of these management patterns will suffice here.

The F and M programs are handled by INS and The Department of State (DOS). Educational institutions on the INS-approved list are permitted to issue the I-20 form to foreign students to indicate admission to the institution. The student, with the I-20 in hand, then applies to a consular officer for a F-1 visa, which, if obtained, he uses to gain admission at a port of entry. The M program operates in much the same way. A student wanting to change schools, or to work during a post-degree training period, needs to secure INS approval.

All parts of the H program involve both INS and State, and the Department of Labor plays a role in some parts of it. Labor's strongest hand is in the farm program, H-2A, where it helps decide the number of workers to be admitted for a particular farm and then inspects the working and living conditions on the farm. Labor plays a lighter role in the H-1B and H-2B programs, where it sets the prevailing wage for the jobs in question; this was a passive process in the past (with DOL doing little other than collecting paper on the subject) but has become a more vigorous activity in the last couple of years. Labor has no role in the small H-3 program for industrial trainees. An employer in all of these programs must file a petition with INS for the worker in question and, if the petition is approved, the worker then goes to a consular officer for a visa and then to a U.S. port of entry.

The J-program is handled by the United States Information Agency (USIA), by State, and by INS. USIA approves a list of institutions that may participate; they, in turn, issue the IAP-66, the certificate of eligibility for exchange visitor status; the alien then takes the IAP-66 to a consular office, which (usually) issues a J-1 visa that the alien then presents to an INS officer at a port of entry.

The L program is handled by INS and State. The multinational corporation files a petition with INS and, if approved, this leads to a visa issuance by a consulate. If the would-be L-visa holder is in the United States legally, then INS can adjust the status here.

POLICY CHALLENGES

There are four domestic impacts of nonimmigrant programs:

1. The short-term impact of the program on the United States while the non-immigrants remain in that status (or in some other nonimmigrant classification);

2. The long-term impact on the size of the nation's population created when some of the nonimmigrants adjust to PRA status;

3. The long-term impact when other nonimmigrants opt to stay in the United States in illegal status, a factor that is sometimes ignored;[6] and

4. The long-term impact made on the labor market by those staying in the United States.

In addition, one could discuss a fifth impact, that on international relations. Ideally nonimmigrants have a good time in the U.S. and return to their homes with good images of this country and a desire to buy its exported goods. That would suggest that we: (1) try to make sure that the nonimmigrants are happy in the United States; and; (2) that they return when their visa expires. This is an intriguing line of thought, but probably marginal to this task.

The logic of the four kinds of impacts and the four major programs suggests a sixteen-unit matrix, and this can be seen in Table 3.2. The descriptions of the impacts are my own sense of the situation and are designed only to set the framework for the discussion that follows. There is no opportunity in this chapter to present detailed documentation on the costs and benefits of each of these programs. The objective is to sketch what appear to be problem and nonproblem areas prior to a discussion of what might be done to resolve the problems.

Short-term impacts. In general terms, all of these nonimmigrant programs seem to be performing well for the institutions that designed them: corporations; the educational establishment; and the immigration bar.

Further, with some exceptions in the H programs, the corporations and educational institutions inevitably obtain what they seek from these programs. Colleges issuing I-20s, for instance, do not have to fight to get their students F-1 visas; it is almost automatic. As we have pointed out elsewhere, the universities and the corporations are the effective gatekeepers in nonimmigrant programs for science and engineering; people they want are allowed to come to this country, most others are kept out; INS simply rubber-stamps the gatekeepers' decisions (North 1995:37–67).

In some cases, there are few, if any, disadvantages to the society or to elements within it. There may be some adverse effects on U.S. citizen executives in the L program, but I have not heard of them. Easy access of foreign students to American undergraduate education is a good thing for the nation's foreign relations and for the American students who rub elbows with the overseas students. There are doubts, however, about who is really paying how much for this exchange.

There are some labor market problems implicit within several of these programs, however. In some, the interests of American workers (including student workers) have been ignored out of deference to corporations and universities. (How to strike the right balance among these domestic interests, of course, is a challenge to the Commission and to the Congress.)

The levels of labor market difficulty with the eight specific nonimmigrant programs could be arrayed in the following manner, with the most troublesome at the top of the list:

H-2A (farm workers). This program simply transfers funds from American farm workers to agri-business; it is small but a disgrace.

H-1B. Group entries, as in the case of computer programmers, are needless and lead to worker exploitation; single entries are less harmful but need to be reexamined.

J-1. The problem with this program is the total lack of labor standards; many admitted under its provisions are, in fact, full-time workers.

M. This is a small program and its short-term labor market impacts are mild.

F. The short-term labor market impacts are mild.

Table 3.2
The Impacts of Four Nonimmigrant Programs on Four Aspects of America (A Proposed Conceptual Framework)

Nonimmigrant Classes/ Domestic Impacts	F & M	H	J	L
Short-term impact while nonimmigrant status remains	Bland to good on the educational system; minimal on labor market; minimal impact on business	Adverse impact on many labor markets; no impact on educational system; good for business	Some adverse impact on a specialized labor market; good for the educational system; minimal impact on business	Bland on the labor market; none on the educational system; good for business
Long-term impact on size of immigrant population	Mild impact (see data below)	Mild impact	Minimal	Minimal
Long-term impact on size of illegal alien population	Of some concern	Of some concern	Not significant	Not significant
Long-term impact on labor market	Bland, scattered	Of some concern	Bland, small, scattered	Bland, small, scattered

64

Ratio of Adjustments in the Four Classes of Interest to Total Immigration, 1985–1994

	F & M	H	J	L
Adjustments, 1985-1994	243,000	182,000	40,000	63,000
Percentage of Total Immigration	2.5%	1.9%	0.4%	0.7%

Sources: Adjustment data are drawn from Table 3.1 and its sources; impact descriptions are those of the author.

H-3. This is a small and bland program.

L. This program has no noticeable labor market impacts.

Unfortunately, I have done no work at all on the 15,000-a-year H-2B program; it brings a largely blue collar workforce into the United States. The workers include, for example, the Jamaican waiters at the Grand Hotel on Michigan's Mackinac Island. I worry about the need for such programs and will leave it at that.

It may be helpful to expand the comments on the two most troublesome of these programs, H-2A and H1B.

As to the agricultural worker programs, I should note that I have had a dim view of them ever since I worked as the Assistant to the Secretary of Labor (then W. Willard Wirtz); my principal assignment was phasing out the *bracero* program, a large-scale farm worker program then lingering on from World War II. We found then, as others have found since, that American employers can do quite well without such programs; that they usually tend to depress wages and working conditions; and that, particularly since the Seasonal Agricultural Workers (SAW) program flooded America's agricultural labor markets, there is no need for temporary worker programs.

My feelings on this subject were, to my great surprise, supported by the recent, grower-dominated Commission on Agricultural Workers. I was sure that the Commission would call for an expanded, easier-on-growers H-2A program, if not a whole new and grower-friendly foreign worker program. Instead it concluded (Commission on Agricultural Workers 1992:133): "Neither an extension of the RAW program nor any new supplementary foreign worker programs are warranted at this time."[7]

The H-1B program presents a much more complex situation. On the plus side, there are times when an employer genuinely needs an alien who is a specialist in something exotic and no one in the U.S. labor market really has the skills. An oil company, for example, may really need a Kazak-speaking petroleum geologist to work in both Houston and Alma-Alta. This kind of need, however, is more rare than industry lobbyists will admit.

Also on the plus (or mixed) side of the ledger, is the use of the H-1B program as a transitional status for a U.S.-trained physicist, for example, who is on his way to PRA status. This allows a talented alien to work in the United States, though it also can add an extra body to a swollen labor force (e.g., the apparent current surplus of Ph.D.'s in science and engineering).

The H-1B program also can be used to bring in large groups of foreign-born workers (such as computer programmers) to do essentially mundane jobs and, often, to displace citizen and PRA workers from these jobs. The employers, given the current minimal levels of labor standards and enforcement, can save substantial funds by providing wages and working conditions that look attractive, say in India, but are well below U.S. levels.

The question then is: How can we preserve the beneficial short-term impacts of the H-1B program while eliminating the well-publicized harmful ones?

In addition to the labor market impacts of some of these programs, there are also some harder-to-quantify impacts on the public purse. Lowered wages and greater unemployment among residents caused by worker displacement in the H and J programs can lead to an unknown amount of lowered tax receipts and increased transfer payments. Further, we have no idea of the amount of public funds spent on educating people admitted in the F and J programs.

Long-term Impact on the Size of the Legal Immigrant Population. Contrary to the somewhat subjective discussion of the short-term impact of nonimmigrants on the U.S., hard numbers in Table 3.2 illustrate the first of the long-term impacts, the demographic one.

A very large segment of the nonimmigrant admissions in the four classes of interest does *not* create permanent, legal additions to the U.S. population. There were more than eight million nonimmigrant admissions during the decade covered by the exhibit and only a little more than one-half million cases of adjusted status. There are two reasons for this, one statistical, the other real. First, as noted earlier, admissions, by their nature, overstate the number of people involved. Second, most nonimmigrants in these classes do not, in fact, stay in the United States.

Looking at the demographic impact of these nonimmigrant adjustments in another way demonstrates that, in the same decade, they accounted for only 5.5 percent of the immigrants to the United States (counting the legalizations under the Immigration Reform and Control Act of 1986 [IRCA] as immigrants). Adjustments from these four classes appear to produce relatively small numbers and a useful segment of the inflow of immigrants. This is a portion of the immigrant population with a great deal of human capital and, by definition, sustained contact with U.S. institutions and systems.

Recent observers have recommended cuts in the number of worker-based admissions. I would, however, look to flows other than these adjustments when making most of the cuts. Substantial reductions in these classes would tend to lower the average educational level of the incoming cohorts of immigrants.

People in the four major nonimmigrant classes of interest, however, are not equally avid to become Americans. The statistics on this point are not the best; for instance, an earlier draft of this paper noted the following comparison (drawn from Table 3.2) between admissions and adjustments in the decade 1985–1994:

Class	Adjustments as % of Admissions
J	1.9%
L	5.5%
F and M	6.5%
H	11.2%

All of these comparisons of adjustments to admissions cover both workers and dependents, as we are discussing the demographic impact of the nonimmigrants.

Reviewers of the percentages above suggested that it would be better to compare admissions in a given year or series of years to adjustments five years later, on the grounds that this is something like the interval between arrival as a nonimmigrant and adjustment of status (for those who follow this course). They also suggested that visa issuance numbers were better than admissions numbers because they approximate more closely the number of people involved in the nonimmigrant population. Good points, both, but they tend to move in opposite directions. The lagging tends to increase the percentages shown above because it relates the number of adjustments to the number of admissions in years when the latter were smaller than in the year of adjustment. The use of visa issuance data tends to move in the opposite direction because the numbers of visa issuances are usually smaller than the number of nonimmigrant admissions.

So, taking nonimmigrant admissions in the four classes for FYs

1985–1989 and the adjustments for the same classes five years later (FYs 1990–1883), I derive the following percentages:

Class	Adjustments as % of Visa Issuances
J	4.0%
F and M	16.7%
L	21.2%
H	38.0%[8]

In both the cruder and in the more careful comparisons, the class relationships are about the same; exchange people are the least likely to adjust, workers are the most, with the student and international executive classes in the middle.

It makes sense that members of the H class were the most likely to adjust; they are employed on a temporary basis by U.S. employers and many are in a trial period. If things go well, the employer will seek a green card for them. My work with foreign-born scientists and engineers suggests that many of the foreign-born, U.S.-trained Ph.D.'s who stay in the United States use the H-1B status as the springboard toward the green card. Most of the H class nonimmigrants adjusting to PRA status do not have the education level of the scientists and engineers, but they do have, by definition, good ties to the U.S. labor market because, in most cases, it is their H class employer who files for the labor certification.

It is not clear why the adjustment rate is not higher than it is for the Ls; they, too, are employed in the United States and the immigration law makes it easy to adjust them to PRA status. Maybe many of them are genuinely multinational people working for multinational corporations, simply spending some time in the United States during a career that will take them to several countries.

The lower rates of adjustment for the student classes does make sense; they usually are not linked to an American employer while here unless they wish to follow an academic career.

Drifting Into Illegal Status. One suspects that some substantial, but unknown, portion of the lower income nonimmigrants in the classes of interest—blue collar workers and vocational students—tend to drift into illegal alien status. Certainly this happened with substantial numbers of the Mexican nationals who came to the United States to work as *braceros* (farm workers) in the 1943–1964 period.

There are, however, no data sets that are helpful in this regard, and the current and recent INS enforcement strategies—with the concentration on the borders and on criminal aliens—suggest that INS deportation data can be of little help. The suspicion lingers, however, that some of the blue collar nonimmigrants, and a few of the white collar ones, stay illegally in the United States.

Long-Term Impact on the Labor Market. In three of the major nonimmigrant classes (F & M, J, and L) I sense that the long-term impact of their adjustment to PRA status is generally bland (perhaps a little less so with J than the others). But I am worried about the lingering labor market impacts of many of the H adjustments.

My understanding is that, when there are *concentrations* of alien workers in a given labor market (be it defined occupationally or geographically), there are likely to be problems of labor market distortion—lower than normal wages, higher than normal unemployment. These problems are likely to be aggravated when the workers involved have few rights or few perceived rights (such as the H-2A farm workers and the newly-arrived Indian programmers).

Further, when these problems exist, there is usually some controversy; the complaints may be ignored by the decision makers, but the complaints are there.

There appears to be little to worry about with the adjusting students or the intracompany transferees on either ground. The adjustees seem to be scattered and the complaints minimal to nonexistent.

But there is plenty of noise about some of the lingering aspects of the H-1B program, at least within the fields of science and engineering. It appears that the whole, seamless web of easy access of talented aliens to U.S. graduate schools, generous U.S. funding for these aliens at those graduate schools, worldwide peace, and (unfortunately) reduced government funding for research and development has led to an overproduction of Ph.D.'s in science and engineering. The H-1B program then facilitates the entry of the foreign-born Ph.D.'s into the U.S. labor market. The only clear beneficiaries of this situation are the institutions doing the training. There appears to be a need to reduce this overproduction; how this should be done—by changing nonimmigrant or other government policies—is discussed later.

HOW NONIMMIGRANT POLICY IS MADE; ALSO, THREE PRECEDENTS, TWO WORKS IN PROGRESS, AND ONE CONTINUING PROBLEM

Nonimmigrant policies are made in the United States by legislators, but in most of the rest of the world this is done by administrators.

Such policies in the United States are highly legalistic, detailed, and subject to substantial reviews by the courts. This is not the case in the other democracies.

In the United States, immigration policy usually consists of four elements: (1) definitions of eligibility for a benefit; (2) statutorily-fixed numerical ceilings on that benefit; (3) waiting lists; and (4) little administrative flexibility except for the possibility, sometimes, of waivers and paroles.

The other two prime, self-recognized nations of immigration (Australia and Canada) have used more flexible targets (annually adjusted) to control the size of immigration and more flexible points systems to decide on whom to admit.

Until recently, U.S. nonimmigrant policy contained no legislated ceilings—if one alien or ten thousand could prove their eligibility, they were admitted. The 1990 Immigration Act, however, broke that pattern by imposing a 65,000 ceiling on the number of H-1B petitions to be issued in a single year.

U.S. nonimmigration policy also is suffused heavily with efforts to create, artificially level playing grounds for U.S. workers and their nonimmigrant peers. Thus, the Department of Labor for years adjusted the H-2A adverse effect wage rate; if a grower could show that he was paying at that rate and was unable to secure needed workers (usually a month or so before they were needed), he could secure the foreign workers he wanted. The artificiality of this process was further accentuated because in real life farm work is compensated by piece rates and the adverse effect wage levels were hourly rates.

Similarly, H-1B employers are supposed to pay their foreign workers at no more than 95 percent of the prevailing wage for the job in question, a shaky concept at best. And why only 95 percent?

I now turn to three interesting precedents in nonimmigrant and labor standards policymaking and to two works in progress.

The Visa Waiver Precedent. Some years ago the United States decided to try an experiment: to retain its general policy of demanding a visa for all incoming nonimmigrants, but to waive it under certain conditions for people from certain nations. The twin driving forces were to make it easier for tourists to come to the United States and to reduce largely useless workloads for the Department of State overseas.

So the United States worked up a (now slowly expanding) list of nations whose residents rarely become illegal aliens; they could come to the United States without a visa if they bought a nonrefundable airline ticket and if they signed away their right to contest a (highly unlikely) INS decision to exclude them on their arrival at a U.S. airport. The experiment has worked well, millions use it, and only a handful have abused it. (I get to the utility of this precedent later.)

The Australian Student Visa Program Precedent. Australia's nonimmigrant program for students makes sharp distinctions, just as the U.S. visa waiver program does. There are "gazetted" and "nongazetted" countries, with the latter having lower incomes than the former and, presumably, higher degrees of abuse of Australia's immigration law.

Australia also makes a sharp distinction between "nonaward" students (those not heading towards a degree) and "award" students. If you are from Tonga and want to take a thirteen-week English language course, for example, you fall into both the nongazetted and the nonaward categories and you are told in a government announcement that your chances of getting a student visa are slim (Commonwealth of Australia 1994).[9]

The California Labor Standards Precedent. The California Department of Industrial Relations enforces the state minimum wage, which is sometimes higher—and always more vigorously enforced—than the federal minimum wage. One of the reasons for the greater vigor of enforcement is that California has found a way to supplement tax funds to support this operation.

Fees and fines collected by the Department of Industrial Relations go into the agency's own budget. An employer of hourly workers, for example, is fined $100 every time a state inspector finds that a worker is on the shop floor but that there is no timecard for that worker (North 1991:54–55).

Work in Progress #1. The U.S. Department of Labor is making efforts to bring higher labor standards into the H-1B program and to penalize abusers of the program.

For example, it worked out a settlement with Syntel, Inc., of Troy, Michigan, in which the firm agreed, among other things, to pay additional wages to previously underpaid H-1B computer programmers, to pay $30,000 in civil penalties, not to hire any more H-1B workers for ninety days, and to invest $1,000,000 in its training programs for U.S. workers (Interpreter Releases 1995a: 1261–64).[10]

Work in Progress #2. Worried by the possibility of terrorist acts by a small minority of foreign students and citing the World Trade Center bombing and the murders at the gates of the CIA, INS has created a Task Force on Foreign Student Data System Reengineering.

The general notion is that the government should keep closer tabs on foreign students and should create a data system that will track them while they are in this country. While the subject is not mentioned explicitly in the draft report of the task force, the thrust of the proposed activities also would tend to discourage F students from drifting, unwatched, into illegal alien status.

The task force makes a number of proposals, in addition to a comprehensive reporting system for individual students, such as:

• Eliminating the power of public schools to issue the I-20;

• Reviewing the list of INS-approved schools from time to time to remove educational institutions that rarely issue the I-20;

• Collecting a fee from each foreign student, via the educational institution, to finance the tighter regulation of the program.

Presumably the task force's program will have no impact on the easy flow of genuine international students (except making it a little more expensive) but will tend to discourage the drift into illegal status. It apparently will have no labor market impacts.

One Continuing Problem. It is always easier to obtain public funding for some activities than others; it is, for example, usually easier to hire more cops than to employ more librarians.

So it is within the Immigration Service. Time and again the Congress will vote to hire more Border Patrol Agents and to equip them with newer and fancier tools, helicopters, sensors, and the like. But it is very hard to obtain what INS gently calls "alien travel money." These are the funds used to buy plane tickets for aliens being deported.

For instance, earlier this year, INS launched a major new initiative to reduce the backlog of asylum applications and to discourage ineligible applicants from filing. The principal new tools were: (1) a de-linking of the application for asylum and the issuance of a work permit, thus eliminating the incentive of an instant work permit when filing for asylum; and (2) the hiring of additional officers and judges to handle the new cases more quickly.

One of the INS assumptions was that with the new system—a multimillion dollar investment—there would be more people being found ineligible and, thus, deportable. Although the system came into being on January 4, 1995, and was due to start causing some deportations in a matter of months, only $100,000 was made available in alien travel funds for the balance of the fiscal year.

The lack of alien travel funds is a recurring problem within INS; I remember some years ago the investigators in the New York District Office were told: Concentrate your enforcement activities on locating two types of illegal aliens, ship jumpers and stowaways. I asked if they were especially dangerous and was told, "No, but the carriers have to pay for their removal and the district is out of alien travel money for the rest of the fiscal year." I return to this point later.

GENERAL RECOMMENDATIONS

Bearing in mind the previous discussion, I have several general recommendations for the reform of the work-and education-related nonimmigrant programs.

1. Limit the number of nonimmigrant classes. The more classes, the harder they are to administer; the more classes, the more loopholes; the more classes, the more confusion in the using publics, institutions, and aliens.

2. Limit the number of government agencies involved. Many nonimmigrant programs now involve the Departments of State, Justice, and Labor; the multidepartment involvement is not desirable but it is, in the short-term, probably unavoidable. What can be done, however, is to eliminate the United States Information Agency and its control over the J-1 program. USIA has said it wants, desperately, to get out of the au pair program; let us assent to that—and more—and remove USIA from the supervision of all exchange programs. If it wants to operate an exchange program of its own (under the general eye of INS), that is all right.

3. Enforce the rules. In addition to fewer programs and fewer agencies, it is vital that we have more governmental control over the nonimmigrant programs to discourage the slippage of legal aliens into illegal status and to protect against labor market abuse.

4. Raise enforcement funds from those using the programs. Individuals, and particularly institutions, using nonimmigrant programs should pay fees to support enforcement measures. INS has, over recent years, raised a great deal of money from individual aliens seeking benefits, and it is starting to collect some fees at the borders. Good. It also should begin to charge break-even fees on some transactions, such as the issuance of the I-20, to fund enforcement within the F program. The California Department of Industrial Relations has set the precedent for such fees.

Further, and for a different reason, INS should start charging substantial fees for accepting (not necessarily for approving) H-1B petitions. The notion here is that the employer will probably pay more attention to his options within the American labor market if there is an upfront fee, of say 10–25 percent of the H-1B worker's wages.[11]

5. Make distinctions, painful though it may be. It makes sense to concentrate resources where there are problems and to invest lightly in nonproblem areas. It also makes sense, as in the U.S. visa waiver program and in Australia's foreign student program, to make distinctions among nations, and, as in the case of Australia, among educational programs. (Remember the nongazetted, nonaward students.) The United States also should make distinctions among types of work and types of corporations—we know that some are much more troubling than others.

In the H-1B program, for example, we do not do the obvious; we do not set much more stringent standards for group usages of the program than for singleton usages. If, as some have suggested, binational corporations in the temporary worker business are more likely to cause problems than domestic corporations, we should not shrink from focusing on the former, even though one set of executives may be foreign-born while the other is native-born.

6. Introduce the nonrefundable, life-time, round-trip air ticket. To ease the return of aliens when their visas are over and to fund their departure if they become deportable, the United States should impose a universal requirement on all nonimmigrants arriving by air (and sea). That is, they must buy a nonrefundable, round-trip ticket that is good for the rest of their lives.

Why should any one arriving on a nonimmigrant visa object? They have, after all, sworn that they are *not* going to stay in the U.S. Why not use the visa waiver precedent in this regard?

The presence of the ticket (probably both a hard copy and a record in a computer) would mean that the alien could always afford to return to his or her homeland. Broke in the United States? Tempted to take a job illegally to raise some money to go home? Don't bother, you have that lifetime return ticket waiting to fly you back home. The ticket also would mean that alien travel money never again would be used to transport overstays, those funds could be focused entirely on those entering without inspection (EWIs).

The airlines, of course, will object. It would add an externally caused complication to their internally caused tangle of ticket prices. They would have to train their computers and their staffs to handle a new set of variables.

But it would allow them to raise their international fares and to keep the extra money as an interest-free loan, a short-term one in some cases, but a very long-term one for someone who successfully entered the United States by air and then became a long-term undocumented alien.

7. Cease legislating immigration via treaties. While the Free Trade Agreement nonimmigrant provisions have made major changes in the way we make policies in this area, no substantial adverse impacts have been seen—yet. But the whole notion of giving a set of diplomats control over migration policies is startling to say the least. There are no congressional hearings and no organized input from interest groups; migration decisions are buried deep in agreements that deal largely with totally different and more pressing issues. Further, the whole process is in the hands of a department (State) that is always emotionally distant from the lives of working Americans.

The Commission should take a stand that Congress should *never* again let immigration or nonimmigration policy fall into the hands of the treaty makers.

8. Create a whole new nonimmigrant system. Legislative policy-making in the United States—at least before January, 1995—was usually a piecemeal process. Laws and systems would evolve slowly and change a little bit at a time. With that in mind, the final section of this report makes a series of suggestions about modifying (or in some cases dropping) the current group of nonimmigrant programs.

But supposing we could ignore the current litter of nonimmigrant programs and create a new system from scratch. What would it look like?

Let us limit this exercise to the five nonimmigrant categories discussed above (as well as the new Os, Ps, and Qs).

Instead of these eight classes, with their subclasses, I propose:

- Students and scholars
- Temporary workers
- Transitional workers
- Intracompany transferees

In general terms, Students and Scholars (S&S hereafter) would be a merger of the F, M, and Q programs with most of the J program.

Temporary Workers (TW) would cover most of the H programs, the workers now within the J program, as well as the Os and Ps.[12]

Transitional Employees (TE) would be people holding short-term jobs in the United States but on their way to PRA status; most people in this category currently are a subset of the H-1B class.

Intracompany Transferees would be essentially the current L program, which would not be changed.

S&S would be administered by INS alone; the Department of Labor would set labor standards and help enforce the other three programs in cooperation with INS. USIA would not be involved, and State would continue to play the visa issuance role.

There would be no need for labor standards in the new S&S program because, except for incidental work by undergraduates, all working graduate students, postdocs, and faculty on short-term assignments would be regarded as workers in the TW class.

Labor standards would be set for the TW, TE, and intracompany transferee classes. (The last named could get along with a simple minimum wage for multinational executives, say $40,000 a year, to rise annually with inflation.) And with labor standards being set by a single agency, institutions would not have the opportunity, as they do now, to comb through various categories seeking the best deal (or the lowest wages).

The TE class would be set up deliberately as a way station to green card status. It would recognize and preserve the most useful part of the

H-1B program, while separating it from the group admissions aspect of the current program.

Demetrious Papademetriou and Stephen Yale-Loehr have suggested an interesting way to select members of the TE class; successful candidates would have to earn enough points in a system that also handles labor-related permanent immigration.[13] A point system could be managed by the government in such a way as to minimize the current glut of science and engineering Ph.D.'s, for example, and yet open the doors for more of them should the need arise later. More significantly, it would cause corporations to hire from among a group of aliens with characteristics needed by the nation in the long haul—as opposed to choosing H-1Bs to meet the narrow needs, sometimes the whims, of an individual corporate manager.

As a part of my larger scheme, then, only TE and intracompany transferees could adjust to PRA status on the basis of labor needs; people in the temporary worker [TW] and scholars and students [S&S] categories could adjust to PRA because of family reasons, as they can now, or to the new TE status should they qualify. One also could come to the United States with a TE visa in addition to adjusting to it from some other nonimmigrant category within the United States.

This would leave us with four nonimmigrant classes of workers and scholars, with an integrated system for the making of governmental decisions, and with a clear-cut set of standards for all involved.

But if all we can do is adjust the current system, the next section provides some more narrow suggestions.

SPECIFIC RECOMMENDATIONS

Within the current framework, I would suggest the following changes.

First, and foremost, adopt the mandatory, nonrefundable, lifetime return airline ticket for all incoming nonimmigrants. If they have such a ticket, they will be a little more likely to return when their visas expire. If they do not return, and fall out of legal status, they can be sent back at no public expense.

Now, regarding the specific classes of interest:

F-1: Academic Students. It is a good idea to keep foreign students coming in, learning in, and then leaving the country. This is what most of them do, and this is to be encouraged.

I am concerned, however, with the question of who is paying the bill and suggest an approach to this problem in Appendix A. I share the view of the INS Task Force that the F program should be tightened administratively and that funds for this be raised by charging a fee for the issuance of the I-20.

In addition, there is something that INS and the Department of Education (DOE) should do that I believe is not yet in anyone's plans. DOE has identified a group of educational institutions where students have a high rate of failure in repaying DOE loans. My suspicion is that these are the kinds of institutions (often proprietaries, often providing vocational training) that do not provide foreign students a good education, either, and that F and M students in these places are more likely to drift into illegal status than other foreign students. DOE and INS should get together and jointly assure that these institutions no longer can issue the I-20 (or the M program's version thereof) nor use the federal loan program.[14]

H-1B: Specialty Occupations. This is a large program with many nooks and crannies. Sometimes it is used for the actual importation (from overseas) of individual workers with remarkable skills for short-term assignments in the United States; sometimes it is used to hire individual talented workers already in the United States in another status; sometimes it is part of a many-stage process by which a foreign-born, U.S.-trained worker moves towards PRA status (as is often the case with scientists and engineers). All of these uses are acceptable to commendable.

The worrisome part of the same H-1B program is its use to bring in *groups* of journeymen technicians and computer programmers at relatively low wages; such workers depress wages and working conditions in the United States and often displace U.S. workers. This part of the program should be eliminated or severely curtailed.

For detailed suggestions as to how to do this, see Appendix C.

H-2A: Farm workers. Abolish the program.

H-2B: Other Temporary Workers (mostly blue collar). I worry about the exploitive nature of such programs here and abroad but have no firsthand knowledge of this particular program and, hence, make no suggestions.

H-3: Industrial Trainees. This appears to be a small and noncontroversial program, so reform energies should be directed elsewhere.

J-1: Exchange Visitors. Again, as with the F-1 program, it is a good thing that a cosmopolitan mix of people is coming to the United States to study, confer, and work with their U.S. peers on a wide variety of subjects and in a wide variety of institutional settings.

Within this useful program, however, there are places where non-immigrant graduate students, postdocs, and others are treated very badly. There are no labor standards in the J-1 program, though many people in the program work for wages and do so for years at a time.

Labor standards should be introduced into this program as it stands or, perhaps better, exchange visitors, who are in fact workers, should be moved out of this program and into a temporary worker program run by the Department of Labor. The universities, of course, would not like that, and the people who would benefit—the foreign scholars and their U.S. peers—are hopelessly ill organized for such a struggle with the splendidly organized educational establishment.

M-1: Vocational Students. It probably was a good idea—if against the thrust of the suggestion that there are too many programs—to separate vocational schools from academic ones.

Someone should examine this program to see if it is worth continuing. Caution is suggested by the general record of private, for-profit vocational schools.

What clearly must be done, as suggested with the F-class institutions, is for INS and the Department of Education to share information on marginal institutions and for both to move swiftly against those entities that either create a high percentage of illegal aliens or whose students fail to repay DOE loans.

Adjusting from Nonimmigrant to Immigrant Status. This subject is at the edge, perhaps beyond our charge. But, with the seamless movement from one nonimmigrant status to another and then on to PRA status that I found so common among the scientists and engineers, perhaps a final set of comments is in order.

I am concerned about the apparent current overproduction of Ph.D.'s in science and engineering and worry that the current easy adjustment from nonimmigrant to immigrant status will aggravate that surplus, given the large number of highly qualified, foreign-born Ph.D.'s in the country and in our educational pipelines.

On the other hand, reduction in research and development investments at the federal level, which would slowly reduce the surplus,[15] seems a terrible idea, and barring Ph.D.'s and other highly educated aliens from immigrant status simply would press down the average educational attainment levels for the arriving cohorts of immigrants.

Several other suggestions have been made about how to cope with this surplus. One I favor has the disadvantage of being very slow-acting: impose on federal research grants a quota on nonimmigrant graduate students—to no more than, say, one-third of the graduate students funded. This would, over time, reduce the number of nonimmigrant Ph.D.'s educated here at our expense and probably would push the universities to look a little more carefully at the domestic talent pool. It also would allow the continuation, at slightly lower levels, of a useful pattern—the training of some of the world's best minds in some of the world's best university laboratories.

Another option would move much more quickly: impose a two-year overseas requirement before any adjustment could be made from nonimmigrant to immigrant status. This is a dusting off, expansion of, and enforcement of the old two-years-overseas rule, which once played a major role in the J program but since has been watered down by a series of waivers. The problem with this is that it would be immediately disruptive, in that for two years no one in the current path from nonimmigrant to immigrant status could make that move.

Yet another proposal would be to levy a substantial fee on adjustments from nonimmigrant to immigrant status of, say, 25–40 percent of the individuals' salaries.[16] This seems to make sense; corporations and universities probably would ask for fewer adjustments and those that they did seek would be the very best. The change would be more gradual than the abrupt imposition of the two-year rule, but more assertive than my suggestion of a one-third limit on funding of nonimmigrant graduate students. The combination of both of these proposals (the one-third quota and the stiff fee) would continue a useful international educational program but limit its impact on American labor markets.

APPENDIX A: A NOTE ABOUT WHO FINANCES FOREIGN STUDENTS IN THE UNITED STATES

One of the difficulties with working with nonimmigrant policies vis-à-vis foreign students is the abundance of misinformation distributed by the educational establishment on who pays the bill for educating foreign students in this country.

It will be difficult to impossible to make appropriate policy in this area as long as the impression remains that American universities— like Iowa's soy beans and Hollywood's movies—are major earners of export dollars. I do not think this is the case; the data offered to support that case are faulty (North 1995:77–85).

What policymakers need, and do not have, is a nationwide set of per-student estimates of the elements listed below. They will, of course, differ from institution to institution, but if we had them for a good sample of America's colleges and universities, we would have a better sense than we do now of who really pays for foreign students. The per-student, per-year estimates we need are:

1. Public moneys subsidizing the institution;
2. Private moneys (such as earnings on endowments) doing the same;
3. Public and private funds subsidizing individual foreign students (on average);
4. Moneys earned in the United States by such students during college years and spent on college-related expenses;
5. Moneys brought to the United States from overseas to support the education of such students.

Were we to have this information, then we would know the extent to which foreign students were supporting their education with money from foreign sources. We would probably find that numbers 1 + 2 + 3 + 4 (U.S. sources of funds) in most circumstances overwhelmed item number 5 (foreign sources) because of the hidden subsidies that wash over much of higher education in this country, benefiting foreign and domestic students alike.

But the educational establishment does not approach the question in that way. It does so in a way that produces headlines like this: "Foreign Students Pump up Economy" (*USA Today* 1995). This uncritical story was a rewrite of an Institute of International Education (IIE) press release on the subject.

Let's switch gears for a moment and assume that someone decided to conduct a survey on what the voters thought of President Clinton (instead of who pays for the education of foreign students). The pollster would ask his question (dealing with only part of Clinton's work) and would provide four alternative responses.

The question: "Voters think Bill Clinton is doing very well with his foreign policy, don't they?"

The alternative answers:

——"Yes, he is doing very well."

——"Yes, he is doing well."

——"He's doing okay."

——"No, he's not doing well."

The question in our metaphoric survey is not to be asked of people generally; it is to be asked of Democratic precinct captains.

A survey with such loaded methodology would not be used by the most desperate of political consultants, but that is *exactly* what IIE does annually.

It does not seek information on the whole question, on the relative significance of the five previously cited flows of funds. Nor does IIE seek hard data on this subject from university budget officials or from the students themselves, the people who would know best; no, it asks for perceptions on this point.

It does not ask the perception question of neutral observers, either; it seeks the perceptions of the foreign student advisers—the moral equivalent of polling the Democratic precinct captains.

Finally, after loading the design of the survey, IIE also loads the ballot. Following the question (primary source of funds) it provides the potential answers:

"Personal and Family"

"U.S. College/University"

"Home Government/University"

"U.S. Government"

"Private U.S. Sponsor"

"Private Foreign Sponsor"

"International Organization"

"Current Employment"

And, lo and behold, every year the patterns of the response fall al-most perfectly into place, mirroring the sequence of potential responses, with the answers being respectively 66.2 percent, 19.0 percent, 5.2 per-cent, 1.4 percent, 2.8 percent, 2.0 percent, 0.5 percent, and 2.3 percent (IIE 1992).[17]

I have called this to the attention of IIE by letter,[18] and, sought, on three different times, to interest three different editors of the *Chronicle of Higher Education* (which ran a long, careful report on our recent book), but no one would touch the presumably interesting, perhaps explosive, question of how IIE was loading the survey's dice.

I had been vaguely aware of the *Open Doors* survey results on this point for years, and had accepted them unthinkingly. Then I ran into a completely different set of results on this subject.

These were from the *Summary Report 1991: Doctorate Recipients from United States Universities* (NRC 1993:18)[19] The National Re-search Council (NRC) had asked the same fuzzy question. (Regarding the primary source of funding—why Ph.D.'s can not be asked about the *percentage* of their funding from various sources is beyond me.) The NRC answers were totally different from those elicited by the IIE:

Population	Primary Source of Funding	
	Personal	*University*
All foreign students (IIE)	66.2%	19.0%
Nonimmigrant Ph.D.'s in physical science and math (NRC)	4.0%	89.1%[20]

There are three reasons for these differences: first, science and en-gineering students are more likely to receive funding than others; also graduate students (as IIE's own data suggest) are more likely to be assisted than undergraduates. But the third reason relates to the fun-damental point made earlier—NRC asked the question of people with direct, unbiased knowledge on the point, the graduate students them-selves.

A Suggestion. It would be useful to have a better notion than that provided by IIE's flawed data and by NRC's narrow data (on Ph.D.'s only) regarding who pays for the higher education of nonimmigrants in this country.

While a total census of the finances of foreign students would tell us exactly how these matters play out, a far more modest study could provide us with the basics needed. What I would suggest would be a sample of some 40 to 60 institutions of higher education, with the appropriate mix of private and public entities, those large and small, those rich and poor, and those with large and small percentages of nonimmigrant students.

The research would involve four tasks: first, and easiest, an analysis of the extent to which public and private funds were used in a recent year in each institution to fund the education of all students, foreign and domestic; the basic question, what portion of the total cost of a year's education (including room and board) was subsidized? This would cover items number 1 and 2 (see above).

The second task would be a files search in the student aid or foreign student office of a sample, say 25, of the foreign students on campus. This should provide information on the extent to which individual assistance was offered to the students in the sample and the extent of on- and off-campus employment.

The third task would be to calculate the total cost of a year's education for the average foreign student, including institutional subsidies, tuition paid, and room and board. From this one would deduct the subsidies, loans made to these students from U.S. sources, as well as financial aid and wages for employment; the residue presumably would represent the moneys coming to the United States as a result of the arrival of the nonimmigrant student.

The fourth task would be to interview a subsample of the foreign students studied through the file searches to check on the accuracy of the files search process.

Perhaps GAO or the Department of Education could be encouraged to mount such a study as the Commission ponders the nation's nonimmigrant policies.

APPENDIX B: A NOTE ABOUT THE U.S. ISLANDS

While the Commission presumably is spending 99.5 percent of its energies on the immigration challenges to the 50 states, it should not

lose track of the difficult immigration policy questions of the U.S. islands in the Pacific—Guam, where the mainland immigration law applies, and American Samoa and the Commonwealth of the Northern
Mariana Islands (CNMI), where the law does not, but should.[21]

While the mainland has some controversial nonimmigrant worker
programs (computer programmers and sugar cane cutters, for example), they are models of generosity compared to the way that foreign
workers are treated in American Samoa and, particularly, in the Marianas.

The exploitation in CNMI's sewing factories is well known on the
mainland—the miserable wages, the life behind barbed wire, the long
hours, the terrible working conditions and the products all labelled
"Made in the U.S.A."

Perhaps less well known are these two simple facts: (1) there are
more guest workers in the Marianas than citizens; and (2) Congress
can restore its control over the CNMI immigration policy by merely
passing a statute.[22]

The exploited workers in CNMI are mostly women and primarily
from China and the Philippines. They are different from the citizen
population in the Marianas, the Chamorros. And, under current CNMI
law, they never can become citizens of the Marianas or of the U.S.[23]

Further, there are elements of sexual exploitation in CNMI that have
not surfaced with mainland temporary worker programs. The largely
Chamorro male CNMI immigration service is notorious for the way
that many of its officers harass the nonimmigrant women; some of those
women wind up as prostitutes. It is grim situation.

The problems in American Samoa are less publicized and less brutal.
Among other things, the exploited class at the moment is another group
of Samoans, citizens of Western Samoa; the migrants speak the same
languages as, and intermarry with, the dominant population. Western
Samoans do the dirty work in the fish-canning plants in Pago Pago,
while American Samoans have the softer jobs in the overstaffed local
government. Western Samoans cannot become citizens of American
Samoa, or more formally, U.S. nationals, but their children can, provided they were born in the U.S. territory. Both CNMI and American
Samoa have real *nonimmigrant* policies—in that they do not have significant provisions in their local immigration laws for immigrants, only
for guestworkers.

While there is extensive unemployment in American Samoa, the local government recently has approved the importation of several hundred Chinese women to work in a new, offshore-owned sewing factory; their stated role is to be instructors in industrial sewing, but they will stay for years, housed in a company barracks. It is well known that it takes only a couple of weeks, at most, to teach someone how to use these machines. The Chinese will be a docile workforce; they will be used to press the Samoan workers to greater heights of productivity as they sew in the labels: "Made in the U.S.A." The mainland minimum wage of $4.25 does not apply in either Samoa or CNMI; the local minimum wage levels are much lower than in the 50 states and much less well enforced.

Meanwhile, in the third remaining U.S. island in the Pacific, Guam, the INA controls, but there are strong local traditions of heavy use of the H-2B program in construction and in the services. (Guam, like CNMI, is a tourist attraction to a subset of the Japanese population—the ones with enough money to travel, but not enough to travel very far.)

Many interest groups in Guam would like the island to control its own immigration policy; there is a strong desire for more cheap labor, in the CNMI tradition, and a strong nationalist desire *not* to grant citizenship to newcomers.

I have been covering immigration and labor market trends in these islands—from Washington—for a decade as the American correspondent for Fiji's *Pacific Islands Monthly*. My advice is to see to it that Guam stays under the wing of U.S. law on this point and to encourage the Congress to restore its domain over the Marianas' immigration policy. It also might be a good idea to let the American Samoan government know that Washington is watching its handling of its foreign workers.

APPENDIX C: DETAILED RECOMMENDATIONS ON THE H1-B PROGRAM[24]

As noted earlier, the Department of Labor has proposed some useful initial steps towards reducing some of the abuses in the H-1B program. It needs to go much further, but first it must acknowledge the basic difference between the use of the program to bring in single workers—and groups of workers. The latter is *always* more harmful both to resident workers and to nonimmigrant workers themselves.

To this end, DOL and other government entities should take the following steps:

Fee structure. There should be a graduated fee schedule—the more nonimmigrant workers an employer wants, the more each costs. Fees should be levied on all applications, whether or not they are approved.

Differential Scrutiny. As a matter of conscious practice, the Department of Labor should announce that it will pay much more attention to applications for groups of people than single applications.[25]

If an application for more than ten workers is received from a single facility, for example, DOL investigators should make site visits, preferably unannounced, to talk with individual workers, both foreign-born and native-born (away from management's eyes and ears) about wages and working conditions. The fees to be paid by those seeking H-1B applications should be used to fund these investigations.

Notice. To make sure that all taxes are paid and to make certain that arriving H-1Bs know exactly what their actual pay checks will be, employers seeking three or more H-1B workers in the course of a year should be obliged to have an exchange of correspondence with their would-be workers outlining wages and deductions. Currently there is no obligation on the part of an H-1B employer to tell his nonimmigrant worker about the extent of federal income tax, state income taxes, FICA, and Medicare deductions, nor about the standard 30 percent deduction required by IRS for nonresident aliens.

Further, copies of these exchanges of correspondence should be filed by the employer with:

- All pertinent federal, state, and local taxing authorities;
- Unions, where present;
- Pertinent technical or professional organizations, and;
- The trade press.

Prevailing Wage. The arrangements currently made for determining the minimum wage are inadequate, as is the puzzling requirement that the employer has to pay only 95 percent of whatever is found to be the prevailing wage. Why not 105 percent to encourage the employer to pay attention to resident workers, be they citizens or legal immigrants?

Instead of using the hard-pressed and underfunded State Employment

Security Agencies to establish prevailing wages, why not use the generally available, occupationally specific salary surveys of the various professional and engineering societies?

In this scenario, if the employer wanted to hire a chemist with a bachelor's degree and two to four year's experience in 1997, for example, the employer would be required to pay the prevailing wage for such workers as established by the American Chemical Society's annual salary survey, or $35,000. Chemists with a master's degree, two or four years after the B.S., would get $40,500. The ACS survey, as currently conducted, does not provide a prevailing wage for a new Ph.D., but a chemist with a doctorate five to nine years after the B.S. received $52,000 in 1997 (Heylin 1997).

These salary surveys reflect the workings of the national labor market and presumably would be regarded as appropriate by the workers involved. The salary scales are easily obtainable by employers (from the trade press) and are not vulnerable to manipulation; neither statement can be made about the current system.

Why not use 105 percent of these prevailing wages in setting salaries for nonimmigrant workers? In that way all concerned could be assured that wage levels would *never* be depressed by the use of nonimmigrant workers. Even at 100 percent of the salary-survey wages, employers could argue that they were not paying below the prevailing levels (even though tapping into a foreign labor force might well, ultimately, depress wages generally).

The 65,000 Limit. The 1990 Immigration Act, for the first time, established a numerical limit on the approval of a set of nonimmigrant petitions, in this case for H-1B visas. Given a piece of legislation that generally was a disaster for American workers competing with foreign-born workers, this was a remarkable provision.

Now that there is some possibility that the limit actually will work to reduce the growth in the number of nonimmigrant workers, the immigration bar and their corporate allies are sure to seek to repeal or soften this provision (*Interpreter Releases* 1993:1438–39). These efforts should be resisted stoutly. If there is a prospect of reaching the ceiling, INS should allocate the limited number of petition approvals near the end of the fiscal year by granting them to employers offering the highest wages.

NOTES

1. Excluded from this essay are the O, P, Q and R classes. These are new, relatively small, and quite specialized, dealing as they do with, among others, entertainers, the more prominent athletes, and people in religious occupations. The total number of admissions in these classes came to 34,443 in FY 1993, compared with 171,829 admissions in all the H subclasses for the same year. Similarly excluded for the same reasons are the relatively new class of Free Trade Agreement nonimmigrants.

2. For a comprehensive, recent analysis of the labor market roles of all the nonimmigrant programs, see Leibowitz 1994.

3. Admissions figures are for an event—someone passing through a port of entry—while the adjustment data count the number of people moving from one immigration category to another. A single nonimmigrant can record several admissions in a given year or only one for a long-term stay in the United States; in the classes of interest, the norm is for several admissions for every individual granted a nonimmigrant visa. Adjustments, however, except for very unusual circumstances, are once-in-a-lifetime events. Hence the admissions and adjustment numbers are not comparable.

4. F-1 students may work on campus with university permission and off campus with INS permission.

5. For more on the often very low salaries paid in the postdoctoral positions, see North 1995:91–95.

6. For example, this possibility is not explored in the otherwise useful paper: Bratsberg 1995.

7. The RAW (Replenishment Agricultural Workers) program was a short-term element of the Immigration Reform and Control Act of 1986 (IRCA) that was never implemented; it would have brought in additional farm workers (presumably from Mexico) had the Departments of Labor and Agriculture determined that there was a shortage of farm workers. The Departments found, in the late 1980s and early 1990s, that there was no such shortage. The RAW program is no longer part of the law.

8. Data for visa issuances were drawn from *Report of the Visa Office, 1988*, table XVI(B) and for adjustments from sources cited in Table 3.1. One of the problems with the visa issuance data system is the fact that in two of the years covered the Department of State failed to record the number of blue collar H visas it issued (then H-2s) and in the other two years recorded only a tiny fraction of them. To adjust for this, I took half the H-2 admissions reported by INS in those years and added those numbers to the number of H visas that DOS did record. (Thus, I estimate one H-2 visa equivalent for every two H-2 admissions.) The rationale for this ratio is that most of these H-2s were farm-workers and there is a pattern of repeated employment of specific workers in

that program. Regarding sugar cane cutters, for example, the U.S. employers and the Jamaican government had directly opposite views on this turnover. The Jamaicans wanted to spread the work among the rural poor, the employers wanted to hire back those workers known to be energetic (and docile); so they split the difference, with 50 percent of each cohort of cane cutters being new-comers and 50 percent being predesignated experienced cutters. One wonders if DOS recognized the implicit symbolism of its statistical policy in those years, i.e., that farmworkers do not count.

9. I am grateful to Christopher Smith, Counsellor and Consul at the Aus-tralian Embassy in Washington, for providing me with this publication.

10. For an earlier report on a similar subject, see: *Interpreter Releases* 1995b:1–4.

11. If these fees were to be levied, there needs to be a mechanism to see to it that the employer, not the newly hired foreign worker, pays the fee.

12. Os are workers of outstanding ability, Ps are entertainers and athletes, and Qs are a group of culture exchange people. These categories were added by the 1990 Act.

13. This proposal has appeared in several places, among them: Papademe-triou & Yale-Loehr 1995:1473–80. See also the chapter by Papademetriou in this volume.

14. Late in this writing I recalled the McDonald's amendment to INA, set-ting up a special work program with that kind of firm for F students. I also recall that the Bureau of International Labor Affairs (ILAB) at DOL has studied this matter. I would hope that the Commission has seen that report, which, I think, was discouraging in tone.

15. By reducing the funding of such research, the number of foreign-born graduate students funded to study in this country would be similarly reduced.

16. The Department of Labor wants to use such fees for training Americans in the apparently needed skills; I would lean to the use of most of such money for the enforcement of labor standards in nonimmigrant programs.

17. See, for example, page 149 for the questions asked the foreign student advisers and page 37 for responses. The same ballot pattern and roughly the same responses can be seen in other editions of this annual report.

18. I suggested that the least IIE could do would be to change the sequence of the multiple-choice responses from year to year, as responsible pollsters do, but there was no answer.

19. The nonimmigrant Ph.D.'s in life sciences (7.0 percent) and in engi-neering (8.6 percent) reported slightly higher dependence on personal resources than those in the physical sciences.

20. Most of this consists of federal research dollars spent through the uni-versity and is identified by the Ph.D.'s as university, not federal, moneys.

21. The INA covers Puerto Rico and the U.S. Virgin Islands; international

migration to Puerto Rico is minimal and, although the Virgin Islands once had a controversial temporary worker program, that matter was resolved long ago. While there are universities in Puerto Rico, the Virgin Islands, and Guam, I have not encountered any discussion of the foreign student programs as a problem on any of these islands. CNMI and American Samoa do not have four-year colleges and, besides, they have much more rigorous deportation policies than the mainland, so, if they have problems with foreign students, they presumably do something about it.

22. The CNMI Governor, Froilan Tenorio, is making a much stronger effort to limit the abuses in the nonimmigrant program than his predecessors, but he wants CNMI to continue to make immigration decisions.

23. The imbalance of power between the citizen population and the guest workers in CNMI is more like the situation in the Trucial Sheikdoms than it is on the U.S. mainland. For instance, there are frequent stories in the local press of Chamorro families *on welfare* hiring (and failing to pay) nonimmigrant servants (see, for example: Phillips 1995). Governor Tenorio has been trying to end this practice.

24. Adapted from North 1995:171–73.

25. One potential problem, of course, is that mass users of H-1Bs will seek to camouflage their activities by creating subsidiary corporations, assigning workers to subcontractors, and the like.

REFERENCES

Bratsberg, B. 1995. The Incidence of Non-return Among Foreign Students in the United States. *Economics of Education Review* 14 (December):373–84.

Commission on Agricultural Workers. 1992. *Report of the Commission on Agricultural Workers*. Washington, DC: Available from the U.S. Commission on Immigration Reform.

Commonwealth of Australia. 1994. *Student Entry to Australia*. (PT981i September). Canberra.

Heylin, M. 1997. Job Situation for Chemists Takes a Turn for the Better. American Chemical Society Web Site http://www.pubs.acs.org.

Institute of International Education (IIE). 1992. *Open Doors 1991–1992*. New York: IIE.

Interpreter Releases. 1995a. DOL Reaches Settlement in H-1B Enforcement Action: ALJ Confirms Notice Requirements. (September 18):1261–64.

———. 1995b. Labor Department Publishes Final LCA Regulations. (January 3):1–4.

Leibowitz, A. 1994. *Temporary Entrants: The U.S. Nonimmigrant Structure*.

Washington, DC: Department of Labor, Bureau of International Labor Affairs.

National Research Council (NRC). 1993. *Summary Report 1991: Doctorate Recipients from United States Universities.* Washington, DC: National Academy Press.

North, D. 1991. *IRCA Did Not Do Much to the Labor Market: A Los Angeles County Case Study (Immigration Policy and Research Working Paper 10).* Washington, DC: Department of Labor, Bureau of International Labor Affairs.

———. 1995. *Soothing the Establishment: The Impact of Foreign-Born Scientists and Engineers on America.* Lanham, MD: University Press of America.

Papademetriou, D., and Yale-Loehr, S. 1995. Putting the National Interest First: Rethinking the Selection of Skilled Immigrants. *Interpreter Releases* (October 30):1473–80.

Phillips, D. 1995. No Maid for Welfare Recipients. *Saipan Tribune* (October 13):5.

USA Today. 1995. Foreign Students Pump Up Economy. (November 9).

Chapter 4

Nonimmigrant Visa Policy of the United States

CHARLES B. KEELY

The use of nonimmigrant visas by foreigners to reside and work legally in the United States has burgeoned in the last decade. Further, the interconnections between nonimmigrant visas—including educational, training, and occupational categories—and permanent residence is widely noted, the object of criticism, and a topic of recent legislative initiatives in the Senate.

The objectives of this analysis are to provide: (1) perspectives about the history, interconnections, and implications of current nonimmigrant visa policy; (2) criteria for developing nonimmigrant visa policy for contemporary realities, and (3) an outline of a nonimmigrant policy.[1]

PERSPECTIVES ON NONIMMIGRANT VISA POLICY

The interrelations between nonimmigrant and immigrant visas. It is easy to forget that current views about nonimmigrant visa policy and practice were not always the conventional wisdom. For example, during discussions of the 1965 amendments to the Immigration and Nationality Act of 1952 (the McCarran-Walter Act), the connections between educational and labor-related nonimmigrant visas on the one hand and permanent immigration on the other was not a major issue. The concept that nonimmigrant and immigrant visas for occupational skills should be seen as a whole, rather than two separate spheres of activity, was not part of the discussion 30 years ago. This is not such a surprise. The level of globalization of the economy and of firms[2] and the extent of international labor markets were in their infancy compared to today. In addition, temporary labor in the mid-1960s still meant unskilled, primarily agricultural labor. The United States ended the *bracero* program in 1964. In that context, temporary laborers hardly conjured up images of managers developing overseas markets for new products or researchers for communication technology.

When the 1965 Act replaced national origins with the visa preferences as the dominant selection criteria, little thought was given to the interconnections among student visas, exchange visitor visas, labor-related nonimmigrant visas, and immigrant visas based on occupational skills. That is not to say that absolutely no connections were noted. For example, a two-year return requirement was mandated for J-visa holders in order to avoid distorting the intent of exchange programs to train professionals in the context of development aid. In addition, the extent of adjustment cases among legal immigrants became a matter of comment, as if in some way adjustment, as opposed to first-time entry, was a perverse way to become an immigrant to the United States. In fact, in the past it was necessary for some immigrant visa recipients to leave the United States and travel to another country to pick up a visa and then go through the fiction of entering the country as a "new entrant" (and not a visa adjuster).

Now, when it is commonplace to note the interconnections between nonimmigrant and immigrant visa categories, the odor of corruption attached to visa adjustment persists. The implication is that it is not right if the proportion of adjustments versus new entries is "too high." The justification for this bias is not articulated, but the transformation of a statistic into a substantive conclusion about the national interest persists, even among informed and intelligent observers.

Another instance of noting the connections between nonimmigrant and immigrant visas was in the context of "brain drain" discussions.[3] The main focus was on the recruitment of highly skilled immigrants, but it was sometimes noted that the recruitment often took place among foreign students trained in developed countries rather than recruitment of advanced professionals in their own country.[4]

Despite instances of making connections between nonimmigrant and immigrant policy, the linkages had little practical impact on policy development in the period immediately following the end of the national origins quota system and the emergence of the preference system as the dominant mechanism for immigrant visa distribution.

Labor certification, the adversarial model, and the growth of the organized immigration bar. The 1965 Immigration Act had a profound effect on judgments about the consequences for the American labor force of immigration based on occupational skills. The 1965 Act changed labor certification from a passive to an active program. Under the 1952 Immigration and Nationality Act, persons admitted under a labor preference from an oversubscribed country were subject to review by the Secretary of Labor only if there was a complaint or if a single employer petitioned for 25 or more visa applicants. In high-quota countries like the United Kingdom, Ireland, and Germany, no review was necessary because there was no need to have recourse to the preference system to gain access to easily available visas. In short, in the very few cases where the preference system even came into play in oversubscribed countries, an occupational preference applicant could enter unless the Secretary of Labor took affirmative steps to prevent entry on the basis of a complaint or the large level of petitioning by a single employer.[5]

Under the 1965 amendments to immigration law, the emphasis of labor certification changed as the preference system became the dominant selection mechanism. A petitioner for a labor-related preference and all nonpreference applicants, including all Western Hemisphere applicants who were not the spouse or minor child of a citizen or legal permanent resident alien, could not receive a visa unless the Secretary of Labor approved via the labor certification process. The support of organized labor for immigration reform leading to the 1965 Act was obtained by inclusion of a labor certification process that required approval by the Secretary of Labor before a visa could be issued for any nonfamily immigrant visa. The labor certification process introduced in the 1965 Act institutionalized anxiety about the impact of immigration on the labor force. Dimensions of the economy were pitted against one another in an adversarial way, as if labor force development is a zero sum game. Any help to meet employers' felt needs was presumed to be achievable, albeit usually at the expense of U.S. workers. However, this anxiety was focused only on immigrant visas and did not extend to nonimmigrant visa practices.

One result of this innovation was the expansion of the organized immigration bar. Labor certification cemented the practices surrounding labor-related migration into an adversarial relationship. The role of lawyers in immigration proceedings grew tremendously, initially around administrative processes related to labor certification. The organized bar led the charge to introduce the L visa (intracompany transferees) in 1970 as a "noncontroversial amendment" to deal with the virtually undisputed needs of multinational corporations to engage in management trainee programs, management internationalization, and so on in order to open new markets. The rhetoric reflected a view that these were cases of "real" need. These were serious corporations that did not throw money away frivolously on international moves of key personnel. They were not sleazy schemers trying to circumvent the intent of the law and hurt American workers. In effect, the justifications of the purported need for L visas reinforced the perception of a need for strong vigilance about labor-related visas.[6]

The immigration process was progressively captured by the legal profession. In addition, corporations, educational and nonprofit research institutions, and other organizations developed trade associations regarding international personnel. No longer was immigration to the United States a matter of filling out forms and producing documents to prove marriage, educational achievement, or other bases for petitioner status. Not just employers, but private voluntary agencies increasingly provided legal services as a basic need of their clients to navigate an adversarial bureaucracy. Refugee admissions likewise became enmeshed in the culture of the legal profession. Lawyers are deemed a virtual necessity in presenting an asylum petition.

The adversarial process, dominated by attorneys on both sides, is now so ingrained that it is virtually naive to suggest that it could be otherwise. Perhaps it cannot, given what we have done in the last three decades. But it was not always so. Despite the jokes, there is, of course, nothing wrong with lawyers, per se. On the other hand, it is not an unalloyed benefit to transform civic interactions and citizens' petitions into legal battles, with the culture of the adversarial system dictating procedures and behavior.

The presumption of labor self-sufficiency. Like it or not, the assumptions surrounding immigrant and nonimmigrant petitioning for labor-related entrants are that applicants and employer sponsors are suspect. Even if honest, their petitions remain questionable because of a presumed harm of immigration based on labor skills to the U.S. labor force in general and to vulnerable American workers in particular. A presumption persists that a country, particularly a populous country like the United States, is or should be self-sufficient in regard to labor. The assumption of labor autarky is compounded by a view of the labor force as static, a fixed pie. Immigrants presumably take places that Americans can, or should be able to, fill if only employers would do their part to recruit properly and to create opportunity.

Questioning these assumptions is suspect as self-serving propaganda on behalf of employers. To suggest that immigrant workers may produce jobs is sometimes judged, in the most charitable phrasing, as wishful thinking. But clearly, foreigners who install and train American workers on the use and maintenance of advanced knitting machinery, for example, maintain jobs in clothes manufacturing. An American equivalent is U.S. personnel of advanced aircraft residing temporarily overseas to train others in maintenance of American jet aircraft. If General Motors (GM) sponsors 25 German engineers/designers to assist in product development for the German auto market, those immigrant workers may help produce many American jobs to manufacture components for cars destined for the German market with its particularly stringent performance demands about cars. Is it good policy to say that such migration takes jobs from American engineers/auto designers and should be prohibited or should the focus be on the particular talents and familiarity with the demanding criteria of German auto buyers and the potential for U.S. exports if GM autos command more of the German market?

It is difficult to adjust uninformed perspectives on the issues of job creation, export development, and other aspects of economic policy and their relation to international labor recruitment. Even if a more balanced perspective received some attention, difficulties would persist in changing viewpoints now so deeply ingrained in public policy, in the legal practice of an organized immigration bar in the public and private sector, and in policy rhetoric.

Regulating international migration, subsidies, and free trade in services. Government regulation of markets often results in subsidization of segments of a society. Tariff and nontariff barriers to protect domestic firms are obvious examples. Inefficient, as well as nascent, industries are protected from foreign competition. Even though free trade is a generally accepted principle, the mention of protection for nascent industry indicates that free trade is not an absolute principle.

Regulating immigration and the access of foreign labor also is justified as a protection of a domestic market: labor. Regulating international migration has the economic effect of subsidizing domestic labor.

To note this does not lead to a conclusion that, by analogy to free trade, limiting immigration is undesirable. People are not goods and their entry into a society as actors is quite different than importing shoes, vegetables, or automobiles. Freer mobility of labor is politically unacceptable and justifiably so if a government is to protect vulnerable segments of the labor force. Adjustment to freer trade (as for example in reaction to NAFTA in all three signatory countries) is often costly, even brutal, for affected workers. Freer movement of labor would be more so, especially for the least adaptable and less skilled. Free movement of labor has been agreed to and endured only in the context of economic agreements between economically advanced countries of relative economic parity (specifically in the EC/EU and the Nordic countries). Free labor movement provisions in economic agreements among less developed countries either have not been implemented or have been abandoned. To note the political impracticality of free labor movement or the persuasive arguments against such a policy, except in special circumstances, does not negate the fact that it supplies a subsidy to domestic labor.

The issue of labor mobility becomes complicated when the topic of trade in services is discussed. Trade in services often requires the presence of a person to provide the service, whether high-level management consultation, artistic performance, or on-site installation and training for specialized equipment. There are other services that are more flexible regarding performance sites. Take as an example a simple and relatively unskilled service function: data entry. The service can be performed by American workers in the United States. The function can be performed by imported workers in the United States. The service can be exported to a foreign country to be performed by foreign workers in their own country and the transformed data electronically transported to the United States, bypassing even the importation of a data tape or other physical product containing the transformed knowledge resulting from data entry.

It is a small leap to the example of computer programming that has been not only a thorn for nonimmigrant policy and practice, but also a controversial topic for U.S.-based firms regarding employment practice.[7] When Seatrain Corporation moved programming operations to India, U.S. workers lost jobs. Intel justifies movement of some programming operations overseas as a way to allow U.S. workers to engage in the cutting-edge development that requires their advanced skills and justifies their higher pay in a globally competitive environment. The savings in routine programming, the company argues, allows investment in the more expensive R&D work by American workers. If a company wins a contract to develop customized programming services and uses B-visa workers to perform programming routine tasks, is that an abuse or a creative use of existing law to meet an unanticipated situation that combines the elements of contracting out and knowledge-based services? Is it any more of an abuse than the less controversial increased use by foreign-based corporations of E visas for intracompany transferees, a visa category with distinct advantages over the L visa for the firm (but not necessarily for the employees and their family)? Whatever one's opinion about what policy should be in such situations, an honest answer would acknowledge that the law and policy did not anticipate the business situation or the business response that combined the general move to subcontracting and the importation of short-term labor to supply a knowledge-based service.

Regardless of one's opinion about profit versus greed and obligations to shareholders versus obligations to fellow citizens and the country that provides the opportunities to prosper as a firm, the complications for immigration policy introduced by the relation between trade in knowledge-based services and migration, especially when combined with contracting rather than staff expansion, are real. There is no simple solution that maximizes trade in services with virtually no migration. Conversely, open migration will not translate into maintaining a competitive technological edge. A one-size-fits-all policy on temporary labor is an anachronism that ignores the reality of contemporary economics and the process of wealth production and job creation in knowledge-based industries.

High-tech economies, increasing returns and international migration. Dominant economic thinking assumes diminishing returns. The ideas about investment and the creation of wealth were developed at a time when agriculture, extraction of resources, and bulk-manufacture dominated the economy. Diminishing returns meant that the more you did something, the harder it became and the less rewarding it got. As coal was extracted, for example, it became harder to find and take out good coal. As coal became more expensive, hydroelectric became competitive. Coal and hydroelectric competed for shares of the energy market. In such a situation, economic theory and methods predicted an equilibrium and the relative prices of competing energy sources. There is one equilibrium solution until another energy source is found or until the law of diminishing returns leads to one source being so expensive that it commands no market share. At that point, a new equilibrium is needed. The context is changed. High-tech economies are driven more by "congealed knowledge" than by "congealed resources." High-tech products include pharmaceuticals, telecommunications, computer software, aircraft, and electronics. In these high-tech economies the main costs are up front. The cost of production per unit becomes cheaper as volume increases, not more expensive. The first version of Windows 95 cost perhaps about one-half billion dollars. The second cost about $20 for the disk, the manual, and the packaging. The more units of Windows 95 that Microsoft sells, the more it can make per unit. This is an example of increasing, rather than diminishing, returns.[8]

A characteristic of knowledge-based industries is that they enjoy protection for the conversion of their knowledge creations in copyright and patent law and policy. In addition, in these industries, history counts. The first to achieve a discovery often sets a standard that results in other technologies not being pursued or adopted. First discovery or first invention gives a tremendous market advantage. A discovery, if registered, gets some protection that allows bringing a product to market. If that product sets a standard, the return is even greater. Microsoft's advantage with the DOS operating system for computers and the return to the developers of the VHS format that bested the Beta format for home video are clear. Recently, developers of competing standards for compact disks agreed to a common standard that allowed them all to participate in the rewards of a single format for CDs to carry audio, data, and video content.[9]

While the first to market will not necessarily set the standard and reap the rewards of increasing returns, being first provides an advantage. Many examples illustrate that becoming a standard gives tremendous market advantage, if not monopoly. Videotape format and computer operating systems, already noted, are two often-cited examples. Once a standard is adopted, other technology, inherently as good, goes undeveloped, often forever or until its benefit for some other task becomes clear. The adoption of the internal combustion over the steam engine is an example of the neglect of one technology, steam, because another became the standard. Sequential processing rather than parallel processing continues to dominate in commercially produced computers, although advantages of parallel processing for some complicated tasks has led to renewed interest in that technology.[10]

For knowledge-based industries, time is of the essence. Both technology development and product development have an important element of timeliness to them, along with the job creation, export growth, and other consequences of standard setting in a product area if the financial rewards are to be reaped. In those environments, personnel recruitment for R&D, product design, international marketing, and so on do not operate on an assumption that labor is to a large extent substitutable.

Arguments about immigration and labor often operate at a level similar to the development of classical economics in which a worker was a worker and in most cases substitutions were available. This undergirded the assumption that most countries, and especially those with large populations, were and could be labor self-sufficient, except in extraordinary circumstances like total mobilization for war. Thus, in the United States, when Turner published his thesis about the closing of the frontier, arguments for immigrants to fill up the land diminished. When industrial unemployment appeared, the need of immigrant labor was disputed. Contemporary proponents of immigration reduction point to the difference between today and the heyday of immigration into the United States. The labor needs of a postindustrial economy, where intellectual skills are more important, differ from an economy in which agriculture, infrastructure building, and heavy manufacturing dominate and labor is more readily substitutable.

The notion that labor self-sufficiency can be presumed for an economy, particularly one characterized by a heavy reliance on knowledge-based sectors, is questionable. A postindustrial economy needs few or no foreign unskilled and lower-skilled workers. That does not preclude a need for those with very high skills or specialized experience. Quick access to advanced human capital is important for timely development of technology, given the protection of patents and copyright, as well as the relative advantage of early entry into the market for products with competing standards. Similarly, effective marketing in different cultures requires collaboration of international personnel who know various markets and the product line. Perhaps it is necessary to rethink what we mean by labor and our notions about how the economy returns profit on investment, creates jobs, and gets access to personnel. To dismiss calls for migration policy and law that responds to international labor markets as simply the desire of corporations for cheap, even if highly skilled labor, may be a mistake.

U.S. higher education as service export industry and its relation to immigration. The American college and university system is a valuable service export that has downstream spinoffs as alumni/ae of U.S. schools move into responsible positions in the private and public sectors of their societies. More immediately, college and especially postbaccalaureate degree holders provide a supply of potential immigrants based on the advanced or scarce skills that they acquire.

The acceptability of linking international educational programs and nonimmigrant and immigrant policy is questioned for three reasons. First, the objective of providing education in a context of aid for development conflicts with allowing adjustment from a student visa status to a nonimmigrant or immigrant status based on skills. The view makes little distinction between students sponsored by their governments, international organizations, or U.S. scholarship programs aimed at skills for development and independently financed students, even from advanced countries.[11] Second, a cloud hangs over all adjustments of status, as if they pervert the migration system or indicate devious intentions. Third, the assumption of labor self-sufficiency leads to questioning why U.S. students are not in the programs that lead to skill qualifications for nonimmigrant or immigrant status. U.S. educational capacity seems to feed a supply-side process. Educational programs cater to foreign students (and may not be otherwise viable). The availability of these students to industry leads to reliance on recruiting foreign students, with the justification that Americans with the requisite skills are unavailable.

While educational programs that enroll high proportions of foreign students can be self-serving for both the universities involved and employers, that is not necessarily the case.[12] Recourse to foreign graduates is not inherently negative. There is no a priori reason to apologize for seeing foreign graduates as a pool for the United States of potential immigrants or temporary workers with very high skills. What perhaps is needed in regard to nonimmigrant and immigrant visa programs is a balance between control and facilitation mentalities. Disturbing development aid goals makes no sense, for example, but neither does a requirement that foreign degree holders from American universities leave the country for three to five years in order to eliminate their recruitment as nonimmigrant workers or immigrants. Such a policy overlooks other benefits, long-and short-term, of an active education export sector for the U.S. economy and international relations.

Conclusion. These disparate comments about the history, characteristics, and assumptions that accompany discussion of nonimmigrant visas do not command universal assent. They are presented to stimulate discussion and to question many of the assumptions and much of the conventional wisdom surrounding nonimmigrant visa policy discussions that pass for facts. As a result, these observations do not translate effortlessly into a nonimmigrant worker policy. They provide guides for criteria to sustain a nonimmigrant policy that recognizes that competing interests cannot be simultaneously met and that the structure and operation of the economy and labor force have changed and continue to develop. The next section outlines criteria to use in the development and evaluation of proposed nonimmigrant visa policy for occupationally-related reasons.

CRITERIA FOR DEVELOPING A NONIMMIGRANT VISA POLICY

Acknowledge competing interests and conflicting values. International recruitment of labor may have differential impacts on different parts of the U.S. economy and even on different segments of the labor force. General Motors recruitment of German engineers/auto designers can be used as an example. Suppose that the request to recruit 25 Germans was denied and that GM went ahead with product development to increase German market share with U.S. engineers. In that case 25 "American" jobs were saved. Suppose, however, that the result of that product development was lower penetration of the German market than would have taken place if the German personnel were allowed into the United States and that, as a result, 400 U.S.-based jobs were not created to manufacture components for cars destined for German retail. There are competing interests between 25 engineering jobs and 400 manufacturing jobs, as well as lower U.S. exports, lower reputation for U.S. products as well engineered in the important German market, and lower profit for GM. Any policy on international personnel and the immigration system must acknowledge that such trade-offs are inherent in such a system, that judgement is required, that solutions cannot always be legislated in advance.

Decision-making processes authorized in legislation, however, can tip the balance regarding which interests and values are likely to be favored. Quite simply, export promotion might be favored if "international personnel recruitment" decisions were in the Commerce Department rather than protecting American jobs by "labor certification" decisions remaining in the Labor Department. Note how even the phrases in quotation marks in the previous sentence put a different spin on a decision whether to permit issuance of an immigrant or nonimmigrant visa based on occupational skills. To pretend that no one will be advantaged or hurt by how the process is organized or what decisions are made is wrongheaded. There will be winners and losers regardless of the proposals made or the policy finally adopted and implemented in legislation and regulation. Those winners and losers are not confined to capital versus labor. In the GM engineer example, the creation of 400 manufacturing jobs is sacrificed for 25 higher-skilled, probably nonunion, higher-payed, and most likely less-disadvantaged U.S. college graduates. Deflecting foreigners from the labor force is not as clear-cut as sometimes presented.

Set labor-related migration to meet domestic goals as the context for nonimmigrant visa policy and integrate policy for visa categories within the nonimmigrant domain and between immigrant and nonimmigrant categories. The criterion of recognizing and addressing interrelations is founded on the contention that all immigrant and nonimmigrant admissions for labor force reasons ought to be included in a unified policy. The controlling reality is labor force recruitment and insertion, not administrative and legal distinctions between visa categories and immigration statuses. The recent growth in the use of nonimmigrant visas and the underutilization of occupationally-based immigrant visas under IMMACT 90 legislation indicate that recruitment behavior by the private sector and legislative assumptions vary. Legal distinctions drawn for administrative and legislative purposes have been regarded as set in concrete. The adversarial process ingrained in immigration practice has not resulted in a cooperative and collaborative fashioning of legislation in which government, employers, and labor contribute. Collaboration does not imply agreement on all issues. But policy based on assumptions made by members of Congress, their staffs, and nonbusiness "experts" does not guide international labor recruitment practices. The result of the adversarial process is that employers and their lawyers analyze legislation and devise ways to use it or to get around it to meet their objectives. This is done not just by marginal employers. This is mainstream practice; everybody involved in immigration policy knows it.

What ought to guide policy development is the need of the economy for both timely availability of certain skills and for protection of U.S. workers. Those needs can be translated into various mechanisms for permitting recruitment of noncitizens, when appropriate, in nonimmigrant and immigrant statuses, including adjustment of status. The movement from one status to another ought to be based on meeting labor force goals—including labor protection—not on an arbitrary concept about the propriety of adjustment of status by foreign students, intracompany transferees, or any other nonimmigrant or immigrant. Even so radical a departure from current practice as requiring work experience under a nonimmigrant visa as a condition for obtaining a labor-related immigrant visa ought not to be rejected on principle.

The unbundling of family and employment visa preferences in the 1990 Immigration Act eases the process of tackling skills-based entry in its entirety as the domain to be addressed. The configuration of immigrant and nonimmigrant statuses based on skills becomes a tool to achieve goals, not separate domains in which the immigration status dominates the labor force goals.

Regard adjustment of status as an opportunity, rather than as a restraint. The design of a labor-related program ought not to try to minimize (nor maximize) adjustment of status. The capacity to adjust ought to be seen as neutral in itself and used to the extent that it may further the policy goals of accessing foreign labor at minimal harm to U.S. workers. Adjustment from a student, training, or exchange visa ought not to be excluded outright. Particular conditions may attach to some student visa holders, depending on their sponsorship, for example. Entire visa classes as currently configured should not be excluded.

Distinguish between knowledge-based workers performing nonroutine tasks that result in otherwise unavailable goods (products, exports, technology, scientific knowledge, etc.) and other workers. If the concepts of increasing returns and congealed knowledge make sense, then workers who perform nonroutine knowledge-based services merit particular attention. Current immigration policy acknowledges the exceptional worker and people of world-class talent. A computer programmer of exceptional creativity demonstrated by prior output and reputation is not a run-of-the-mill programmer with a B.S. degree. The latter ought not be allowed into the United States on nonimmigrant or immigrant visas to compete with competent U.S. programmers. To be sure programming, even of routine kinds, is no mean skill, but it is widely available in this country. A superstar, however, may merit a visa. Similarly, the United States has many trained chefs and there is no reason to recruit even specialty chefs for a particular cuisine. Trained chefs can receive the additional training to perform tasks for whatever cuisine is desired. This does not preclude the truly world-class chef from occasionally receiving a visa.

One can multiply examples. The criterion should be clear. Knowledge-based services of a nonroutine nature ought to result in visas. By implication, routine, knowledge-based services and personal services should not command U.S. immigrant and nonimmigrant visas, except in the rarest cases of truly world-class practitioners.

View higher education as a labor resource. If the policy focus is on labor force needs and both nonimmigrant and immigrant visas are seen as instruments to achieve policy goals, then the service export sector of higher education ought to be seen as a resource. It is counterproductive to adopt an arbitrary policy that any foreign student ought to be required to return to her or his own country. It makes no sense to erect barriers to entry into the U.S. labor force for any foreign student graduate of a U.S. university that are greater than for a foreign graduate of a foreign degree program. All foreign students are not enrolled in U.S. educational institutions for economic development goals. All foreign students are not supported by government scholarships. If there are problems or abuses in visa adjustment from a student or training visa, the solution is not wholesale discrimination against foreign students. Permitting adjustment does not imply a right to adjustment or the suppression of such other goals as protection of domestic labor.

Do not rely on immigrant and nonimmigrant visas for labor-related migration as a revenue-generating scheme. The concept of imposing a tax on applicants or sponsors for labor-related visas is government extortion. If the Commission or the Congress thinks that a visa for labor-related migration is detrimental, it should not make it available to those that can afford an official bribe. To pretend that such funds are needed to underwrite training or retraining programs by the federal government, after years and billions of dollars on training, is a sham. The problem of black youth unemployment, for example, has not been lack of funds for youth training. Similarly, a pot of money funded by a fee for a labor visa will hardly translate into higher enrollment of disadvantaged American youth in nursing programs. To implicitly promise such results from a fee for a labor visa is disingenuous. Further, in proposed legislation the Department of Labor has unfettered discretion over the use of such funds for DOL programs, including for example, summer jobs programs. As worthy as summer jobs programs may be, their connection to a fee for labor visas as a means to reduce reliance on foreign labor or to increase domestic preparation for high-skilled jobs is charitably described as a stretch.

INTERNATIONAL LABOR MIGRATION POLICY OUTLINE

A design for nonimmigrant visa policy ought to be couched in the wider idea of a policy for controlled recruitment of needed and useful noncitizen labor that does not harm the domestic labor force. The "do no harm" injunction has to be understood in a way that allows for some cases of adjustment in the U.S. labor force. However, displaced workers must be placed in equivalent paying jobs with all relocation costs paid and new jobs must result if the visa is to be granted.

A characteristic of labor visa policy ought to be a continuation of labor certification to assess that the foreign workers are complementary or, if replacements, that they nevertheless produce more jobs because of the special skills of the incumbents and that displaced workers get new, equivalent jobs. Certification should continue to ascertain that wages and standards are not undercut.

A new balance must be struck between labor force protection and enhancement of the economy through judicious recruitment and use of noncitizen labor. If decision makers are incapable of accepting that no country on the cutting edge of competitive, high-tech industry is labor self-sufficient, then this set of presentations will fall on deaf ears. If decision makers think it impossible to design regulations that distinguish among workers and their capacity to create jobs or reject the idea that all workers are not equal in their contribution to job creation, wealth production, or potential contributions, then a one-size-fits-all policy should be adopted that fundamentally limits all labor migration to a minimum.

Confine restriction of adjustment of status to achieving articulated goals. Conversely, permit adjustment of status within nonimmigrant categories and to immigrant categories, unless a specific goal dictates otherwise. For example, require students, trainees, or exchange visitors sponsored by their own government, the United States, or multilateral organizations and agencies (e.g., UN agency scholarships or fellowships) with funds meant to develop skills for development to provide evidence of work in their home country for a number of years before becoming eligible for adjustment of status to a work-related immigrant visa.

Eliminate distinctions in nonimmigrant visas for intracorporate transfer between U.S.-based and foreign companies. This may require analysis of trade and investment treaties to renegotiate provisions conforming to the realities of global firms. Broader international discussion of this issue may be needed in multilateral and even nongovernmental forums to develop common understandings and practices about international migration in the contemporary world.

Limit an immigrant visa for occupational skills to persons whose skills are unavailable in the United States, or who have a demonstrable level of attainment that is recognized as world class, or who have a combination of skills and experiences and a connection to a corporation that justifies working in the United States as part of a career advancement that is a normal business practice. Do not impose fees on the immigrant or sponsor. No specific recommendation regarding annual allotments is made.

Require nonimmigrant labor visa applicants to demonstrate competence or experience unavailable in the United States or involvement in normal corporate career development for intracompany transferees who have a connection with the company for a year or more. Allow sponsoring institutions training and exchange visas for promising talents, demonstrated by scholastic records, letters of established referees, and ordinary review procedures by the sponsoring institution. Competitively chosen postdoctoral fellows are an example.

Do not bar nonimmigrant visa holders who develop a level of expertise to qualify for an immigrant visa from adjustment by the mere fact of their having held a nonimmigrant visa.

Evaluate the time limits on nonimmigrant, labor-related visas by analysis of industry practice, the history of prior nonimmigrant, labor-related visa holders (what proportion adjusted to permanent resident, went to a non-U.S. position in the corporate sponsor, etc.), and practice by other countries. The issue of time limits requires attention not only to length, but also to renewals and recertification.

In concert with other countries, move to a policy that permits an accompanying spouse a work permit in the United States. Spousal work prohibitions are anachronistic and, given current realities, more often than not sexist in their impact.

Have one immigrant visa category for occupationally-related applicants in a labor-related visa package that incorporates nonimmigrant and immigrant visas. This would require sponsorship by the employer and labor certification about availability or the world-class credentials and prevailing wage and conditions issues as is done currently. Nonimmigrant visas would have:

1. *Students,* perhaps divided into (a) government or multilateral agency sponsorship as a development program and, therefore, a limit on adjustment and (b) nonsponsored;
2. *Exchange visitors,* again with an (a) and a (b) category for governmental, development-oriented sponsorship related to adjustment;
3. *Intracompany tranferees,* eliminating the current distinction involved in L and E visas;
4. *Temporary visitors for business,* the current B visa, with a prohibition against performing work as part of a joint venture or subcontract except to manage the joint venture or job for the B visa period; and
5. *Distinguished workers who are eligible for an immigrant visa but do not wish or require one* (similar to the current H-visa holder who may be recruited by a new employer but have a limited-time horizon for work in the United States).

No changes are proposed in the current arrangements for performers and professional athletes, news media, representatives of international organizations, and so on. No limits ought to be imposed for nonimmigrant visas at the outset, but levels ought to be monitored and Congress encouraged to review and evaluate trends.

The general thrust of these proposals is that nonimmigrant visas be available for recruiting world-class people to take up a new position in the United States, for intracorporate transfers by current staff, for education and training, and for short-term business trips. Education, experience, and training in the United States may qualify a person for an immigrant visa and high attainment should qualify a person to become a permanent resident. Conversely, people with skills that can be reproduced easily or that are available in the United States should not be given visas. The labor force is protected by the retention of certification regarding availability, qualifications, and labor standards.

The attempt in this review and recommendations is to balance reasonable need and reasonable protection under current circumstances that include international recruitment as a normal and necessary aspect of international competitiveness. The United States should expect and demand reciprocal access from other countries. Access to the U.S. labor force should be limited to those whose skills are in short supply, who produce jobs, exports, and advances in the growth sectors of the economy in knowledge-based industry, and whose entry is useful because of reciprocal obligations regarding multinational corporations and keeping U.S. companies competitive. This view accepts the role of education and training as integral to knowledge-based industrial growth and competitiveness. At the same time, current procedures to protect the U.S. labor force should remain in place. People who would receive visas under these proposals not only would not harm the American labor force but would energize job creation through discovery and product development and opening of new markets to American goods and services.

NOTES

1. This chapter focuses on temporary visa categories that permit a visa holder legally to reside and work in the United States and on categories connected with formal education and training. Visitor visa holders (tourists) are not discussed.

2. In the 1960s, the focus was on multinational, rather than global, firms. The distinction is between a multinational firm still anchored in the country of its founding, but with operations in a variety of countries (e.g., Swiss Nestle, American Ford, German Siemans, Dutch Phillips, Canadian Seagrams) and a global firm in which the founding country connection becomes more and more tenuous. The decisions on investments, assets, accounting, and so on are made in a way the laws of the country mandate as a condition of business. A global firm is the logical outcome economically of multinational operations. An example of the problem of determining whether a firm is one or the other is

reflected in the difficulty in deciding what is an "American" automobile if content is the criterion. Most examples of what were considered multinational firms would now be seen as global firms.

3. Brain drain rhetoric persists even though internationalist arguments have all but prevailed among economists. The idea that change of immigration policies in developed countries could appreciably affect the labor force development policies of developing countries, much less affect economic performance in any but the most marginal and indirect way, has gone the way of doctrines about centrally planned economies.

4. It is somewhat ironic that the phrase "brain drain" originally was used to describe the United Kingdom's post-World War II loss of physicians and other professionals to the United States.

5. Recall that the preference system hardly affected the vast majority of immigrants under the national origins quota system maintained in the 1952 McCarran-Walter Act. Under that law, the overwhelmingly dominant criterion for admission to the United States was place of birth. All else paled in comparison to the importance of national origin for an American immigrant visa. Continued assertions that the 1965 Act changed the emphasis from occupational criteria to family criteria in the preference system are beside the point and mislead. National origins so dominated choice of immigrants that the preference system had virtually no impact on the selection of immigrants under the McCarran-Walter Act. To note the change in the preference systems of 1952 and 1965 is formally correct but irrelevant for the practical effect on policy outcomes.

6. Immigration law prescribes that the consular officer must presume all applicants for visas, including visitor or other temporary visas, are actually intending immigrants. The next step to a presumption that all petitions and statements, whether made by a U.S. citizen sponsor or an alien applicant, are fraudulent is not such a huge step.

7. An important aspect of the controversy about computer programmers entering the United States, especially on H1-B visas, is the spreading practice in the American economy of contracting out. Like leasing of equipment, contracting out reduces investment costs and allows for flexibility regarding labor costs. Workers need not be added to the payroll. Lesser skilled workers do not benefit from spread effects of the more costly salaries and benefits that large firms, which have a spectrum of skills in their work force, usually pay. A janitor in an IBM facility, for example, benefits from the spillover of IBM practices in ways not available to a counterpart in a janitorial company that employs primarily unskilled workers. Contracting out exists independently of immigration. Methods to lower labor costs, which is another way of saying recruitment of cheap labor, is not confined to importing labor. Combining contracting out

and foreign labor may maximize labor cost cutting. To block low-wage labor importation, however, will not end or counter the independent effects of contracting out for goods, equipment, or services.

8. Economists trying to develop theory and methods to deal with assumptions of increasing returns and the possibility of more than a single equilibrium solution are dealing, in technical jargon, in dynamic stochastic discrete choice models, sometimes more simply referred to as path dependent models. The discussion in this section relies on a profile of one of the principal economists (Arthur 1994a; 1994b) in this area.

9. Ironically, the VHS will decline and eventually go the way of 78 rpm phonograph records to be replaced by the disk, smaller than the old Beta video disks and not exactly the same technology, but a disk nonetheless. Note also that the triumph of the disk means that digital tapes for audio reproduction will not be widely marketed.

10. The pioneer ENIAC computer was a parallel processing machine.

11. Proposals have been made requiring foreign students to return home for one to three years, making no distinction on source of funding.

12. Some of the characterizations of higher education in the debate over foreign students and immigration have the flavor of the criticisms leveled at private voluntary organizations (PVOs) in the refugee field in the early 1980s. PVOs often performed resettlement services for the federal government when people were admitted as parolees and before any Congressional authorizations to pay for those services. In effect, the private sector advanced money with no guarantee of repayment in every case. When some PVOs developed contingency funds through savings from prior grants, they were accused of being "Refugee, Inc.," as if PVOs and their parent organizations were getting fat at the public trough. The university in western tradition has always being internationalist. Scholars were and are recruited for talent, regardless of nationality. The most cursory overview of American experience, especially in this century, confirms the continuation of that tradition. It has been beneficial for basic national defense and the economy. Similarly, students have been international. The University of Paris student body in the Middle Ages was organized by "nationes," broad groupings by area of Europe from which they came. Foreign students attend U.S. universities for many reasons besides development-related aid programs and many are not sponsored by government or multilateral organizations. To equate foreign student training with a new-found way for higher education to be self-serving is historically ignorant. A better case has to be made than mere notation of a correlation of foreign students in universities and recruitment by corporations to hand down an indictment of U.S. higher education. To prohibit recruitment of superstar engineering students from elite graduate schools by Raytheon or Motorola for advanced communications technology research as a way to counter degree mills in the private sector special-

izing in elementary computer programming or cosmetology is myopic. In the name of the national interest, such policy opposes the nation's true interests.

REFERENCES

Arthur, W. B. 1994a. Profile. *Bulletin of the Santa Fe Institute* (Winter):5–8.
————. 1994b. *Increasing Returns and Path Dependence in the Economy.* Ann Arbor: University of Michigan Press.

Part II

Workers

Chapter 5

The New High-Tech *Braceros*: Who Is the Employer? What Is the Problem?

MICHAEL P. SMITH

The California economy is undergoing basic changes as a result of rapid downsizing in the U.S. defense industry, a global corporate trend to restructure operations and become more flexible, the deployment of manufacturing and processing functions of the state's highly vaunted high-tech industry to other states and nations with weaker regulatory environments, a volatile economy, and growing job insecurity. These developments constitute a wider context helping to explain the anti-immigrant backlash now occurring in California and elsewhere. One facet of that backlash has been a call from diverse quarters, including environmental organizations, professional associations representing U.S. skilled workers, and grassroots anti-immigrant groups (see Bellinger 1993:69–70; Carey 1993) for a reexamination of 1990 changes in U.S. immigration law (IMMACT) that increased the number of highly skilled nonimmigrant workers that U.S. employers could hire for "temporary" periods of as many as six years under the H-1B visa provisions of current immigration law.

The political-economic trends now condensed under the rubric "global restructuring" (Feagin & Smith 1987:3–34; Dicken 1992) locally have produced an uneven, volatile, and fluctuating labor market demand for highly skilled professional and technical workers in the California economy of the 1990s. Existing empirical studies are few and none have been drawn with sufficient detail or categorical occupational focus to map precisely the impact on the skilled labor markets in the state's economy of the use of nonimmigrant workers drawn from the global workforce. To be sure, a central issue of concern to workers and federal and state regulatory agencies in California is the possibility that the presence of highly skilled foreign workers made available by current provisions of immigration law compounds an already unfavorable labor market for U.S. skilled workers. How well founded is this concern? This chapter seeks to separate this question from the wider questions of job loss caused by such other processes as growing corporate downsizing, defense industry restructuring, and the overproduction of scientists and engineers by U.S. universities.

The claim has been made that the use of nonimmigrant workers is a cause of both job displacement and wage depression among U.S. skilled workers. How valid is this claim? How does the answer vary by type of skilled occupation? What has been the impact of the employment of nonimmigrant skilled workers in the sector of the California economy that has been most heavily reliant on the use of H-1B temporary skilled workers since 1990, namely, the computer industry in Silicon Valley? This chapter seeks to shed light on each of these key questions.

The chapter is divided into four parts. The first section provides a contextual overview of the changing California economy. The second section details the study methods used in the larger qualitative research project from which this chapter is drawn. The body of the chapter then focuses on the central question raised in the title: ''The New High-Tech *Braceros*: Who is the Employer? What is the Problem?'' Finally, to underline the importance of investigating broad questions, such as immigrant labor displacement on a case-by-case basis, selected comparative data are presented to show that other employment sectors, in this instance university teaching and research and the biotechnology sector, operate quite differently from the computer sector and offer quite different answers to the questions at hand.

THE CHANGING ECONOMIC CONTEXT OF RECEPTION

As the California economy plunged in the early 1990s, people and businesses began leaving the state in unprecedented numbers. According to the California State Department of Finance, 600,000 Californians left the state in the fiscal year ending June 30, 1993. Every county in the state except San Francisco lost population. Two-thirds of the out migration occurred in the five-county Los Angeles metropolitan region, where defense cuts were most pronounced. Despite the declining economy and the overall out migration, 200,000 legal foreign immigrants entered California in the following fiscal year.

In Silicon Valley, the early 1990s was a period characterized by efforts by major employers in the computer industry to downsize, streamline, and outsource operations. According to industry analysts, this restructuring of operations was, in part, driven by the impact of defense cuts on the computer industry but also by such factors as: (1) the overall maturation of the industry; (2) a desire of firms to shift from the manufacture of mainframes to desktop computers; (3) the pressures of competition from new entrants into the global marketplace; and (4) an ensuing personal computer price war that cut deeply into profits. The chief labor market effect of these developments was to reduce opportunities for full-time employment in computer-related jobs in Silicon Valley.

An early strategy used by computer industry firms in the 1980s was to move low-wage manufacturing jobs offshore or to other states with weaker regulatory environments while retaining high-pay programming and engineering jobs for Silicon Valley. By the early 1990s, this approach was superseded by a newer computer industry strategy of relying more extensively in Silicon Valley itself on temporary employees, including foreign computer consultants, to perform an increasing number of project-specific operations. The downsizing of the permanent workforce resulting from these strategies allowed major computer manufacturers to shed thousands of permanent jobs in both Silicon Valley and worldwide. By the end of 1993, computer firms headquartered in Silicon Valley were able to cut between 15 and 25 percent of their permanent worldwide workforce while maintaining productivity, although not always market share.

Silicon Valley's Santa Clara County was one of the worst hit parts of Northern California throughout the period. The county's employment in computers and office machinery plunged from 73,600 in 1990 to 43,000 in September 1994. The shakeup of the computer industry labor market in Silicon Valley continued throughout 1994 as a major new round of mergers and acquisitions enabled firms, particularly in database software and on-line services, to reduce workers and return to profitability.

Paradoxically, industry analysts point out that the demand for software engineers in Silicon Valley was high throughout the downsizing period and continues to be high today. A recently released study by the public-private Joint Venture Silicon Valley Network points out that from 1989 through 1993, computer software engineering emerged as the region's biggest job generator (Sinton 1995). Software employment in Santa Clara County actually grew by 9,556 jobs during this period, although this growth did not compensate for the loss of 17,332 defense-related jobs and 11,775 semiconductor hardware jobs during the same period. This appears to be a result not simply of the shift from hardware to software development, but also a reflection of consistently high demand for *temporary* software engineers, programmers, and coders as companies laid off full-time employees.

The decline of the defense sector has been a related factor contributing to the erosion of high-skill, high-wage jobs in California. Clearly, the state has taken the brunt of the nation's defense layoffs, suffering 25 percent of all jobs lost nationally in the defense sector (National Commission for Economic Conversion and Disarmament 1994). Although the three metropolitan labor markets studied in the larger research project from which this study is drawn—Silicon Valley, the San Francisco Bay area, and greater Los Angeles—have been affected by defense downsizing, major defense and aerospace related layoffs and plant closures have been especially severe in Los Angeles because of the dependency of that region's economy on the military budget as a central engine of economic growth. Between 1989 and 1993, 240,000 jobs disappeared in Los Angeles county. The once seemingly recession-proof aerospace and electronics industries abruptly reversed course and the construction and real estate industries floundered with them. In 1993 alone, 110,000 high-wage, defense-related jobs were lost to the Los Angeles economy (Smith 1996).

The loss in California of highly skilled jobs through federal government budget cuts, corporate downsizing, and consolidations and mergers in the defense, electronics, and computer industries was paralleled by a major belt-tightening of the University of California and state college systems. This university downsizing was necessitated by cuts in state funding for higher education in the face of declining state government revenues produced by the prolonged recession. In California, the public university downsizing policy was characterized by the introduction of incentives to encourage early retirement of tenured faculty members, increasing reliance on temporary lecturers to teach some vacated courses, the cancellation of other courses, and an increase in both class sizes and the time required for students to complete their course requirements.

Among the rare exceptions to the adverse employment trends in California during the early 1990s were the biotechnology and health services sectors. In these sectors, skilled research and service jobs increased throughout the period, even in southern California.

INVESTIGATING NONIMMIGRANT EMPLOYMENT: STUDY METHODS

In a comprehensive qualitative field research study, commissioned by the U.S. Department of Labor (Smith & Ciepiela 1995:1–57), I directed a study team that investigated the process and efficacy of the Alien Labor Certification Program and the Temporary Worker Visa Programs used to bring foreign professionals into skilled labor markets in California. Our recently completed research focused on the computer software and hardware engineering industries in Silicon Valley and on the biological and chemical industries, universities, and medical centers in the San Francisco Bay Area and greater Los Angeles. These locations and employment categories were chosen because, in the two years preceding our study, our selected sample of employers in these regional labor markets, including private firms, universities, and medical centers, were found to have the highest numbers of Labor Condition Applications (LCAs), permanent labor certification applications, or both in the state of California. By this selection method, five skilled occupational sectors in California were found to rely heavily on foreign worker immigration programs in general and the H-1B visa category in particular. These included computer software and hardware engineering, electrical engineering, university teaching and research, biotechnology research and development, and medical research and services. Our larger qualitative ethnographic study generated substantial evidence concerning the nature and extent of job displacement by highly skilled foreign workers in each of these occupational sectors in California.

Qualitative and historical data for this study were gathered during 1994 and early 1995 primarily by conducting qualitative, open-ended interviews with all parties involved in the recruitment, employment, and regulation of foreign nonimmigrant skilled workers. Ethnographic interviews also were conducted with samples of both U.S. and nonimmigrant skilled workers affected by this employment process. Our overall sample thus included: U.S. employers; foreign workers; U.S. workers; officials from the Regional Office of the U.S. Department of Labor (DOL) and the Immigration and Naturalization Service (INS) immigration attorneys; and representatives of professional associations and unions whose members were impacted by the process. Our study goal was to compile a balanced set of viewpoints enabling us to assess the impact of the 1990 IMMACT legislation on the business and personnel practices of U.S. firms, on the employment opportunities of U.S. skilled workers, and on the selected U.S. labor markets during an ongoing period of global economic restructuring and economic recession and corporate and university downsizing in California.

Our study sample of *employers* included interviews with 58 individuals representing 37 employers in Northern and Southern California. These data were supplemented by twelve participant observation interviews conducted with all categories of employer at a two-day seminar in San Francisco sponsored by the American Council on International Personnel (1994) for employer immigration representatives. Employers thus comprised the largest and most diverse segment of our sample. Among these, the computer industry, which forms the central focus of this paper, was the most extensively and intensively investigated. Our computer industry sample included 39 individuals representing 22 computer and engineering firms and five computer consulting businesses.

To elicit the views of *immigration attorneys*, most of whom represented employers seeking nonimmigrant skilled workers, we interviewed ten attorneys in sessions lasting from one to two hours. We also attended several panels on H-1B visa issues at the annual meeting of the American Immigration Lawyers Association held in San Francisco during the period of our study. Attorneys were asked to describe their experience with the 1990 IMMACT regulatory changes as well as their clients' needs for sponsoring foreign workers.

Our sample of *workers* included fifteen skilled U.S. workers and twelve foreign nonimmigrant skilled workers, one of whom represented an Indian professional association. Sixteen of these interviews were in-depth qualitative ethnographies of respondents' work histories and contemporary experiences in the globalized labor market. Eleven additional interviews were conducted by a combination of e-mail correspondence and telephone interviews with highly skilled U.S. and foreign workers who are members of two computer user groups of highly skilled workers.

To supplement the perspective of workers we interviewed six representatives of *professional associations and unions*. These respondents varied in terms of their organizations' active involvement in issues of immigration and labor market conditions for their constituencies. Two associations represent computer consultants and have been actively lobbying the DOL and the INS for more vigorous enforcement of IMMACT prevailing wage provisions and more rigorous determination of "shortage" occupations. The other four representatives of engineering trade associations and unions, while less directly involved in such questions, nevertheless provided insightful analyses of how changing structural conditions in the global economy have affected labor market conditions, particularly in the computer and engineering fields.

Finally, our sample of *government regulators* included seventeen respondents. The interviews with federal regulators included sessions in San Francisco with a supervisory immigration examiner from the INS, a top administrator in the DOL Western Regional Office, and an INS case officer who screens permanent residence applications of H-1Bs. At the state level we conducted group interviews on three separate occasions in Sacramento with eight certifying officers and six labor market information specialists from the California Employment Development Division (EDD). These respondents were asked their perceptions of local labor market and wage conditions, the efficacy of the LCA and labor certification processes for protecting U.S. jobs and wages, and the impacts of the 1990 IMMACT legislation and DOL regulatory practices.

In sum, our research strategy was twofold. Immigration attorneys and federal and state regulatory officials were asked largely to describe in detail the actual implementation of the nonimmigrant temporary employment provisions of the 1990 IMMACT legislation, particularly the H1-B visa process. Employers, workers, and trade association representatives were asked for their opinions in a wider-ranging series of questions. In addition to their views of the immigration law provisions relating to nonimmigrant workers, these included the following:

- The supply and demand of labor in their industry;
- The effects (positive and/or negative) of foreign workers in their industries with respect to such things as job competition, quality of work, and cultural diversity;

- The standard educational and professional training (and retraining) required for affected occupations;
- Prevailing wages for particular occupations and industries;
- Prevailing job search strategies and the operation of professional networks among both foreign and U.S. workers; and
- The effects of current macroeconomic conditions and recession on the ability to find employment in the affected industries.

It is this second set of questions and respondents that forms the basis of the findings and policy recommendations presented below.

NONIMMIGRANT COMPUTER WORKERS: WHO EMPLOYS? WHO BENEFITS? WHO PAYS?

How do the Silicon Valley employers, computer consulting businesses, domestic and foreign workers in the computer industry, and representatives of professional associations and unions whom we interviewed view the uses of nonimmigrant "temporary" workers in the computer industry? How do these findings address the issues of job displacement and wage depression? What policy implications follow from these qualitative findings?

Silicon Valley Employers' Perceptions

In light of the increased globalization of economic and cultural relations, it is hardly surprising that, in addition to the computer industry per se, employers as different as universities, government agencies, banks, and insurance companies are recruiting the greatest numbers of foreign nonimmigrant computer specialists in California. Because these workplaces differ significantly as forms of economic and social organization, they are recruiting different types of foreign workers, at varying levels of educational backgrounds and skills, for different purposes, and with different time horizons and career pathways in mind. Nevertheless, nonimmigrant foreign workers with computer programming and software design skills have been recruited by all of these employers. It is thus necessary to distinguish among three distinct types of "firms" operating with significant numbers of H-1B nonimmigrant computer workers in contemporary California: (1) computer industry firms per se (including software companies and hardware manufacturers); (2) computer consulting businesses; and (3) the corporate and government clients of computer consultants and consulting businesses.

Based on 39 direct and participant observations and on individual and group interviews with these categories of employer in Silicon Valley, our study found that the bulk of H-1B workers hired by the California computer industry per se have a master's degree in software engineering, design engineering, computer engineering, computer science, materials engineering, and integration engineering with specific product experience. Computer engineering firms hire few Ph.D.'s. They also hire B.S. entry-level workers infrequently, doing so only when the local market cannot supply adequate computer engineering degree holders with experience in their emergent product fields. These firms reported that almost all of their bachelor-level workers are hired locally.

Employers argue that there is a "dearth" of qualified U.S. computer engineers at the master's entry level. Many employers believe that U.S. workers do not pursue master's degrees and that they do not combine computer science and engineering enough to qualify for product development jobs. Consequently, firms explained that they hire these foreign master's-level workers "strictly out of need." Some also feel that foreigners are more attractive employees because they exhibit more "drive" than U.S. workers in searching for jobs. Our respondents do not believe that foreign workers obtained jobs through different recruiting networks than U.S. workers, claiming that they get resumes and referrals through standardized processes of running advertisements, maintaining resume banks, accessing professional networks, and recruiting at universities. Several claimed that they "did not go out looking for foreigners." Most of the foreign workers entering the market at the master's level obtain their degrees from U.S. universities and are hired as F-1 students in practical training. Our sources estimated that more than 70 percent of their H-1Bs were hired as F-1s. Aside from minimum degree requirements, respondents stated that they hired workers based primarily on special requirements relevant to proprietary product development. They argued that they cannot simply retrain employees and stay competitive because computer technology changes too rapidly. The need for "timely product development" forces them to eliminate candidates who do not already possess the specialized experience they require.

Some firms that have engaged in "downsizing" over the last several years stated that they have eliminated some of their foreign workers as jobs dropped off and are trying to redirect other foreign workers away as they focus on outplacement and retraining. Many contended that firms are not enthusiastic about hiring foreign workers because it is expensive. Some of these employers believe that H-1Bs do take U.S. workers' jobs. On the other hand, many contended that their firms benefit from hiring foreign workers by acquiring technical skills quickly, adding cultural diversity to the workplace, and expanding foreign markets. Moreover, they reported that well more than 60 percent of their H-1Bs eventually are sponsored for permanent residence.

Computer Consulting Firms

Our study also included in-depth interviews with representatives of five computer consulting businesses that supply foreign workers to the computer industry, the U.S. corporate sector, and agencies at all levels of government. The consulting firms included four U.S.-based subsidiaries of Indian corporations and one U.S.-owned firm run by an Indian M.B.A. The latter employs both Indian and U.S. computer consultants in relatively equal proportions. All of these firms provide software design services in several profitable niches within the computer industry. These firms offer teams of software engineers, applications programmers, and systems analysts to *two* primary markets: (1) computer manufacturers wishing to develop systems software but without software departments; and (2) large corporations, such as banks and utility companies, developing alternative d-base systems in UNIX and graphic interface windowing environments (GUI).

India now is regarded widely as a leading source of expertise in these areas. The firms that are subsidiaries of larger Indian companies can facilitate both incountry consulting teams and offshore processing teams in India. Representatives of these firms reported a virtual "explosion" in business from major U.S. corporations that are converting data bases from large mainframes to more flexible UNIX d-base systems. According to these firm representatives, the labor pool of UNIX and GUI experts in the U.S. is absorbed and U.S. d-base designers tend to stay away from the more menial coding and testing tasks that the consulting firms execute.

Note that, between 1993 and 1995, the consulting firms whose executives we interviewed have changed their compensation and visa use practices in response to tightening of wage compliance and stricter B-1 visa enforcement. They have eliminated the use of B-1 visas for all but short-term assignments that involve the training of U.S. workers in installed systems (with compensation from Indian subsidiaries). These executives stated that 80 to 90 percent of their foreign consultants enter the U.S. with an H-1B visa for several assignments of varying duration over a term of one to three years. In response to the changing political climate and the increased availability of "temporary" U.S. computer workers with corporate downsizing of the permanent workforce in the industry, one consulting business now hires 50 percent of its consultants locally and several others have plans to hire U.S. consultants. They expect that this will improve their workforce and profile in the industry.

All of these respondents stated that they also have eliminated in-kind payments as components of salary and pay the full cash salaries stated on H-1B and labor certification applications. However, even these firms acknowledged that other consulting firms that supply nonimmigrant computer workers to U.S. employers still count in-kind payments as salary and defend it on the grounds that they must assist Indian workers materially because they have difficulty securing apartment leases and car loans or because they have no local credit. None of the firms stated that they fine consultants who break their contracts. They all acknowledged that some of their workers, in their words, "desert" their companies when U.S. firms offer them employment with permanent residency sponsorship.

Only recently have these consulting firms started sponsoring H-1Bs for permanent residence. Firms currently are sponsoring H-1B workers and claim that the longer-term residence facilitated by the H-1B visa, as opposed to the B-1 visa, is decreasing the flowback to India and inserting these foreign workers into the permanent U.S. workforce.

These respondents firmly believe that U.S. business practices of requiring up-front experience without offering adequate training and nurturing of recent graduates will keep U.S. companies dependent on temporary Indian personnel. While there is no difference in the quality of U.S. and foreign workers, they believe that U.S. companies focus too much on short-term quarterly performance instead of human development, thereby creating a pool of U.S. workers with requisite degrees—but without experience—who are viewed as functionally unqualified for time-intensive product development.

Skilled Worker Perspectives

Our ethnographic interviews with U.S. and foreign workers in California included interviews with a sample of eight foreign and eight U.S. skilled workers, mostly employed in the computer industry. Additionally, relying on the Internet, we conducted eleven other focused but open-ended interviews by e-mail and telephone. This generated data from eight additional U.S. workers and three additional nonimmigrant workers. As our Internet call for interview respondents was sent out nationwide to two skilled-worker user groups, eight of the eleven workers we attracted by this method worked in states other than California, mostly in the fields of university teaching and postdoctoral research.

The Foreign Workers' Perspective

In our California sample we interviewed directly eight foreign workers, one of whom represented an Indian professional association. Four of the Indian consultants came to work in the U.S. on H-1B visas sponsored by Indian-based consulting firms in Silicon Valley. All followed a similar pathway to gain employment as H-1Bs. They had prior experience working for the parent company in India and expect to return to the Indian operations after completion of their U.S. assignments unless they apply for permanent residence. Currently, only one intends to pursue permanent residence. These respondents have bachelor's degrees in computer science and electrical engineering from Indian universities and specialize in writing software for relational databases (UNIX), products being developed extensively for major corporations within and outside the computer field.

These consultants described their work in the United States as providing software services that complement existing U.S. software programmers and engineers within company-specific contexts. They do not believe that they displace U.S. workers but rather offer ''made-to-order skills'' that enable U.S. firms to acquire necessary expertise quickly and economically by eliminating the need for recruiting, retraining, and reshuffling workers.

These foreign consultants are split on whether the supply of qualified U.S. computer workers meets the demand in the industry. Those who do not believe there is a shortage of qualified U.S. workers claim that H-1B consultants are hired because they can be acquired more quickly than U.S. workers as consulting firms keep diversified pools of consultants on hand. All of them believe that the demand by U.S. firms for Indian consultants will remain high as long as firms continue to treat their workforce as a short-term "dispensable" cost measured by quarterly statistics and insurance premiums. They criticized U.S. firms for neglecting the training and development of professionals in exchange for drawing upon a revolving and temporary workforce that itself feels no need for loyalty to firms and only seeks higher wages.

While none of the foreign nonimmigrant respondents who work for computer consulting businesses believe they are being paid below prevailing wage, they concur that they are paid "on the low side" because they do not have degrees from the United States, usually receive entry-level pay, and do not have access to the investment and bonus benefits of other U.S. skilled computer workers.

The testimony of four other H-1B direct hires by computer industry firms illustrates a second major pathway for foreign skilled workers to enter the U.S. labor force, particularly the computer and engineering labor force. These respondents received bachelor's degrees in their home country, then enrolled in U.S. universities as F-1 students for graduate study in computer science and various engineering fields. After graduating, they obtained full-time jobs in Silicon Valley firms as F-1s in practical training. They later changed status to H-1B with sponsorship from the hiring firm.

One of this latter category of nonimmigrant workers firmly believes that there is a definite shortage of U.S. computer and engineering workers who have master's degrees and that foreigners make up for that gap in the marketplace. He added that U.S. workers are not highly represented in graduate-level programs, that close to 90 percent of professionals with advanced computer and engineering degrees are foreign, and that foreigners also are filling more faculty positions in these areas. Three of the four respondents following this employment pathway reported that they feel that the U.S. firms they worked for actually preferred to hire nonresident aliens. One believes her firm managers hire nonresidents because they pay low salaries and often require ten-hour work days with no overtime compensation.

The View of American Workers

We interviewed a total of fifteen U.S. workers. Eight of these worked in California. These included computer consultants, full-time employees in the computer industry, and postdoctoral researchers working and seeking employment in both university and industry settings. We also interviewed seven U.S. workers from outside California who are members of the Young Scientists Network computer user group. There is general agreement from the U.S. skilled-worker respondents that their labor markets are oversupplied, that jobs are scarce, that unemployment and underemployment are more common, and that wages have stagnated. Two of the computer consultants interviewed worked as full-time employees in the defense industry in southern California until the early 1990s when they were laid off and began working as contractors. Other macroeconomic factors aside, respondents believe that, in light of economic conditions, foreign workers contribute to job displacement and wage depression. This sentiment was strongly echoed in the area of postdoctoral research in universities and industry by the seven U.S. members of the Young Scientist Network whom we interviewed by Internet.

Computer consultants feel they are being displaced by a growing number of foreign consultants in the industry since the early 1990s. They believe the 1990 immigration legislation helped to encourage the expansion of foreign-based consulting firms that now underbid U.S. firms for contracts with major U.S. corporations. These workers also pointed to outsourcing of certain kinds of computer programming as an accompanying cause of job insecurity. The U.S. computer consultants feel that cost and time savings are the major factors driving corporate contracting of H-1B consultants. The full-time computer worker, who has worked in the industry for eight years and who is also a project manager, reported that her firm has been replacing full-time workers with temporary contractors. One of their major contracting firms is an Indian-based company that supplies them with workers upon request. Several projects operate completely offshore through the parent company in India, while others in the United States are entirely staffed by H-1Bs. She claimed that the availability of workers in the United States is not the issue, but rather time and money are, as the firm can hire new H-1Bs as early as the next day and foreign workers are paid "far below" fees and salaries paid to U.S. workers.

U.S. computer consultants also blamed the federal tax code for worsening their prospects for job security and prosperity because it prevents them from operating independently from third-party contractors and from charging higher fees. They feel this tightening of tax regulations by the federal government is particularly damaging in light of current immigration policy that they believe facilitates the growth of foreign-based computer consultancies operating in the market.

Given these conditions, all of the computer-related respondents concurred that their job searches take much more time and do not necessarily result in satisfactory employment situations. A worker consultant who looks for jobs in the newspaper, at job fairs, and with the help of "head hunters," described the systems as "hit and miss" because jobs are snapped up almost immediately. Like other consultants interviewed, he contacted up to 30 consulting firms in seeking a placement. Another respondent commented that he and his fellow workers often take jobs for which they are overqualified because of the prevalence of programmers. Another expressed frustration at answering advertisements that seem to require wide ranges of skills and experience that he described as "humanly impossible." These jobs require sophisticated languages that he feels are rarely used in programming but are the basis upon which he is rejected for an interview.

U.S. computer worker responses also stood in contrast to the commentary from U.S. firm representatives regarding the need for acquiring specialized skills through the H-1B and labor certification processes. This sentiment was particularly prevalent among workers in the computer and engineering fields who perform relatively standardized work that does not require a high degree of specialization. The consensus among computer and engineering workers is that the skills foreign workers bring are no better than those available locally. Two of the computer consultants also stated that they do not believe that Indians have a corner on the market for skills in UNIX-based relational databases, a claim articulated consistently among the Indian-based computer consultant interviews.

Workers generally also disagreed that U.S. firms need to hire foreigners with up-front skills because they cannot afford the time or money to train U.S. workers at the outset of projects (i.e., that they need to "hit the ground running"). They believe very firmly that retraining and general adaptation to specific company products is standard operating procedure in the industry. This means that no computer worker is ever completely ready to enter a job without some training in and orientation to new and customized systems. They disagreed that foreign workers do not require the same preproject training and investment. In summary, every worker interviewed holds that pure cost reduction, i.e., "profit" is the primary reason firms hire foreign workers.

Interestingly, U.S. computer consultants characterized their role in the computer industry in terms similar to those of the Indian consultants—providing complementary skills to existing product teams. Like foreign consultants, they make their skills quickly available and engage in continual retraining to maintain a wide range of skills built up through work at multiple companies. Therefore, they believe that U.S. firms hire foreign consultants because they cost less, not because they provide substantively different or better services than U.S. consultants.

These U.S. respondents, particularly those who work in the computer consulting fields, believe that foreign consultants are being paid "well below" prevailing wage rates. Most respondents quoted hourly wage figures for foreign consultants that were as low as one-half of the standard hourly fees for the industry. Their views contrasted sharply with the information provided in interviews with the managers of foreign-owned computer consulting businesses. The foreign workers we interviewed in this field were not always aware of prevailing hourly fees for the kind of consulting work they did, but some stated that they believe they are being paid "somewhat less" than comparable U.S. software consultants and all place themselves at the "low end of the scale."

The View from Professional Associations and Unions

In addition to employers and workers, we interviewed representatives from six professional and union associations. As already noted, these respondents varied in terms of their associations' concern about and active involvement in issues of immigration and labor market conditions for their U.S. worker constituencies. The two associations that represent computer consultants have been lobbying the DOL and the INS vigorously over the past two years, fighting what they see as policies that bolster foreign competition and abuse of wages and working conditions in the consulting field, including widespread use of the B-1 visa and the continued practice of paying below-market hourly wages to foreigners despite the LCA provisions implemented by IMMACT 1990. They argue that foreign workers are paid "far below" prevailing wages in computer consulting. This, in turn, constitutes unfair competition and drives down hourly consulting rates for U.S. computer consulting businesses and displaced computer engineers who have become consultants by default.

These representatives faulted the U.S. Department of Labor and the California EDD for contributing to this problem for three reasons. First, they believe that the LCA process is unenforceable in the third-party consulting environment because it masks the real employer. As the LCAs cannot be posted in the actual workplace, they end up being posted in the administrative offices of consulting firms. This undermines their potential effectiveness, as U.S. workers never see them. Second, computer consultants are hesitant to make formal complaints about depressed fees because they have very little job security in the consulting environment. Third, they argue that EDD generates too low a prevailing wage figure for consultants because it averages together the salaries of full-time workers with the fees of consultants who generally lack fringe benefits and thus command higher hourly rates than full-time workers.

The other representatives of engineering trade associations and unions that we interviewed were less immediately involved in the particular issues raised by U.S. consulting firms in California. Nevertheless, these respondents stressed the adverse impacts of defense downsizing, corporate strategies of hiring temporary, debenefited workers, unfavorable tax policies for consulting businesses, and the overall national recession as adversely affecting the life chances of their members. (For factors related to the global flow of engineers see National Research Council 1988.)

While they were unable to account precisely for the relative employment impact of these structural factors as against immigration policies toward skilled workers, they nonetheless argued that:

- There is a trend for what one respondent described as "U.S. job shops" to be underbid by "foreign job shops" because foreign workers will accept lower wages and, thus, foreign job shops can underbid competitors;

- That foreign workers are hired not because they possess special skills unavailable locally but because they are cheaper;

- That foreign workers do contribute to wage depression by entering the U.S. market at a time of unfavorable labor market conditions for U.S. engineers;

• That the current "oversupply" of engineers is causing the most talented workers to leave engineering and enter other fields like law, business, and finance.

These organizational representatives of U.S. highly skilled workers shared the perception of the foreign workers we interviewed with respect to U.S. corporate practices regarding labor training and human resource development. One even said the U.S. corporations "think of workers as throwaway items." Note also that some of these respondents regarded *outsourcing* as a far greater threat to U.S. engineers and computer professionals than competition from H-1B nonimmigrant workers. They pointed out that software programming already is being outsourced "over the wire" and that design functions may soon follow the same route. Implicit in this concern is the danger that enforcement targeted at foreign "job shops" may only accelerate the trend of American corporations outsourcing contracted work to the foreign consultants' offshore firms.

COMPARING NONIMMIGRANT RECRUITMENT ACROSS SCIENTIFIC OCCUPATIONS

As suggested above, in light of the increased globalization of economic and cultural relations, it is hardly surprising that "employers" as different as computer and engineering firms, biotechnology companies, and public and private universities are recruiting the greatest numbers of H-1B temporary scientific workers in California. Because these "workplaces" are historically specific institutional settings that differ significantly as forms of economic and social organization, they are recruiting different types of foreign "temporary" workers at varying levels of educational backgrounds and skills, for different purposes, and with different time horizons and career pathways in mind. While space does not allow a detailed discussion of each of the other scientific occupations included in our larger study, it is, nonetheless, important to offer a brief discussion of our key findings regarding nonimmigrant recruitment in a selection of the other fields we studied to illustrate the specificity of our findings regarding the computer industry, to capture the complexity of developing global labor markets, and to add depth to our overall analysis.

The Biotechnology Industry

In our larger study we interviewed five representatives of three high-end H1-B user biotechnology companies in San Francisco and Los Angeles. Each of these firms hire "temporary" foreign workers almost exclusively in research and development. They actively recruit high level Ph.D.'s from the global marketplace as research project managers and postdoctoral researchers with specialized expertise in ongoing firm projects. Beyond this, they recruit all other scientists and assistant scientists locally, except when particular support people are requested from foreign labs by their H1-B project directors.

The transnational talent pool of scientists in biotechnology is small and close-knit. Recruitment relies heavily on international professional networks. The recruitment process for project managers is very thorough, with firms spending as many as six months to find an exact match of expertise. The population of foreign professionals in California biotechnology firms tends to be very diverse with no nationality constituting even close to a majority. This finding underlines the professional nature of recruitment networks and the limited impact of ethnic recruitment networks in this scientific field. These firms afford two possible pathways from H-1B status to permanent residency. Some of the scientists recruited are offered sponsorship upon their initial employment as a recruitment incentive. Others are afforded the possibility of this option after a trial period ranging from six months to two years.

Perhaps not surprisingly, in light of the above recruitment process, the biotechnology firms whose representatives we interviewed are not experiencing any problems with the H-1B process. As they recruit top scientists and pay high salaries, they do not experience any "prevailing wage" problems with state regulators. Although they did complain that the labor certification process has been slowing down and becoming increasingly "aggressive," these firms have been successful in using the "outstanding" immigration category to recruit the vast majority of their foreign scientists. They argued, and offered evidence to support their claim, that far from causing any labor displacement of U.S. Ph.D. scientists, the research and product development projects they create actually expand job opportunities for domestic biotechnology specialists because of the firms' practice of rounding out research project teams directed by foreign scientists through local recruitment.

Although our findings are limited because of the small size of our firm sample, the biotechnology firms we did select were the highest users of H-1B scientists in the state. Moreover, the recruitment processes described for each firm were remarkably consistent with each other. The findings suggest that neither wage depression nor job displacement is a serious problem in this scientific occupation. If this is the case, there is little need to consider any sweeping policy change for this sector. Put colloquially: "If it ain't broke, don't fix it."

University Teaching and Research

Our employer sample of university administrators of immigration programs included eight individuals representing the state's four largest university users of H-1B visas for their faculty and research staff: two large public universities; one large private university; and one moderate-sized elite private university. We also addressed the employment conditions of Ph.D. scientists in university teaching and research with a sample of nine U.S. respondents and three foreign respondents with doctoral degrees, drawn from both our ethnographic and Internet samples of scientific "workers." To supplement these qualitative interviews, we attended a half-day meeting of the Bay Area Foreign Scholar Advisors, representing the four universities in our sample and twelve other public and private universities throughout California. Finally we conducted participant-observation research at a half-day workshop held at one of our major public universities for foreign Ph.D.'s moving into U.S. labor markets.

The universities we sampled hire foreign workers mostly as faculty and postdoctoral researchers. The averages derived from data provided to us by the four largest university users of the H-1B visa category were 30 percent faculty and 70 percent postdoctoral researchers. All of the faculty are selected by a scrupulous process for the recruitment of tenure-track employees and nearly all are sponsored for permanent residence as a condition of employment. The use of H-1B visas for this category of employees functions largely as a "holding pattern" while permanent residency approval is sought. In contrast, postdoctoral researchers generally are sponsored for H-1B visas with departmental approval and verification of the availability of three years of research funding. The two principal pathways by which foreign doctoral-level scientific workers receive H-1B visas are conversion from F-1 and J-1 visas. University representatives reported that the positions filled by the J-1s and F-1s are advertised for general recruitment before foreign candidates are approved for H-1Bs to allow access of others in the market to the positions. While foreign-born faculty and postdoctoral researchers are spread throughout departments, university employers reported that there is some clustering in engineering, computer sciences, business, and medicine and among Indians and other Asians.

University immigration administrators expressed great concern over the issue of prevailing wage determinations. While the EDD, the California State Employment Security Agency (SESA), employs a national survey, *Academe*, our four sampled California campuses argued that the survey generates excessive salary quotes for junior faculty because it amalgamates faculty salaries for all levels without recognizing traditional tenure step systems. Employer respondents were adamant that the EDD fails to understand how universities function and disregards their own wage scales that reflect statewide salary conditions and the multiple layers of university rank and step systems. Further, they pointed out that conducting ad hoc local wage surveys is not a feasible way for them to offer alternatives to the amalgamated *Academe* surveys because often the university is the only institution of its kind in its local labor market.

The university administrators with whom we spoke advanced the argument that they should not be subject to H-1B regulatory constraints at all because universities, as institutions, always have sought, and indeed require, foreign scientific professionals for intellectual exchange and to fulfill their research and academic missions. As nonprofit organizations in the service of the advancement of knowledge, they further argued, they should not be expected to compete with corporate professional salaries in private industry. They advocated instead the creation of a special H-1C visa category for universities that does not have a numerical cap, stringent wage verification procedures, or severe penalties.

The employment conditions of the Ph.D. scientists whom we interviewed in our university sample of scientific occupations varied greatly, ranging from full-time, tenure-track faculty members and research scientists to postdoctoral researchers working in their fields, to those working in temporary positions outside the field of their Ph.D.'s. Despite notable differences in personal work history, these respondents converged in describing four contemporary trends in their respective scientific fields: (1) an oversupply of Ph.D. scientists in their labor market; (2) reduced opportunities for permanent positions in university teaching and research; (3) a resulting substantial prolongation of time spent as low-paid postdoctoral researchers prior to entry into their field, where they are treated as temporary workers with reduced or nonexistent benefits; and (4) a growing abandonment of some highly oversupplied fields by Ph.D. scientists for better paying work in other fields that do not require the graduate education they spent so much time and money to acquire.

While the U.S. respondents with Ph.D.'s acknowledged the positive impact of foreign scholarship on university life, they also worried about competition from foreign Ph.D.'s for increasingly elusive faculty positions. Some of our respondents reported that U.S. scientists with doctoral degrees shy away from university-based research positions because of low wages, thereby selecting themselves out of the market. Some of the U.S. Ph.D.'s we interviewed, who have entered other fields in private industry, said they were forced out of this market by a combination of low wages, extreme overproduction of both U.S. and foreign Ph.D. scientists by American universities, particularly in physics and mathematics, and exploitative working conditions in postdoctoral research labs. They argued that foreign Ph.D.'s are willing to accept such conditions because they see low-paid postdoctoral research as a key pathway to a green card. A few of our U.S. respondents have accepted work in fields completely unrelated to their fields simply to earn a living wage. Two high energy physicists, for example, have gone into computer programming and managing a biology laboratory because they cannot find any work in their own fields. Several others in our sample were encountering extreme difficulty securing any but the most temporary, insecure, and nonbenefited university postdoctoral research positions.

Further exacerbating this problem is the practice by universities in California and elsewhere of downsizing their operations and increasing their use of temporary employees, both domestic and foreign. As there are no established Dictionary of Occupational Titles (DOT) codes for postdoctoral workers, universities can offer very low salaries to postdoctoral researchers, often financed by soft money. They also can offer limited fringe benefits and remain unchallenged as U.S. scientific workers continue to exit this market, discarding their long human capital investment in Ph.D. study, while foreign postdoctoral researchers remain quiescent, and, sometimes, even accept exploitative working conditions. We were told, for example, of Chinese postdoctoral medical researchers in a major California university who were hired as quarter-time researchers under prevailing wages but who spent more than 50 hours per week in their labs in hope of obtaining sponsorship and remaining permanently in the United States with green cards.

University representatives have made a coherent case in support of the general proposition that universities are permanently in need of a steady infusion of foreign talent to engage in their basic tasks: cutting-edge research; the general advancement of scientific knowledge; and the production of new knowledge that has general public benefit. They argued that they should be exempt from the stringent regulations that apply to profit-making businesses regarding H-1Bs and labor certifications. Based on the findings of our study, the case for their argument is considerably stronger in the case of their recruitment of full-time, tenure-track faculty members than in the case of part-time faculty and temporary postdoctoral researchers.

In the former case, the universities engage in extensive formal search requirements, multiple interviews, and, at the time of our study, the need to conform to strict affirmative action guidelines. In this search they clearly are advantaged in obtaining the best available talent worldwide by the great oversupply of Ph.D.'s that they have generated, particularly in some scientific fields like mathematics and physics. While their graduate degree programs may be faulted for insensitivity to existing labor market conditions, when they recruit new tenure-track faculty, the quality of candidates' research and, to a lesser extent, their teaching skills are paramount. Thus, the recruitment by universities of permanent teaching and research faculty tends to be driven by an open search for the best talent worldwide, rather than by a desire to reduce costs.

In contrast, in the case of university postdoctoral researchers, wide discretion is left in the hands of principal investigators, often operating on soft money from external grants. These "employers" depend on a steady infusion of relatively low-paid postdoctoral researchers to keep their research going. Hiring often is done by means of personal social networks, both professionally and ethnically based. The quest for excellence often is superseded by the mutual cultivation of mentor-mentee relations between principal investigators and postdoctoral candidates. The search for candidates is limited as well by the differential willingness and ability of U.S. and foreign Ph.D. researchers to work long, often uncompensated, overtime hours for relatively low salaries.

In view of the above findings, our larger study makes three policy recommendations:

• That immigration policy makers limit any proposed establishment of a less restrictive scientific worker immigration category for universities, such as a proposed H-1C visa, to full-time, tenure-track, teaching and research occupations;

• That, in enforcing existing regulations, state and federal regulators of prevailing wages pay attention to the reasonable arguments university representatives have made concerning the uniquely layered and segmented tenure-step systems that constrain the salaries that can be assigned within the full-time, tenure-track teaching and research system; but that

• Because of the potential for general wage depression, abusive working conditions for foreign postdoctoral scientists, and job displacement of U.S. scientific researchers in the postdoctoral occupational category, the regulatory process should concentrate scarce enforcement resources upon and insure prevailing wages for the postdoctoral researcher occupational category. Creating such a less-restrictive visa category for faculty employment would complement this recommendation by freeing up resources to be deployed in the job category where they are most needed.

THE NEW HIGH-TECH *BRACEROS* REVISITED

Having focused this chapter largely on the processes of nonimmigrant recruitment and employment in the computer sector, what are the policy implications and recommendations that follow from our findings? First and foremost, computer software work is complexly articulated in distinct occupational niches in the United States and world economy and should be understood and dealt with as such. When designing policy change it is thus crucial that the "real employer" of nonimmigrant skilled computer workers be recognized and addressed in the future.

We have seen that one of the key changes in the computer industry springs from its corporate restructuring by expanding the number of temporary workers while reducing its full-time workforce. In the industry itself there is a labor surplus, not a shortage, as software engineers leave full-time employment in computer companies, particularly defense-related firms. At the same time, occupational data show that the positions of software engineer, programmer, and coder are growing at a rapid rate both in California and nationally. How do we explain this anomaly?

The answer is twofold. First, computer firms in Silicon Valley are shifting from hardware to software applications, downsizing their permanent workforce in Silicon Valley and worldwide, and relying increasingly on contract labor to perform software design, programming, and coding functions. Second, corporations of all kinds outside the computer industry are picking up many of those displaced from the industry as well as hiring H-1B and U.S. computer consultants as temporary workers to help them to downsize and create a more flexible workforce. Both primary data drawn from our interviews with U.S. and foreign workers and employers and abundant secondary documentary sources (e.g., ICIM International 1992:1–4; APL Management Consultants 1992:1–4) reveal that the downsizing firms relying on computer consultants run the gamut of the U.S. economy, including finance and banking, real estate, accounting, manufacturing, public utilities, pharmaceuticals, health care, the travel industry, and even government agencies at all levels.

Thus, the key question is: "Who is the employer?" The real employers of the computer workers in these occupations are neither the U.S. consulting companies nor the foreign-owned "job shops" that supply workers, but rather the clients who subcontract their services. It is the downsizing corporate and government clients who are generating the demand for temporary software consultants to assist them in restructuring. The "job shops" and consulting businesses are merely middlemen responding to the demand generated, especially from large corporate firms. The DOL tendency to regard the "job shop" as the "employer" plays into the hands of the real employers, as subcontracting is a device used to avoid legal responsibility for wage compliance and visa petitioning. Ironically, downsizing—both within and outside the industry—has reduced employment of full-time computer software engineers, programmers, and coders, thereby expanding the supply of potential consultants even further. The combined effect of this dynamic has been to depress hourly fees in this field—in some cases even lower than seven years ago.

A second irony is that state and federal regulatory agencies have spent a great deal of time trying to separate out "job shops" from "legitimate consulting businesses" (see, for example, Zachary 1995: A2). We have found that consulting agencies and "job shops" do differ from each other in the rates they pay their consultants, which, based on qualitative data from interviews, can be quite significantly lower for foreign H-1B consultants. However, we do not find the distinction to be centrally important except to the extent that wages are affected. Foreign competition does lower the prevailing wage of software engineers, programmers, and coders, particularly at the lowest levels. However, the more salient issue is that *both* types of consulting businesses merely are supplying the overarching corporate (and, to a lesser extent, government) demand for more efficient ways to organize work, reduce their obligation to provide fringe benefits to full-time workers, and create a more flexible global workforce.

Defense-related firms clearly have failed to retrain their existing workforce in the face of the need for conversion to civilian production. Evidence from the professional association representatives and even the foreign workers we interviewed indicates that nondefense-related industries tend to be equally inattentive to such long-range considerations as worker retraining and human resource development. In the epoch of global restructuring earlier corporate strategies of building allegiance from permanent workers by human development policies have been replaced by a race to become more flexible in the global marketplace by relying on an expendable workforce of temporary workers and shrinking an increasingly insecure permanent skilled workforce. Among computer software engineers and programmers, permanent job displacement has expanded the pool of computer consultants, increased the search time for contracts, and reduced the time available to keep skills up-to-date in a rapidly changing field.

POLICY RECOMMENDATIONS

In light of these developments, the following policy recommendations address the real problem at hand:

• Regulatory and enforcement mechanisms should focus on the "real employer," i.e., the clients of contract workers, including holding them accountable for paying prevailing wages to nonimmigrant workers and for retraining displaced American workers;

- To this same end, the Education and Training Administration (ETA) in the U.S. Department of Labor well might focus its efforts on creating retraining opportunities for displaced U.S. workers;
- Displaced skilled workers also should be offered tax credits or deductions to cover the costs and time of retraining.

As a corollary to these interrelated policy recommendations, as H1-B consultants do appear to contribute to wage depression, it is finally recommended:

- That the DOL focus its efforts on monitoring this aspect of the so-called computer "job shops" to insure that they pay their workers prevailing wages, rather than targeting them as the sole culprit responsible for U.S. worker displacement.

CONCLUSIONS

By and large, high-skill workers in the computer field have been displaced by corporate downsizing, both inside and outside the computer industry, not by competition from foreign H-1B workers. There is no doubt that expanding the size of the labor pool by the entry of H-1B software engineers, programmers, and coders increases the difficulty U.S. computer consultants are experiencing in finding a steady supply of work. Yet, they are finding work, as the demand for temporary computer software consultants remains high. The main problems U.S. computer consultants face are stagnant consulting fees and a highly competitive environment for consulting work that contributes to continuing income stagnation. The complaints U.S. workers voice about foreign competition stem from the fact that, in the current political climate, this is an issue they can do something about by acting to "stop immigration." But the structural displacement produced by downsizing is a much larger problem—in the computer field and elsewhere—that can be addressed by serious efforts to enforce prevailing wage standards and develop proactive policies to retrain an increasingly insecure segment of the U.S. workforce.

In the final analysis, because of the growing reliance of U.S. industry, commerce, and government on outside consultants, it is important to map the complexity of the emerging consulting sector of the U.S. and global labor market. In today's age of flexible production, all categories of employer are turning increasingly to consultants to perform project-specific operations. This study focused intensively on computer consulting as a business and software engineers as workers. But the policies and practices identified in the foregoing analysis may be applicable more generally to address the rising tide of temporary consulting workers nationally and worldwide.

Despite this likely convergence, it is important to raise a cautionary note by recalling our comparative analysis of the recruitment and employment of nonimmigrant scientific workers in other fields. Clearly, global recruitment and employment processes in biotechnology research and development, university teaching and research, and computer software engineering operate in fundamentally different ways. Thus, to design reasonable policy responses to contemporary conditions, policy changes concerning nonimmigrant employment regulations need to be considered carefully, on a case-by-case basis, both across scientific fields and between different job categories within particular sets of workplaces. To do otherwise is to fly in the face of the complexity of the global world we have created and the transnational networks that now sustain it.

That very complexity poses the paradox now facing national regulatory environments in today's global economy. By allowing a steady flow of highly skilled specialty workers to enter the United States for relatively long temporary periods at prevailing wage standards, contemporary immigration law has made regulatory officials responsible for administering a de facto guestworker program. If regulators set prevailing wage standards too low, they become subject to the political charge that they are running a "high-tech *bracero* program" that hurts American workers. On the other hand, if they set them unreasonably high or make domestic access to nonimmigrant workers too bothersome for U.S. employers, they run the risk that U.S. firms presently employing nonimmigrant workers simply may switch from a policy of importing skilled temporary workers to one of exporting the work that they do to knowledge production sites in less-developed countries like India and Pakistan or in Eastern Europe where needed skills and technological means of communication already are concentrated. In the field of computer consulting such outsourcing already is happening. If the pace and scale of outsourcing is accelerated by cumbersome or exclusionary immigration policy, both regulators and policymakers will be held politically responsible for creating a "high-tech *Maquiladora* program." In our contemporary political climate, the paradoxes of economic globalization indeed are coming home to roost.

NOTE

I wish to acknowledge the contribution of my research assistant, Marie Cie-piela, who coauthored the larger report on foreign worker specialty employment (Smith & Ciepiela 1995), parts of which were drawn upon in writing this paper.

REFERENCES

American Council on International Personnel. 1994. *Employer Sanctions, Avoiding Discrimination in Hiring, Immigrant and Non-Immigrant Visas: Two Day Seminar.* February 7–8, San Francisco.

APL Management Consultants. 1992. Export of Software Products from Pakistan. Promotional correspondence for subcontracted outsourcing of software programming projects. (October 22).

Bellinger, R. 1993. Fed Plan to Ease Aliens' Hiring Slammed. *Electronic Engineering Times* (March 10).

Carey, P. 1993. H-P in P.A. Sued over its Use of Foreign Workers. *San Jose Mercury News* (October 8).

Dicken, P. 1992. *Global Shift.* New York: Guilford Press.

Feagin, J. R., and Smith, M. P. 1987. Cities and the New International Division of Labor. In M. P. Smith and J. R. Feagin, eds., *The Capitalist City: Global Restructuring and Community Politics.* Oxford: Blackwell.

ICIM International. 1992. Promotional correspondence profiling ICIM's on-site computer contract programming, turnkey consulting, and offshore software development. (November 5).

National Commission for Economic Conversion and Disarmament. 1994. *Report of the National Commission for Economic Conversion and Disarmament.* Washington, DC: U.S. Government Printing Office.

National Research Council. 1988. *Foreign and Foreign-Born Engineers in the United States.* Washington, DC: National Academy Press.

Sinton, P. 1995. Silicon Valley's Economy Growing. *San Francisco Chronicle* (January 9).

Smith, M. P. 1996. Looking for Globality in Los Angeles. In A. Cvetkovich and D. Kellner, eds., *Articulating the Global and the Local.* Boulder, CO: Westview Press.

Smith, M. P., and Ciepiela, M. 1995. *A Study of Foreign Worker Specialty Employment and the DOL Permanent Labor Certification Program in California.* (Project No. J-9-K-3–0033). Report prepared for the U.S. Department of Labor. (March).

Zachary, G. P. 1995. Curbs on Foreign Professionals Assailed. *Wall Street Journal* (January 13).

Chapter 6

Skill Level and Employer Use of Foreign Specialty Workers

JACQUELINE HAGAN AND SUSANA McCOLLOM

Employers increasingly rely on a well-educated and highly skilled workforce to meet the competitive demands of today's global economy. The Immigration Act of 1990 responded to a perceived shortage of skilled workers by increasing the number of both economic-based immigrant and nonimmigrant visa categories. Most significant and controversial among these changes was the reclassification of the H visa category, which remains since its inception in the Immigration Act of 1952, the largest program supplying temporary foreign workers to U.S. employers.

Originally, the H program was conceived as a mechanism for tapping into a labor pool of temporary foreign workers to meet bottlenecks in the supply of U.S. workers in particular occupations.[1] The 1990 Act streamlined the procedure by which employers gain access to skilled foreign labor by replacing the "distinguished merit and ability" requirement with a simplified "specialty occupation" clause and increased dramatically the number of foreign workers that U.S. employers could bring into their workplaces for periods of as long as six years.[2]

However, following passage of the 1990 Act, the United States, along with a number of other industrialized nations, was swept into a global recession that translated into severe cutbacks in research funding, corporate downsizing, and high unemployment. The hardships of the latest economic cycle reinforced an ongoing trend of significant realignment and reorganization of the production of work. Moreover, such shocks were felt especially hard in the fields of science and technology:

many skilled workers in these areas lost their jobs and well-trained recent college graduates confronted shrinking employment opportunities. Despite this, the number of H-1Bs filed has risen steadily each year since 1990 and they are concentrated in the fields of science and technology. These interrelated developments raised a number of questions regarding the effects of the H-1B program.

In response to these developments, in late 1993, the U.S. Department of Labor (DOL) sponsored several in-depth field studies to examine how the H-1B system works and how it affects the various actors, including domestic and foreign workers, professional associations, government officials, and immigration attorneys. In selecting the research sites, DOL sought states with a high number of H-1B applications in the areas of science and research but with different labor market conditions. The research reported on below was conducted in Texas in 1994, a time of economic expansion following a prolonged recession in the state.

THE ECONOMIC CONTEXT OF FOREIGN "SPECIALTY" WORKERS IN TEXAS

In the 1980s, almost a decade before the rest of the nation, the Texas economy experienced what became a worldwide recession. Beginning in 1982, an oversupply of oil in the world market sent the prosperous Texas economy into a severe five-year recession. Unemployment increased steadily during this period, peaking at roughly 9 percent by 1986 (Smith 1989). Given Texas' historical dependence on oil and petrochemical production, no metropolitan area, industry, or occupational group was spared the recession's repercussions. As the center of the world petrochemical industry, Houston was especially hard hit: the area's unemployment rate stood as high as 13 percent in 1986; declines in manufacturing, business services, and construction resulted in a loss of more than 200,000 jobs in the city between 1982 and 1986 (Hagan & Rodriguez 1992).

In response to the recession, large petrochemical and engineering firms headquartered in Houston initiated a restructuring strategy—a process that continues to the present. Typically, these multinational corporations (MNCs) retained those components of the business that they did best. In most cases, this involved keeping and retraining very highly skilled employees in software design and engineering and outsourcing lower-level tasks, such as programming and coding. The elimination of salaried positions enabled these companies both to maintain production levels and remain competitive.

In some cases, downsizing—or "rightsizing" as it is euphemistically referred to by the corporate executives interviewed—involved laying off more than 40 percent of a firm's work force. This strategy had particularly severe consequences for engineers, computer programmers, and analysts who comprised the information systems and research and development components of multinational corporations headquartered in Houston. Software analysts and programmers, who had earned high annual salaries (as much as $80,000) during the boom years, entered the ranks of the unemployed. Computer consultants, who had carved their own niche in the booming information and support components of the petrochemical industry, no longer were able to secure long-term projects at the high hourly wages (as much as $65) that they once had enjoyed.

A shift from a goods-producing to a service-producing economy, beginning in the late 1980s, started Texas on the road toward economic recovery. By 1990, the Texas labor market ranked third nationally in employment. The unemployment rate dropped to 6 percent by the close of 1990, a level it still maintains (Texas Comptroller of Public Accounts 1996). In 1995, Texas led all states in the number of new jobs added annually; currently Texas ranks tenth in the nation in the rate of employment growth. The state's early emergence from the recession was due, in part, to the development of a more diversified economic base and the continuing relocation of high-tech industries to Texas. While oil and gas production are still an important sector of the state's economy, Texas is now less closely tied than it was to these volatile industries. For example, it is projected that, from 1993 to 2000, employment in the mining industry, especially in the areas of crude petroleum and natural gas extraction and oil and gas services, will decline by as much as 40 percent in some areas of the state. On the other hand, employment in service-producing sectors is large and growing: 96 percent of employment growth in Texas by the year 2000 is expected to occur in service industries (Texas Employment Commission 1992, 1995).

Expansions in business, engineering, and health services drive overall growth in service-sector jobs. While total wage and salaried employment for the state is projected to grow by 16 percent between 1993 and 2000, employment in business, engineering, and health services is projected to increase by 41 percent, 40 percent and 31 percent, respectively. Many of the growth occupations in these sectors are those in the higher-skill and knowledge-base areas. For example, computer-related jobs currently rank first among the fastest-growing skilled occupations. Computer system analyst and computer engineering positions are projected to increase by more than 58 percent from 1993 to 2000. The number of computer programmers also is expected to increase by 40 percent during that period. Other high-growth skilled occupations include science-related jobs in teaching and research, which are expected to grow by more than 30 percent before the year 2000 (Texas Employment Commission 1995).

It was within this context of economic expansion and healthy employment prospects for well-trained U.S. workers in science and research that a team of researchers studied the role of H-1B foreign specialty workers in the Houston and Austin area labor markets. That research forms the basis for the findings and recommendations discussed below. The chapter first discusses the project's methods, its manner of selecting firms in the research, academic, and computer industries, and its mode of inquiry. The chapter then separately presents the findings on, and recommendations for, the H-1B program in research universities and medical centers and in the complex computer industry. The conclusion identifies lessons from the study of the H-1B certification process that can be used to improve the program.

METHODOLOGY

The research reported on below is based on a 1994 field study supported by the U.S. Department of Labor's Bureau of International Labor Affairs and conducted by a team of researchers in Texas. Texas was selected as one of several research sites for the larger study because of its high national ranking in the number of H-1Bs filed and because it is the location of a DOL/ETA (Employment Training Agency) regional office. This agency is responsible for approving the Labor Condition Applications (LCAs) of H-1B petitioners and supplied the Texas team with list of ranking H-1B user firms in the state.

The primary goal of the DOL study was to understand better how the H-1B system works and how it affects those involved. To identify the interplay of the various actors in the H-1B process, the study centered on the firm as the unit of analysis and relied on a qualitative field methodology that was best suited to capture process and variation over time. Open-ended interviews were conducted with all actors involved in the recruitment, employment, and regulation of H-1B workers. The total sample included regional DOL and Texas Employment Commission officials, managers, U.S. and foreign workers in heavy-and light-user H-1B firms, private immigration attorneys, firm representatives responsible for preparing H-1B applications, and representatives of professional associations.

The original firm sample size of thirty included a variety of public and private educational institutions and a range of computer engineering firms. The firms were selected according to their size, public-versus-private status, and variable usage of the H-1B specialty skilled workers in science research and teaching, engineering, and computer-related occupations. Most of the large corporations and engineering firms and a number of the firms involved in computer applications and servicing are located in Houston; a smaller number of firms concentrating in software development are located in Austin. Public and private universities included in the sample are distributed in various cities across the state.

Once in the field, however, we were refused interviews by a number of the employers. Still others blocked access to their employees and their attorneys. By the end of the eleven-month field study, we had conducted 31 interviews with individuals representing 23 firms. In addition, we visited research laboratories of medical centers and universities in which H-1Bs are temporarily employed as postdoctoral fellows and associate scientists and conducted telephone interviews with several of the principal investigators of these research endeavors.

We had the most success in gaining access to workers. Within the 23 sample firms, we interviewed approximately seventeen H-1B foreign specialty workers and thirteen U.S. skilled workers. Most were interviewed a second time by telephone to monitor employment and immigration developments. The occupations of both the foreign and U.S. workers in the sample range from high-level computer analyst and life scientist to computer programmer and university postdoctoral fellow. We attempted to ensure that both foreign and U.S. workers were represented in high-skill and lower-skill professional occupations within the firms.

The U.S. worker interviews were supplemented with three interviews with leading representatives of professional associations for university professors, mechanical engineers, and computer consultants. One respondent is a past president of a national association of computer consultants and active in lobbying efforts for greater enforcement of prevailing wage provisions in the H-1B and permanent certification programs. Additionally, we attended the political action committee meetings of U.S. computer programmers and analysts vigorously lobbying for the elimination of the H-1B program. The U.S. worker perspective was explored further by reviewing dozens of official complaints to DOL from U.S. workers.

Our sample of attorneys includes eight private immigration attorneys, seven of whom represent the sample firms in their petitions for H-1Bs. The study sample also includes a number of government officials charged with processing and regulating H-1B applications. We conducted telephone interviews with regional and national INS representatives charged with screening and processing permanent certification, including those of H-1Bs. We visited the DOL/ETA regional office and interviewed the regional DOL certifying officer, the H-1B officer, and the office computer programmer. The regional office was instrumental in explaining the steps of the certification process. It also provided the research team with updated lists of employer names to use for the selection of firms. The research team also conducted interviews with staff of the Texas Employment Commission (TEC), the state agency responsible for providing prevailing wage data for specialty occupations.

The questions asked during the interviews varied by respondent category. Government officials were asked to describe the H-1B process from the perspective of their official task and to identify weaknesses or bottlenecks in the system with an eye towards improving interagency communication. Wage and hour officials were asked to describe in detail problems particular to the prevailing wage issue in various occupations and industries and variations across public and private firms. Employers, employees and professional association members were asked a series of open-ended questions concerning: (1) the dynamics of the supply and demand of workers and their industry; (2) economic transformations in their industry; (3) company-level restructuring strategies; (4) recruitment methods; (5) prevailing wage issues; (6) workforce composition; (7) changing skill demands; and (8) perceived effects of the H-1B program on their industries. Employees were further asked to track in detail their education and work history. H-1B workers were asked to provide a detailed immigration history, including information on transitions to and from other immigration statuses.

The Texas research team was most successful in gaining access to all involved parties in computer industry firms and in medical and university research settings. The following two sections outline our key findings regarding the usage of H-1Bs in these labor market sectors.

INTERNATIONALIZATION OF SCIENTIFIC RESEARCH: DEMAND FOR HIGHLY SKILLED FOREIGN WORKERS

Within the science and medical areas, our firm list included four very large medical centers and three research universities. Foreign researchers on H-1B visas were found overwhelmingly in the following departments and laboratories: Biochemistry, Molecular and Human Genetics, Cell Biology, and Engineering. They were recruited as research associates and research fellows by departmental heads and principal investigators to work on funded research projects, most of which are federally supported by the National Institutes of Health (NIH) and National Science Foundation (NSF). All are involved in high-level research and development positions on the basis of their highly specialized expertise.

The projects on which H-1Bs work alongside U.S. scientists in these laboratory settings are often at the cutting edge of science and involve research of a defined and complex area (e.g., megabase DNA sequencing of certain chromosomes). Research personnel must be not only highly skilled, but well-trained and well-versed in their area of expertise to meet the deadlines of funded research.

Project directors and department heads argue that there are not enough qualified U.S. candidates that meet these criteria. The following comments by a chair of a Biochemistry Department and by a Professor of Cell Biology explain the difficulty in recruiting qualified candidates:

Having a Ph.D. alone is insufficient to qualify individuals for careers in science. The background and training, as well as the research interests, become very important factors in hiring such individuals because a principal investigator must produce meaningful results within a prescribed period of time. To train and retrain takes more time than is available to most principal investigators.

These cutting-edge research projects do not involve routine experiments, but require continuous probing of the unknown. . . . Such probing requires highly sophisticated experimental techniques that only a few individuals are trained to perform. Therefore only a few qualified scientists are available to hire.

We have tremendous difficulty hiring qualified personnel for postdoctoral fellow positions in my laboratory. We've done local, national, and word-of-mouth searches. Many of the candidates have not been qualified. We require a candidate to have previous training and experience in cell culture and molecular biology. This training is essential to meet NIH deadlines. We simply cannot afford to spend three to four months training personnel when you consider that three-year NIH RO1 grants are due for renewal at the end of twenty-four months; well, it takes two to three months to find and hire someone, another few months to train them.

In all of these departments and laboratory research settings, both foreign and U.S. workers and their employers agree on the importance of H-1B visas in advancing research. Both U.S. co-workers and employers of foreign workers state that without access to the specialized skills of foreign labor, the quality of scientific research in the United States would severely decline. They believe it to be a vital component in the functioning and success of the research process, as the following quotes illustrate:

There is not a large enough supply of U.S.-born students in the hard sciences. The best person should be taken for a postdoctoral position. I would rather be surrounded by the best there is than simply by Americans. It doesn't work in this field to give U.S. workers all of the jobs (a U.S. postdoctoral student in cell biology).

Our research in Cell Biology and Neurology is fundamental to our understanding of learning processes and the diseases that affect them, that is diseases such as Alzheimer's and Parkinson's. We are considered by others in our field as one of the leading laboratories among the international community. If my four H-1B associates had not been able to obtain the visa, it would have had an enormous impact on my research program. Suffice it to say that the quality and quantity would have been substantially diminished, my ability to secure federal and nonfederal funding for the research would have been sharply curtailed, and I believe that my laboratory would not be recognized, as it is, as one of the leaders in our field. H-1Bs are essential if U.S. laboratories are to remain competitive among increasingly sophisticated laboratories in the rest of the world (Professor of cell biology and neurology).

Foreign workers appear essential to the functioning of scientific research in universities and medical centers. Without them, we were repeatedly told, research institutions would lose their competitive global edge in technological and scientific research. All representatives of these institutions, including departmental heads, laboratory advisors, and co-workers agree on the important contributions foreign workers bring to their research environments. Not only does it allow the United States to maintain its competitive edge in the global science and technology community, but it may also provide jobs for U.S. counterparts for collaborative research and technical support positions.

SHORTAGE OF U.S. RESEARCHERS

Employers in scientific research repeatedly commented on the shortage of U.S. graduate students to fill research positions in the hard sciences. There is a declining number of U.S. students entering U.S. graduate programs in science, countered by a simultaneous increase in foreign students—whose nations' educational institutions and economies have grown tremendously over the past few decades—coming to U.S. universities to study science, math, and engineering. Similarly, many new Ph.D.'s, especially U.S.-born graduates, increasingly are lured to the higher salaries and less demanding work schedules afforded by private industry. Foreign-born graduates of U.S. universities, many of whom are on a J-1 student visa, are at a disadvantage when it comes to locating permanent employment in private industry, which appears to favor U.S.-born candidates. The culture of scientific research is far more diverse and flexible; research teams in laboratory environments are typically composed of diverse groups of foreign and national scientists.

Scientists employed in research universities and medical centers, especially postdoctoral fellows, do not seem to be motivated by the often rather meager earnings offered by these institutions. Nevertheless, if the monetary rewards were greater, we might have more U.S. workers seeking careers in hard science. If, somehow, the supply of foreign workers dried up, it might well place upward pressure on wages for principal researchers and, especially, support staff. However, it does not follow that the federal funding that is a major source of U.S. basic research monies would increase to meet that need. Would the for-profit marketplace then be pressured to invest more money in basic research within the U.S. or would it move operations offshore? Further, it is unclear whether the declining number of U.S. researchers in the sciences is merely a problem of financial incentive. The declining number of U.S. scientists is, some argue, more fundamentally a result of changing secondary school curriculum, attitudes towards the rigor of scientific work, and a lack of federal support for science education.

Departmental heads and educators acknowledge that foreign students attend and support our universities because of the premier research and learning opportunities available. They subsequently compete to work in university and medical center environments because of their advanced technological environments and opportunities to work on cutting-edge research projects with some of the best scientists in the world. Employers fear that it is only a matter of time before graduate programs and research laboratories in their home countries reach sufficiently sophisticated levels to keep foreign researchers home or to draw those in the United States back home. Department chairs and laboratory advisors express their good fortune in having foreign researchers as part of their research teams and fear the day when foreign researchers and scientists will no longer seek research opportunities in the United States. These same fears were expressed by several U.S. postdoctoral fellows working in a biochemistry lab at a prestigious medical center. As one recent graduate explained:

There is a new trend among graduates in Chemistry. While many of the U.S. graduates increasingly favor private industry employment, more and more foreign-born graduates are returning home once they complete their education and training.

Professors in several of the study universities told us that this pattern is increasingly adopted by Korean-and Taiwanese-born doctoral graduates of U.S. science and engineering programs. Indeed, the return migration of foreign scientists to their homelands made national news in 1994 when distinguished chemist Yoan Lee, a long-time U.S. resident and Nobel Prize winner, made the U-turn and headed back home to direct Taiwan's prestigious Academia Suniea, an impressive conglomerate of 21 research institutes.

In sum, the H-1B visa does not appear to be abused by employers in universities and large medical centers. Positions are filled on a competitive basis and recruitment occurs at both a national and, increasingly, global level. Moreover, competition varies by the reputation of the project director and prestige of the grant. Often, interested candidates approach scientists under whom they wish to work. In this context, professors lacking an established research record have the most difficulty locating qualified candidates. Salaries are low compared to those in the private sector, especially for postdoctoral fellows, whose salaries are largely determined by federal funding sources and can run as low as $21,000 per year. Despite these meager earnings and uncertainty of employment once the H-1B runs out, many foreign postdoctoral fellows continue, at least for now, to be drawn to the technology and research opportunities available in U.S. research institutes, especially the opportunity to work with distinguished scientists on prestigious grants. As we might expect, some H-1Bs are drawn to the United States because of the lack of research opportunities back home. For these workers, the elusive green card eventually becomes a common goal. As one H-1B postdoctoral fellow working in a robotics research laboratory told us:

In Tunisia [his home country], there is a glut of scientists with Ph.D.'s from American universities, but no research opportunities for them back home. Many of us came on J-1 student visas. Our education was paid for by our government or yours. But how could they expect us to return home to nothing once we had been exposed to the most advanced research in the world?

More common, however, are statements by many who predict a future in which more Yoan Lees will return home to work in high-tech companies and research institutes created by their governments. The ability of U.S. research institutes to continue to recruit workers from an international labor pool of highly qualified persons remains an open question. This issue, while rarely raised in immigration policy debates, permeated our interviews with research personnel. As the U.S. government hints at divestment in science research, the so-called Tigers of Asia (Singapore, South Korea, and Taiwan) continue to plow billions of dollars into the development of technical and research institutes. In the absence of renewed federal support for scientific research, what we might increasingly see is the return migration of many American-educated scientists and engineers. Such a scenario would signify a dramatic reversal in the direction of the scientific brain drain that historically has favored the United States.

Since at least World War II, foreign scientists have contributed to scientific advancement in the United States and our central position in the international scientific community. Many convincingly argue that to maintain this position in the context of a shortage of U.S. qualified scientists and increased global competition, especially from our Asian neighbors, research centers must have the means to recruit and appoint foreign scientists efficiently. The H-1B appears to be the best mechanism to achieve this goal.

REORGANIZATION OF HIGH-TECH WORK: OUTSOURCING COMPUTER PROGRAMMING

With the increased computerization of work, it is not surprising that we found both foreign and U.S. computer analysts in various types of firms that cut across industrial categories. Foreign H-1B computer programmers and analysts and their U.S. counterparts whom we interviewed occupy positions ranging from low-level data entry positions in the petrochemical industries, to sophisticated software designers for high-technology MNCs. Assessing the role of these foreign workers in the U.S. labor market and their impact on labor displacement and U.S. wages is complicated by a number of major recent changes in the computer industry.

The organization of computer work has been changed dramatically and complicated by corporate downsizing and the increased demand for computer skills in all sectors of the economy. Many of the firms in which we conducted our field investigations, as might be expected from the history presented above, initiated dramatic downsizing during the late 1980s and early 1990s. Downsizing in the industries employing computer workers affected workers in different ways: many salaried workers were laid off permanently; computer consultants, who had worked for premium wages during the boom years of the 1970s and 1980s, faced wage depression resulting from an oversupply of computer workers and greater competition from outsourcing agencies.

We encountered a number of U.S. programmers and analysts who are out of work, mostly as a result of downsizing, not H-1B competition. These workers have not maintained the skill level required by advancing technology in today's computer industry. In many cases, they cannot afford the retraining costs. Thus, they are forced to compete with recent graduates with better skills or with foreign workers willing to work under the types of conditions that prevail in the industry today.[3]

CLIENTS, CONSULTANTS, AND JOB SHOPS

The way in which computer work is organized has become increasingly complex. The key employers of foreign and U.S. computer programmers and analysts include: (1) client firms, large corporations that since the late 1980s advent of downsizing outsource the bulk of their software development, especially programming tasks; (2) consulting firms that have for several decades provided high-skill software development and application services to large corporations; and (3) outsourcing agencies or "job shops," new, but fast-growing competitors in this profitable and competitive labor market niche. In contrast to the high-skill services provided by consulting agencies, job shops appear to supply the client with a lower range of skills, primarily in programming and some software application.

In our firm sample, the clients typically were large petrochemical corporations that underwent considerable downsizing in the late 1980s and early 1990s. They employ only a small minority of highly skilled H-1B engineers and software design specialists in their workplaces. Foreign and U.S. workers are recruited and paid on a competitive basis. We located several consulting firms that had serviced two of the client sample firms and one job shop that was a major outsourcing firm for the largest client in our sample. We interviewed workers, both U.S. and foreign, employed by these firms.

The computer consulting firms we studied in Austin and Houston provide services to client firms. They primarily use their own employees on a salaried or an hourly consulting basis and usually perform the work at the client site. The four consulting firms we studied primarily are involved in very advanced software design, production, and application. Two of these firms used to provide low-end software application services to client firms but claim that they are no longer able to compete at this skill level with outsourcing firms. We heard this story more than once. None are heavy users of H-1Bs although they employ a number of foreign-born, as well as U.S. analysts. The employers interviewed allowed access to current employees. Both foreign-born and U.S. workers are paid comparable high salaries or hourly consulting fees, depending on the arrangement made between the employee and employer; employers repeatedly commented that they try their utmost to find the best workers and pay maximum wages regardless of a worker's nationality. Interviews with workers confirmed their employers' statements. Given that the firms we studied rely on highly specialized skills in software design, employer recruitment and worker salaries remain very competitive. A more varied sample, including consulting firms involved in the low-end of software application, might yield very different results.

Large corporations increasingly have become clients of job shops. Downsizing in these large petrochemical and medical corporations has resulted in a reliance on both local consulting firms and outsourcing agencies to supply or perform that component of the production process that primarily requires low-level computer skills and does not require on-site supervision. The production processes in the information and research divisions of these firms do not require full-time, permanent employees. Often they need certain types of computer-related skills only on a temporary basis. These needs increasingly are filled by outsourcing agencies (job shops) that are the main employers of H-1B visa holders. Most of the work done by the H-1B workers is at the job shop, not the client site, which distinguishes them from consulting firms that are more likely to provide services at the client site. This a key distinction between the two service providers; job shops have a great deal of autonomy in structuring the work process.

As mentioned above, employers of two of the consulting agencies we interviewed claim to have been undercut by outsourcing agencies that pay lower wages to their employees and are able to bill their clients less without cuts to their own profits. Our interviews with U.S. computer programmers who work for clients under these various managements indicate that the current trend is towards increased reliance on the services of job shops. A small minority of U.S. workers recognize that the real employers in this computer game are the clients, i.e., the large corporations that use job shops to meet the needs of a flexible production process and, in some instances, as a dodge to avoid legal accountability. Managers in large corporations were proud to tell us that they employ very few H-1Bs, "only those with exceptional skills." Yet, this complex way in which computer work now is organized makes it very difficult to determine who truly employs computer workers. We believe this is an extremely important issue, as the ultimate employer should be held accountable for the employment conditions of U.S. and foreign workers. To date, the media have focused on job shops—in fact, the suppliers—while ignoring the larger firms—the clients who create the demand for these low-level "production" type positions.

SWEATED LABOR AT THE ENTRY LEVEL?

Job displacement and wage depression are potentially important issues within some parts of the computer industry. This is especially the case regarding lower-level programming and coding positions in job shops. Outsourcing firms employ both highly skilled programmer analysts and low-level coders and programmers. Highly skilled programmers work as salaried employees or contractors; in either case, H-1B worker earnings do not appear significantly lower than those of their U.S. counterparts. In contrast, we found a great discrepancy between the wages paid to foreign and U.S. workers in such low-level positions as coding, programming, and routine applications. We interviewed four H-1B worker programmers who were paid salaries almost $10,000 a year less than their U.S. counterparts in the same firm. Another job shop pays H-1Bs, who are on call for six days a week for one firm, salaries; they pay U.S. coworkers, who work at a variety of sites, hourly consulting fees. At neither place do the working conditions of the H-1Bs appear to meet those attested to by the employer, thus creating a two-tiered employment system in the industry. Further, these positions—that at most require a B.A.—do not involve the application of specialized skills that justify the temporary hiring of an H-1B worker. The following case illustrates our point.

We gained access to a job shop that was a major supplier of programming services for one of the largest clients firms in our sample. Most of its workers are Filipino computer programmers who were recruited abroad by the outsourcing firm's headquarters in New York. Word of mouth from other programmers lured these programmers to a well-known and quite fashionable Manila hotel where they all gathered in a seminar room and were "courted" by the recruiters—offered handsome salaries averaging $33,000 a year with benefits (compared to $400–600 per month in the Philippines), a relocation fee of several thousand dollars, a one-way ticket to the United States, initial housing, and the opportunity to lease a car through the company. In exchange,

they had to sign a contract stating that they would work for the firm
for a minimum of eighteen months, during which time the firm promised to petition for their permanent residence status.[4] None of the workers interviewed has received permanent certification, but they are
reluctant to broach the subject with their employer for fear of loosing
their job and, thus, their H-1B visa.

The Filipino programmers work in an underground, high-tech sweat-
shop, located on the basement level of the modern skyscraper in which
the outsourcing firm is located. In the shop's front room, three Anglo
supervisors sit at widely spaced desks. In an adjacent back room of the
same size, approximately 20 Filipino employees work in cubicles. All
the H-1B Filipinos we interviewed at this outsourcing firm are on salary
that they believe is at least $10,000 less than their American counter-
parts. This is difficult to determine precisely since the latter are sometimes paid on a consulting-fee basis. Consultant positions generally are
more lucrative than salaried ones in computer work and also are more
desirable because of the greater autonomy provided to the workers.
Nonetheless, the H-1B workers are willing to take less in earnings in
exchange for the promise of a green card. For these workers, the H-
1B definitely is seen as a pathway to permanent residency (even though
some state that they plan to return to the Philippines). Upon receiving
permanent labor certification, all workers intend to move out of this
firm because of the poor working conditions and ambiguous policy
decisions. Their most frequently cited reasons include too much supervision, a pattern of arbitrary promotions, and a practice of not paying
workers for overtime. They complain that, while American workers
always go to the client's site, foreign workers rarely do so. On those
few occasions when they are sent to the client's site, they told us, they
typically are accompanied by an Anglo employee who interfaces with
client representatives.[5]

The H-1B workers also feel that their jobs could be done by U.S.
workers. The majority told us that their previous work experiences or
skills used in the Philippines are not applied in their positions at this
outsourcing firm. In one case, a worker, who was recruited with the
understanding that she was being hired because of her skills in CO-
BALT programming, has been with the job shop for two years and has
never used these skills. On the contrary, the firm trains the foreign
workers; the majority of these workers claim they learned entirely new
skills to fit clients' needs. At the same time, these Filipino workers see

themselves as more desirable than other foreign workers because of cultural similarities, including English fluency and colonial linkages. In summary, the possibility for abuse of H1-B workers exists in these low-level computer positions.

Moreover, at least in the case of Houston, the market has not provided training and employment opportunities for U.S. workers structurally displaced by downsizing strategies. Our findings suggest that, in cases where firms (all types) use outsourcing agencies for low-skill level computer programming and coding, the potential for wage depression and some job displacement may exist.

POLICY RECOMMENDATIONS

1. Given the increasing globalization of scientific research, coupled with the enormous contributions foreign scientists have made to U.S. research institutions, we recommend that efforts be made to facilitate temporary positions in these settings. Specifically, we recomend:

Creation of a special H category for research universities and institutes. This category should not have a numerical cap to assure the continued entry of high-level foreign scientists into research institutions. Creation of this category could make the paperwork process less cumbersome for institutions' administrative personnel, usually the Directors of International Services[6] who have little training in immigration procedures and less burdensome for foreign workers, especially post-doctoral fellows.

2. Corporate downsizing has had an impact on American workers' earnings and job security. Nowhere is this more observable than among workers in computer-related occupations. Downsizing and the use of temporary workers is increasingly observable in other industries as well. While it is impossible to turn the tide of market forces, a few suggested changes could minimize the potential for the abuse of the H-1B worker and for the negative impact of restructuring on American workers, specifically computer programmers and analysts:

The U.S. Department of Labor should monitor closely the supply of U.S. workers in low-level computer positions. In the absence of a real occupational shortage, perhaps the educational requirements for H-1Bs should be increased from a bachelor's to a master's degree. We found that it was H-1B workers with less training who are most likely to face workplace abuse. Clearly, there are special skills and techniques that highly skilled foreign workers possess. We have, however, come across too many foreign H-1Bs with only bachelor's of science degrees who are performing tasks that can be easily done by U.S. workers.

Emphasis should be given to retraining unemployed workers who are displaced during corporate downsizings. In the absence of federal funding for this retraining, we recommend giving tax breaks to unemployed U.S. computer workers to help support their personal retraining costs.

The client company, as well as the outsourcing agency, should be held accountable for the working conditions or violations of the terms of the H-1B visa. The abuse of H-1Bs is most prevalent in the joint ventures of client and outsourcing firms. Greater regulatory efforts on the part of the Department of Labor could track the employment history of firms, not industries, to capture the effects of downsizing and corporate leasing of services on U.S. workers.

CONCLUSIONS

Given what looks like a robust labor market in Houston for computer analysts and programmers and for high-level researchers in faculty positions, we initially were at a loss to explain what we encountered in the field: unemployed and underemployed computer programmers and analysts and an increasingly tight labor market for faculty positions. We also were perplexed by professional association reports of increasing unemployment among scientists, engineers, and computer analysts. The only way to explain what looks like a simultaneous surplus (unemployment) and shortage of workers (projected demand) is by the increasing prevalence of spot shortages in particular high-skilled occupations within science and technology. Unfortunately, we were unable to locate any objective data to illustrate clear instances of spot shortages resulting from an uneven mix of supply and demand.

What we did encounter in the field, however, were displaced older computer analysts who were not retrained to compete in this rapidly changing technological environment and unemployed computer analysts who would not work for wages less than they had received during the boom years. At the same time, we also encountered employers scraping to locate competent computer analysts to work with an emergent complex computer language such as C++. Similarly, we came across positions at universities that had gone unfilled for months or years because the department was looking for someone with a particular skill, e.g., an engineer skilled in robotics development.

These seemingly contradictory and divergent employment trends among skilled workers are not so perplexing once we look beyond immigration policy and focus on the implications of corporate downsizing and global labor markets for skilled workers. While corporate downsizing in Texas cut across all industries, it had particularly severe consequences for computer programmers, system analysts, and engineers employed in the research and development and information services divisions of many large petrochemical firms headquartered in Texas. These skilled workers, many of whom had carved out their own niches in the petrochemical industry and were commanding unprecedented high salaries during the oil boom years of the seventies and eighties, found themselves either unemployed or unable to command their previous consulting fees. Although the Texas economy has taken a turn for the better in recent years, skilled workers encounter much greater competition than before as a result of a burgeoning consulting sector that increasingly services client firms. Faced with increasing competition and stagnant wages, many disgruntled workers target the H-1B program as the source of their problems.

This is not to say that corporate downsizing alone is responsible for the displacement and wage depression of skilled computer programmers and analysts in Texas labor markets. The growth of the consulting sector in Texas labor markets also has created greater competition among these skilled workers. Within this sector, some consulting firms capitalize on the H-1B program to bring in foreign workers to perform entry-level tasks that could be done by native workers with a bachelor's degree.

The recruitment and employment conditions of skilled H-1B workers in science and research operates at a very different level. Candidates for these high-level research positions are carefully recruited on a competitive basis and paid the prevailing wages. In these research settings, the H-1B program achieves its intended policy goal, providing employers with immediate access to the best and brightest among an international labor pool of highly qualified scientists and researchers.

While the focus of this study is limited to the recruitment and employment experience of engineers, computer programmers, and scientists and researchers in less than 30 firms in Texas, the findings strongly suggest a more general trend. Despite an apparently "robust" Texas economy with a high demand for technical and professional workers, the labor market opportunities for most will remain limited. The most qualified and most experienced segment of the workforce will be the most prepared to escape the consequences of increased restructuring of the workplace. They are the ones most able to take advantage of the demands and opportunities of a dynamic global market that increasingly is driven by rapid research advances in technology and science requiring new, specialized skills. Slight increases in the number of temporary foreign workers in U.S. labor markets, as provided by the H-1B visa, appear to have little effect on these structural changes in the organization of work. Further restrictions and regulations in skilled immigration, however, might well have dramatic effects. Restricting employer access to temporary skilled foreign labor might expand U.S. corporate offshore production to include highly skilled production in recently established research sites in Asia and elsewhere. Extreme caution must, therefore, be exercised when contemplating changes to existing policy.

NOTES

1. In addition to the H-1B subdivision (the H-1A being discontinued), the H program includes three other types of temporary foreign worker categories: the H-2A subcategory is reserved for temporary agricultural workers, the H-2B for temporary nonagricultural services not exceeding a year, and the H-3 for a relatively small number of certain trainees.

2. A specialty occupation under the 1990 Act is one that requires the practical and theoretical application of specialized knowledge and attainment of at least a bachelor's degree in the specified specialty.

3. Many displaced U.S. workers, unwilling to accept the possibility that downsizing has depressed wages, attribute declining opportunity and wages to foreign workers.

4. This was the time required for the initial cohort of recruits; subsequent cohorts had to promise to work anywhere from two to three years.

5. As these foreign workers come into contact with their U.S. counterparts in the industry, they express increasing interest in becoming contract workers, positions seen as more lucrative and autonomous than salaried positions.

6. In Texas, the Attorney General's Office does not allow public institutions to hire lawyers for this purpose.

REFERENCES

Hagan, J. M., and Rodriguez, N. P. 1992. Recent Economic Restructuring and Evolving Intergroup Relations in Houston. In L. Lamphere, ed., *Struc-*

turing Diversity: Ethnographic Perspectives on the New Immigration. Chicago: The University of Chicago Press.

Smith, B. 1989. *Handbook on the Houston Economy.* Houston: Center for Public Policy, University of Houston.

Texas Comptroller of Public Accounts. 1996. *Texas Economic Quarterly* (January).

Texas Employment Commission. 1992. *Industry and Occupational Projections to the Year 2000.* Austin: Economic Research and Analysis Department.

———. 1995. *Discovering Your Future: Industry and Occupation Projections to the Year 2000.* Austin: Economic Research and Analysis Department.

Chapter 7

Nonimmigrant Visa Programs: Problems and Policy Reforms

GREGORY DeFREITAS

Any attempt to improve this country's nonimmigrant policy first must be clear about the basic purpose of that policy within the broader context of the national immigration system. The principal goal of the immigration system has, for at least 30 years, been the humanitarian one of reuniting families and providing safe haven to refugees. Some have argued that this emphasis has been excessive, resulting in declines in the skill levels of recent cohorts and in worsening competition with native workers. They favor making economic characteristics of prospective immigrants a much more important criterion for admission.

As an economist, I find such proposals tempting but ultimately wrongheaded. My own research and reading of the latest empirical literature convinces me that immigration has, at least at current levels, had relatively small net impacts on overall domestic wages and employment (DeFreitas 1995). This does not lead me to favor unrestricted admissions, nor does it mean that we should neglect to evaluate carefully and be ready to make adjustments for the economic impacts of future migration streams.[1] But humanitarian goals remain far preferable to any strategy (probably futile) of making immigration another lever of economic policy. In the event that proposed reductions in annual entry slots are enacted in the near future, it seems to me far more important to preserve ample family and refugee visas than to earmark scarce visas based solely on an applicant's occupational skills.[2] Moreover, a basic national employment goal should be eventually to fill any

short-term skill shortages through training or retraining of native workers rather than relying on foreign professionals.

Since most economic research has focused on the impacts of immigration on unskilled or semi-skilled labor markets, relatively little is
known about the domestic consequences of importing large numbers
of skilled workers. We do know from the 1990 census that more than
one-tenth of U.S. scientists and engineers are foreign born, well above
the immigrant share of the population (Bouvier & Simcox 1995). There
are more immigrants in professional occupations (1.35 million) than
there are African American professionals (1.1 million). And it is clear
that well-educated immigrants have carved out niches in certain well-
paid occupations. For example, more than one-fifth of U.S. physicians
are now foreign born, and the fraction is much higher in such specialties
as immunology, neurology, and pediatrics. About 12.3 percent of all
engineers are immigrants, with a disproportionate foreign presence in
education and in private research and development. The foreign born
account for 9 percent of registered nurses, of whom nearly one-half are
from a single country, the Philippines. In New York City, it has been
estimated that 20 to 30 percent of nurses are temporary foreign workers
(U.S. DOL 1989). Even in the government sector, there is evidence of
ethnic networks insulating immigrant niches. In New York City government in the 1980s, the foreign born achieved growing concentrations
in technical professions, with competitive equivalents in the private
sector, such as accountants, chemists, and engineers. Nearly one-half
of all new engineers hired by the New York Transportation Department
in the period 1986–1990 were Asians (Waldinger 1994). Immigrants
appear to be attracted to secure, well-paid, public sector jobs, at least
until they can improve their language skills enough and attain the licenses required to enter the private sector.

The studies of immigrant professionals typically conclude that their
rising share of high-level jobs may induce employers to become dependent on foreign labor sources instead of actively recruiting and
training natives for these jobs (see Levine, Fox, & Danielson 1993;
National Research Council 1988; U.S. DOL 1989; Waldinger 1994).
Insofar as this diminishes natives' access to high-skill, high-pay jobs,
the implications for American workers at all skill levels are worrisome.
For it may mean that not only is there competition between native-and
foreign-born professionals, but also that there is some reduction in the
chances of the less-skilled for upward occupational mobility. Until

more research becomes available on this issue, it seems prudent to, at a minimum, resist any attempts to expand the number of employment-based permanent resident slots or even to lower the number somewhat. Nonimmigrant policy reform becomes all the more important as the immigration system undergoes change. The nonimmigrant programs need to meet three goals: (1) to provide American businesses, universities, and cultural institutions access to international talent; (2) to provide foreign visitors access to U.S. schooling and training; and (3) to ensure that pursuit of the first two goals does nothing to expose U.S. workers to unfair competition with foreigners or to reduce their opportunities for training and upward job mobility. In what follows, I briefly discuss some of the main reasons why certain current nonimmigrant programs are failing to serve these ends and make a number of recommendations for policy reforms.

THE H-1B PROGRAM

H-1B temporary visas for specialty occupations have been the source of great concern of late for a number of reasons. First, it presently is completely legal for employers to lay off U.S. workers and replace them with H-1B workers. As recent corporate restructurings, global competition, and defense cutbacks have threatened the job prospects of many American technicians and professionals, more and more cases of alleged displacement by temporary foreign workers have appeared. For example:

- Aggressive downsizing at Digital Equipment Corporation slashed nearly 21,500 jobs between late 1991 and November 1993. But this coincided with the firm applying for more than 1,100 H-1B visas to bring in foreign computer workers.
- In June 1995, at CSX Corporation's Sealand unit in New Jersey, about 100 American computer programmers lost their jobs as Sealand hired an equal number of replacements from India and the Phillipines. Worse still, the U.S. workers were required to spend their last weeks at the firm training their own replacements. Many of these jobs ultimately will leave the country with the newly trained foreigners on their planned return home. Sealand estimated that the export of jobs would save the company 30 percent on salaries (Zachary 1995).
- Likewise, American International Group, Inc. laid off almost 250 computer service workers in its insurance operations in New Jersey. H-1B replacements

were brought in and received their training from the soon-to-be-terminated U.S. employees.

A second source of concern with the program is the apparently widespread abuses by so-called "job contractors." Some of these are alleged to bring large numbers of foreign workers into the country solely to lease them to U.S. firms. They appear to shuttle these workers in and out of the country, especially to fill many computer and health care jobs. The Department of Labor (DOL) has documented numerous cases of job contractors violating the law by paying foreign workers far below the prevailing wage. In the physical and occupational therapy fields alone, nearly 400 H-1Bs recently were found to be owed $2 million in back pay by contractors.

The relative ease with which unscrupulous job contractors have exploited the program highlights another problem. Employers are not required to show that U.S. workers are unavailable for the jobs H1-B workers will fill, nor are employers required to demonstrate that they are seeking to train or recruit Americans for these jobs. In fact, the program is driven largely by employers themselves.

Finally, any program that is supposed to meet only "temporary" employment needs should keep foreign worker stays as brief as possible. Yet, current law allows for a period of stay of as many as six years, well beyond any reasonable notion of a temporary visit to fill a short-term skill shortage. This likely induces some firms to become dependent on a steady supply of foreign workers rather than to seek to recruit natives. Moreover, it is evident that H-1B visas have become a conduit for obtaining employment-based green cards. DOL estimates that more than 90 percent of the recipients of such green cards are already in the United States and that perhaps two out of three of these are already employed (often illegally) by the very firm that files the immigrant petition for them.

These problems lead me to suggest the following changes in the H-1B program. Some of these correspond to recent proposals by the commission and by DOL (Fraser 1995; Reich 1995), but, in general, I favor stronger measures.

RECOMMENDATIONS

1. Restrict the eligibility for H-1B visas to those occupational categories in which DOL verifies that there is a labor shortage. This would

require a new system parallel to the existing labor certification program. The latter long has been far too employer-driven and inefficient, as the DOL itself now recognizes. Hence, the new system must be designed carefully to avoid these past flaws and to exploit better both government and independent economic analysis of local labor market conditions. More resources need to be allocated to improve the availability of up-to-date labor market data for localities, particularly that subset in which most temporary foreign workers tend to concentrate.

2. Reduce the validity period of labor condition applications (LCAs) from six to two years and bar renewal applications. Under recently adopted DOL rules, the validity period for each application was cut to three years, but employers are still allowed to keep an H-1B worker for a total of six years if they submit an LCA for a three-year renewal. Anything more than two years is excessive and encourages some employers to become dependent on foreign labor.

3. Require that all employers filing H-1B LCAs attest that, within the six months before an H-1B worker begins employment, they have not laid off legal permanent resident aliens or U.S. citizens with similar qualifications and work experience in the job for which the temporary foreign workers are being sought; and require that they attest that they will not lay off such legal immigrant or citizen workers within the six months after H-1B employees are hired or leased by the firm and for the duration of the visas.

4. Bar access to H-1B workers where a firm's employees are involved in a labor union election campaign, strike, or lockout. The DOL now supports prohibiting access to such workers during strikes or lockouts, but protection of workers' democratic right to choose collective bargaining representation without interference by their employers also necessitates guaranteeing, once employees have filed an application for an election to choose whether or not to be represented by a union, that foreign workers not be used as a real or perceived threat.

5. Require employers filing H-1B LCAs to demonstrate that they are undertaking substantial and continuous efforts to fill the jobs for which they currently desire foreign workers with U.S. employees in the near future.

6. Require employers of H-1B workers to pay a fee, equal to 20 percent of the value of the total compensation package it will pay to those workers, into a public or private fund certified by the DOL as dedicated to the goal of improving the training and recruitment of U.S. workers into the occupations for which the H-1B workers currently are

being employed. This parallels the proposals of the commission for employment-based immigrants.

7. Raise the standards to be met by "job contractors" to prevent past abuses at any of the multiple work sites that may lease their H-1B workers. Current DOL regulations generally are limited to the place of employment at the time an employer files an LCA. This allows job contractors who place foreign workers with other employers to enjoy laxer controls. The new policy reforms recommended above should be applied to all work sites where H-1B nonimmigrants are working, whether or not they are employed by a job contractor (see discussion in U.S. DOL 1993).

8. Require nonimmigrants holding H-1B visas to leave the United States for a minimum of one year following expiration of that visa and before applying for any permanent residency visa. This will help end the common practice by which H-1B visas are used merely as a holding mechanism while nonimmigrants stay in the United States seeking receipt of green cards. It also should help reduce U.S. employers' dependence on nonimmigrant labor.

OTHER EMPLOYMENT-BASED NONIMMIGRANT PROGRAMS

The wide array of other temporary visas granted for ostensibly employment purposes also bring into the country large numbers of individuals. For example, J-1 visas (for exchange visitors to teach, study, or conduct research) totaled more than 197,000 in FY 1993, and another 43,000 relatives came with them. To coordinate all these programs so as to protect American workers better, I suggest:

9. All other employment-based nonimmigrant visa applications must pass the same labor shortage test recommended (see 1 above) for H-1B LCAs before the nonimmigrant is permitted to work here during the duration of the visa.

CONCLUSIONS

Widespread concern about the nation's worsening income inequality and underemployment have generated renewed debate about the optimal volume and composition of immigration. Thanks to fierce lobbying by business groups and encouragement from economists claiming immigrants' "quality" had fallen, the U.S. government in the 1990s expanded the permanent visa category for people with "needed skills" and granted large numbers of employment-based nonimmigrant visas. This was done with very little research knowledge of the possible consequences on skilled native workers or on the prospects of the unskilled for occupational mobility.

There is evidence that skilled immigrants recently have been hired by firms that were simultaneously cutting their skilled native work force. And many on H1-B temporary visas, after mastering key elements of the work process at U.S. firms, return home to train others to do the same work. This then facilitates the export of jobs abroad by American firms seeking low-cost, high-tech labor. Computer programmers, cinematographers, and aircraft machinists appear to be among those most at risk of replacement. So great has their concern become that it has helped spark at least one strike (Boeing) and led the DOL to undertake a long-overdue scrutiny of the abuses of some job-contracting firms.

These modest steps have provoked an opposition campaign by the National Association of Manufacturers, the U.S. Chamber of Commerce, Microsoft, and other computer companies. They insist that global firms need large numbers of skilled foreigners to stay competitive and grow, thereby enabling them to expand their U.S. base. However, in an era of widespread corporate downsizing, claims of skilled labor shortages have raised growing suspicions. Unlike the early 1980s, the majority of permanent layoffs now are occurring among college-educated employees. The share of job loss accounted for by those earning at least $50,000 has doubled since the eighties. Many scientists, engineers, and computer specialists have found themselves quite vulnerable to cutbacks by defense contractors, high-tech civilian firms, and universities.

What is needed now is more, not less, limitation on and monitoring of skill-based temporary immigration programs. International exchange of ideas and skills still can be ensured by granting brief visas for foreigners willing to train U.S. workers. And the more than 300,000 student visas now granted each year provide ample opportunity for those from abroad seeking access to training here.

Instead of exporting more high-wage jobs or importing professionals to meet supposed "skill shortages," business and government must be induced finally to provide first-class schooling, training, and retraining for the vast numbers of low-wage and underemployed Americans. And, as well, they must help generate enough new high-wage jobs for these workers to fill.

NOTES

1. I have detailed my recommendations for reforming the permanent resident visa system elsewhere (DeFreitas 1995).

2. See the findings of Jasso and Rosenzweig (1995) on the reduction in the occupational differences between employment-based and family-sponsored immigrants within a few years of arrival.

REFERENCES

Bouvier, L. F., and Simcox, D. 1995. Foreign-Born Professionals in the United States. *Population and Environment* 16 (May):429–44.

DeFreitas, G. 1995. *Immigration, Inequality, and Policy Alternatives*. Working Paper #82. New York: Russell Sage Foundation.

Fraser, J. 1995. Statement before the Subcommittee on Immigration of the Senate Judiciary Committee (September 13).

Jasso, G., and Rosenzweig, M. R. 1995. Do Immigrants Screened for Skills Do Better than Family Reunification Immigrants? *International Migration Review* 29 (Spring):85–111.

Levine, R., Fox, T., and Danielson, S. 1993. *Preliminary Findings from a Study of the Impact of the Nursing Relief Act of 1989*. Washington, DC: The Urban Institute.

National Research Council. 1988. *Foreign and Foreign-Born Engineers in the United States: Infusing Talent, Raising Issues*. Washington, DC: National Academy Press.

Reich, R. B. 1995. Statement before the Subcommittee on Immigration of the Senate Judiciary Committee (September 28).

U.S. Department of Labor (DOL), Bureau of International Labor Affairs. 1989. The Effects of Immigration on the U.S. Economy and Labor Market. *Immigration Policy and Research Report 1*. Washington, DC.

———. Employment and Training Administration. 1993. Labor Condition Applications and Requirements for Employers Using Aliens on H-1B Visas in Specialty Occupations and as Fashion Models. *Federal Register* 58 (October 6):52152–61. Washington, DC.

Waldinger, R. 1994. The Making of an Immigrant Niche. *International Migration Review* 28 (Spring):3–30.

Zachary, G. P. 1995. Skilled U.S. Workers' Objections Grow as More of Their Jobs Shift Overseas. *Wall Street Journal* (October 9):A2.

Chapter 8

California's Farm Labor Market and Immigration Reform

PHILIP MARTIN

Agriculture in California has from its beginnings relied on newcomers to the state who had few nonfarm job options to seasonal farm work. For this reason, the state's farmers long have had a keen interest in U.S. immigration policies, usually seeking exceptions to general U.S. immigration policies on the grounds that the nature of California agriculture was such that foreign workers were needed.

Since 1980, California agriculture's most successful influence on immigration policy was reflected in the Immigration Reform and Control Act (IRCA) of 1986. IRCA imposed sanctions or fines on U.S. employers who knowingly hired unauthorized alien workers and offered legal immigrant status to many illegal aliens who worked in U.S. agriculture. The intent of IRCA was to deter illegal immigration, to legalize the status of long-term illegal U.S. residents and illegal farm workers, and to regulate the access of farmers to legal nonimmigrant and probationary immigrant workers. Growers were able to win concessions for because IRCA threatened to stem their flow of labor. The long-standing H2-A program was simplified and a guestworker program, contingent upon a reduction in the supply of labor, was instituted.

More recently, Congress has moved to further strengthen border patrol efforts, as well as sanction enforcement. As a result, and despite strong statements against agricultural guestworkers in June 1995 by both President Clinton and the Commission on Immigration Reform, California farm organizations tried and failed to include a guestworker program in immigration reform legislation moving through Congress.

As in the mid-1980s, the growers argue that, despite employer sanctions and high unemployment rates among U.S. farm workers, at least 30 to 50 percent of their seasonal workers are unauthorized. If effective, strengthened border enforcement sanctions might, they believe, remove these workers.

They argue a guestworker program, one that is flexible and easy to administer, will be necessary in order to make their needed worker numbers and to meet legal requirements for authorized status.

CALIFORNIA AGRICULTURE'S LABOR MARKET

California has the nation's largest and most diverse agriculture. California farmers produce the same commodities that are found in other states—milk, wheat, and cotton—but the distinguishing feature of the state's agriculture is the production of specialty crops: California produces about 40 percent of the nation's fruits and nuts, vegetables and melons, and such horticultural specialties as flowers and mushrooms. These so-called FVH commodities, in turn, represent one-half of California's $20 billion in farm sales, and the orchards, vineyards, and greenhouses in which they are produced are where most farm workers find jobs.

There are many ways to describe a California farm labor market in which 800,000 to 900,000 individuals find at least temporary jobs with 25,000 crop and livestock employers or agricultural service firms, such as farm labor contractors and custom harvesters. One way is to focus on three "C"'s: concentration, contractors, and conflict.

Concentration refers to the fact that most farm workers are hired by a relatively small number of large farms. Contractors refers to the presence in many farm labor markets of "intermediaries" who match seasonal workers with jobs. Conflict refers to the stormy history in which workers protested low wages or poor working conditions but then individually got out of agriculture when their collective efforts to obtain wage and benefit improvements were rebuffed.

Concentration. Agriculture is probably California's largest employer of adult immigrants. According to state Unemployment Insurance (UI) tax records, 24,500 California farm employers paid $4.6 billion in wages to employees in 1990 (Martin & Miller 1993:22). But these farm labor data conceal as much as they reveal. Most of these farm employers or "reporting units" are small; one-half pay less than $10,000 in farm wages. The largest 1,250 farm employers—just 5 percent—pay about two-thirds of California's farm wages.

Concentration is also the rule among farm workers. A "farm worker" is anyone who works for wages on a farm. Farm work is seasonal, and so most farm workers also do nonfarm work or, as many are immigrants, return to their country of origin when there are no farm jobs for them in California. Most workers are in the farm work force for only a short time. More than one-half have less than $1,000 in annual farm earnings which, at $5 hourly, means that they do 200 or fewer hours of farm work, or the equivalent of 5 weeks.

Concentration means that the largest 5 percent of employers, and the 10 percent of farm workers who are employed year-round, account for most of the farm wages paid and earned. The "average" farm employer is very small, while the large farm employers, who hire most of the state's farm workers, each may employ a peak 5,000 workers and have a weekly payroll of $1 million—making them large employers by any definition.

In Figure 8.1, small farms were those that sold less than $50,000 of FVH commodities in 1992—they were 61 percent of all production units, but they accounted for only 3 percent of total sales. At the other extreme, the 39 percent of FVH farms that each sold more than $50,000 of FVH commodities in 1992 accounted for 97 percent of California's FVH sales.

The "average" California farm worker earned about $3,000 from farmers in 1990, but there are few workers with such earnings. Instead, workers tend to fall into one of three groups (Martin & Miller 1993). Just more than one-half are very low earners—earning $1,000 or less for working on one or more farms for a few weeks during the year. About 40 percent, or 360,000, are in the seasonal worker category, earning $4,000 to $6,000 for one-half year's farm work. The third group are the year-round workers who earn $12,000 or more annually.

Who are these large farm employers who hire most of the state's farm workers? A 1992 survey of 900 California farm employers reported that only about 30 percent of all farm employers were corporations, but 60 percent of the sample farms with annual payrolls over $500,000 were corporations, usually family-run (Rosenberg et al. 1995: 14a). An example is the Zaninovich table grape farm in California's San Joaquin Valley, an operation that annually sells about 5 million 25-pound boxes of grapes at an average price of $10 per box; Zani-

Figure 8.1
FVH Farms and Sales in California in 1992

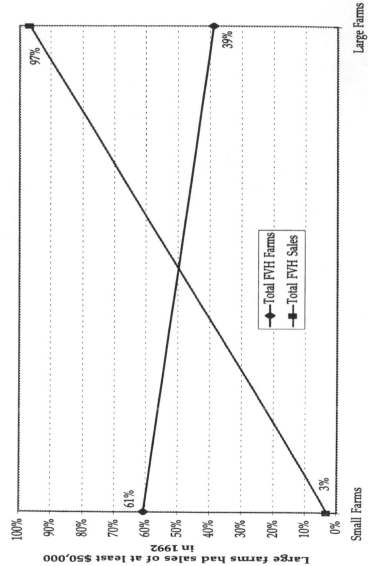

FVH farms have at least 50 percent of their sales in vegetables, fruits and nuts, and/or horticultural specialties. California had 41,521 FVH farms with $9.3 billion in FVH sales in 1992.

Source: 1992 Census Agriculture, U.S. Department of Commerce, September 1994.

novich hires 1,000 farm workers to help generate $50 million in annual grape sales. Fresno-area raisin farms represent the small end of the farm size spectrum. In the most labor-intensive activity in U.S. agriculture— some 50,000 farm workers spread through 200,000 acres of vineyards to cut bunches of 20 to 25 pounds of green grapes and lay them on paper trays to dry into raisins for six to eight weeks each August and September. Workers receive $0.15 to $0.18 per paper tray of raisins cut and laid, and the farm labor contractor (FLC) who typically recruits them receives $0.04 to $0.05 for payroll taxes, business expenses, and profits. Most of the vineyards are small—20 to 50 acres—and workers are often "recruited" with a sign at the entrance to the vineyard saying, in Spanish, "workers wanted."

Workers employed in short harvest crops such as raisins can earn more if they find other farm jobs, such as harvesting peaches and plums before, and olives and citrus after, the raisin harvest. Many farm workers are able to string together a series of farm jobs, but it is not easy for many of them to travel from farm to farm looking for work.

Contractors. Intermediaries who find jobs for farm workers and supervise them while they work, are the second "C" of the California farm labor market; most farm workers find a succession of farm jobs with the help of a contractor intermediary. Contractors are not a new phenomenon; Chinese farm workers in the 1870s designated one person in the crew who could speak English to search for the next farm job for the crew. Over time, farm labor intermediaries evolved from one of the crew to independent businessmen who seek to profit from the difference between what a farmer pays to have a job done and what the worker gets (Fisher 1952; Fuller 1942; McWilliams 1949).

Contractors have been the major farm labor story of the 1980s and 1990s. There were only 935 FLCs in California in 1990 who were registered with state Unemployment Insurance authorities to pay taxes on the wages they paid to workers, but they employed one-third of all farm workers reported to the UI system, and their role in matching farm workers and jobs has been increasing (Thilmany 1995).

Critics assert that there are far more FLCs who are not registered and that farmers have encouraged the rise of labor contracting by switching from hiring workers directly to hiring them through hard-to-regulate contractors. According to farm worker advocates, farmers know that these "merchants of labor" must be cheating the government or the workers, as the FLCs in some cases agree that their workers will do farm work for what appears to be a money-losing fee. Cesar Chavez made the elimination of farm labor contractors one of keystones of his efforts to reform the farm labor market and ensured that the California Agricultural Labor Relations Act (ALRA) in 1975 included a clause that asserted that FLCs could not be employers for labor relations purposes.

The theory was that only such strict farmer liability for FLC labor relations law violations would encourage farmers to be responsible for the activities of FLCs who bring workers to their farms. Many farm worker advocates would like to impose strict liability on farmers for minimum wage and immigration law violations. Under current circumstances, a FLC can be the employer solely liable for minimum wage and immigration law violations, but not for labor organizing violations.

Conflict. The third "C" is the inevitable conflict between employers and workers over a "fair" wage. This conflict can be resolved in three major ways: first, by employers acting unilaterally, as happens in workplaces where the employer says, "Do it my way or leave;" second, by determining a fair wage through collective bargaining; and third, by using government rules that stipulate minimum wages and mandatory benefits for workers. The usual way of resolving work place conflict in agriculture has been for dissatisfied workers to exit the farm work force.

Conflict in farm labor markets has several unique characteristics. Farm employers often band together and set a "standard" wage, thus creating peer pressure to resist worker demands for higher wages or they decide not to use the H-2A program to "prove" that it cannot work in California. In many instances as farm worker leaders have been radical outsiders in conservative rural communities, the entire community, not just the farmers, often was willing to tolerate violations of individual rights to resolve "farm labor troubles." The workers who were dissatisfied with the wages they were offered on farms sometimes faced eviction from their temporary homes, making their choice about whether to refuse to work a decision that affected both their income and their housing.

California Fruits and Vegetables

California has led the nation in farm sales since 1950. While the state has only 2 percent of U.S. farmland; it accounts for more than 10 percent of the nation's farm sales because it produces high-value fruit and vegetable commodities. Thus, California farmers obtain far more revenue per acre than most U.S. farmers. For example, California harvested 1.2 million acres of vegetables and melons in 1990, and they had a farm value of $3.5 billion. Nebraska farmers, by contrast, tilled fifteen times more land but had only about the same level of farm sales.

U.S. agriculture can be profiled as an economic sector producing mostly livestock and field crops. California agriculture is different. About two-thirds of California's 1994 farm sales of $20 billion represents the sale of crops; only one-third represents the sale of livestock products. Within California's crop sector, fruits, vegetables, and horticultural specialties worth $9 billion were three-fourths of the state's $12 billion in crop sales. Field crops, such as cotton, hay, wheat, and rice, are important users of California farmland and water, but they account for only one-sixth of California's farm sales.

California began producing labor-intensive fruits and vegetables and shipping them long distances a century ago, but much of the expansion of California's FVH agriculture occurred since World War II. In some cases there have been truly dramatic production increases: broccoli production grew more than sixfold between 1960 and 1993; almond and strawberry tonnage rose more than fivefold; nectarine and wine grape production more than quadrupled.

The land used to produce fruits and vegetables is valuable. In 1990, for example, land in the Monterey area used to produce vegetables was worth an average $10,000 per acre and vineyards and orchards in the Fresno area sold for $5,000 or more per acre. A rough indicator of the amount of money tied up in California FVH agriculture can be seen in the following estimates: if the value of CA vegetable land averages $10,000 per acre, then 1 million acres of California vegetable land is worth about $10 billion. If the value of fruit and nut land averages $5,000, then 2 million acres of fruit and nut land also is worth $10 billion.

Labor Costs and Harvest Cycles

Most of the fruits and vegetables grown in California generate farm sales of $2,500 to $3,000 per acre. The production of fruits and vegetables is considered "labor-intensive," an adjective that is rarely defined but suggests that the costs of hired workers are the single largest production expense. Labor costs in FVH production range from 20 percent to 50 percent of total production costs—higher than the 20 percent average in manufacturing, but less than labor's 70 to 80 percent share of costs in many service industries.

In most commodities, expenditures for hired workers—seasonal and year-round, and production plus supervisory labor—are about one-third of total production costs. A farmer grossing $3,500 per acre from the sale of table grapes pays about $1,500 to the workers who tend and harvest them. From the point of view of consumers, labor costs are only a small fraction of supermarket prices. In the early 1990s, farmers got about $0.40 per pound for table grapes and $0.13 represented the cost of labor. However, the retail price of grapes averaged $1 per pound, so that farmworker wages represented only about 13 percent of the retail price.

If farm worker wages were to double, if farmers continued to use the same amount of labor as before, and if all of the increased cost of farm labor was passed on to consumers, then the typical wage of grape workers would jump from $6 to $12 hourly. However, the cost of grapes for consumers would rise only 13 percent, to $1.13 per pound.

Labor costs, important to farmers, are much less important to consumers because farmers obtain only about one-third of the typical retail price of a fruit or vegetable. Thus, whether farm worker wages go up or down, they affect only one-ninth of the retail price of a fruit or vegetable.

If farmworker wages were to double, as in the above example, experience shows that most of the adjustments on the farm would take the form of a reduced demand for workers, not an influx of U.S. workers into the farm work force. If wages were higher, farmers would have incentives to find substitutes for farm workers. Perhaps they would use machines to harvest their crops, even if the machine did not pick as carefully as farm workers.

In other cases, farmers might not pick as often or, to make workers more productive, farmers might develop mechanical aids for them. In some cases, higher wages might lead to importing a commodity from a lower-wage country. In short, rising farm worker wages would cause far more changes in the way farmers get work done than in the prices consumers pay for food.

California fruits and vegetables do not ripen uniformly, so the peak demand for labor shifts around the state in a manner that mirrors harvest activities. Figure 8.2 provides one estimate of the seasonal pattern of employment on California farms.

Harvest activity occurs year-round, beginning with the winter vegetable harvest in southern California and the winter citrus harvest in the San Joaquin Valley. But the major winter activity is pruning—cutting branches and vines to promote the growth of larger and more uniform fruit. In fruits such as peaches, pruning accounts for 10 to 20 percent of the seasonal labor required to produce the fruit but, because pruning occurs over several months, there are fewer workers involved. During the rainy months between November and April, employment on farms is only one-half its peak September levels.

Surveys find a declining percentage of migrant farm workers. A 1965 statewide survey of farm workers found that 30 percent migrated from one of California's farming regions to another; a 1981 survey of Tulare county farm workers found that 20 percent had to establish a temporary residence away from their usual home because a farm job took them beyond commuting distance (California Assembly 1969; Mines & Kearney 1982). A national survey of farm workers in the early 1990s found that fewer than 10 percent followed the ripening crops (Gabbard, Mines, & Boccalandro 1994).

There is some worker migration between farming regions organized by employers, such as the lettuce harvesters' move from Salinas to Imperial to Huron, but such employer-organized migration seems to be decreasing. Instead, a lack of housing and surpluses of labor everywhere have discouraged the migration of workers from one farming region to another. Farm labor contractors continue to move crews of solo men from area to area, but there are now far fewer "freewheeling" families travelling up and down the state looking for farm jobs without prearranged jobs and housing than in the 1960s and 1970s. Workers tend to stay in one area of California for three reasons: the harvesting of some crops has been stretched out for marketing and processing reasons; temporary housing for migrants is scarce; and the availability of unemployment insurance and service programs makes migration less necessary.

Many workers still migrate, but they tend to shuttle into the United States from Mexico and then remain in one location rather than to follow the crops after their arrival in California (U.S. Department of Labor 1993a; 1993b). Thus, the reduction in follow-the-crop migration does not mean that there is no migration, only that the nature of mi-

Figure 8.2
Midmonth Estimates of Hired Workers in California Agriculture, 1994

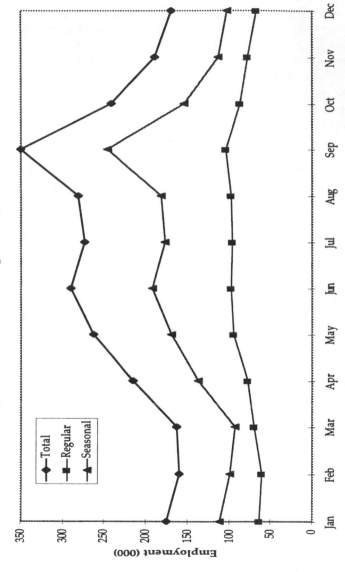

Regular workers are employed 150 days or more by one employer.
Source: State of California, EDD Report 881-M, March 1995.

gration has changed. In theory, migrant camps open for six months annually should experience considerable turnover as families move on to the next harvest. That they do not highlights the importance of housing—the lack of it—in explaining behavior: once a "migrant family" finds suitable housing, it is reluctant to move out and have to search again for housing.

Farm Employment

California farmers employ about 900,000 individuals to fill an average 350,000 farm jobs over the year. Total and average employment have been remarkably stable since the mid-1960s as mechanization that eliminated farm jobs has been offset by expanded production and the switch from farm families to hired workers to do more of the state's farm work.

Mechanization—picking a crop by machine rather than by hand—has reduced employment in many commodities, but the production of other commodities has expanded enough to create new jobs and to stabilize farm employment (Brown 1984). Processing tomatoes provides an example of what happens to farm worker jobs as a result of mechanization (Thompson & Schering 1978). In 1960, a peak 45,000 workers—80 percent of whom were *braceros*—handpicked 2.5 million tons of the processing tomatoes used to make catsup in California.

In 1990, about 5,500 mostly female farmworkers were employed to sort four times more tomatoes (Mamer & Wilke 1990). In this case, mechanization reduced the number of jobs for farm workers and changed the harvesting task from handpicking tomatoes into field boxes to riding on a machine and sorting machine-picked tomatoes.

During the 1960s, many thought that the choice was to mechanize or stop growing hand-harvested crops (Thomas 1985). For example, a major 1970 study predicted that "California farmers will continue the intensive search for labor solutions, particularly mechanical harvesting" (Dean et al. 1970:52). Another 1970 study concluded that "the door to employment is rapidly closing for those persons whose only qualifications for employment are a will to work and enough muscle to compete" (Cargill & Rossmiller 1969:22).

The expectation that soon there would be no need for those who could bring only strong backs to farm work was so widespread that the federal government began programs to help farm workers adjust to the nonfarm jobs they, it was expected, soon would have to seek (Martin & Martin 1994). But the mechanization of the tomato harvest proved to be the exceptional type of labor-displacing change in California agriculture, not the rule.

The publicity, generated in the late 1970s by lawsuits against the University of California for its part in using tax dollars to develop plants and machines that displaced farm workers, reinforced the false sense that soon there would be no need for seasonal farm workers (Martin & Olmstead 1985). In reality, the surprise is how little labor-saving mechanization there has been in California since the 1960s. In 1990, most of the major fruits and vegetables grown in the United States were hand-harvested.

There have been important labor savings in California agriculture, but they are usually less visible than machines replacing hand-harvesters. Changes in production practices for perennial crops have saved labor—such as drip irrigation that saves irrigator labor, dwarf trees and vines trained for easier hand or mechanical pruning, and precision planting and improved herbicides that save thinning and hoeing labor.

As machines and changes in production practices eliminated some jobs for farm workers, there was an important countertrend creating jobs for field workers: field packing. Crops traditionally have been picked by field workers into bins or boxes and then hauled to a packing shed, where nonfarm workers sorted, graded, and boxed the table grapes and broccoli. During the 1970s and 1980s, many crops began to be picked and packed in the field. Picking and packing grapes, vegetables, and melons in the field may not affect the overall level of employment in preparing these crops for market, but field packing increases "farm" and decreases "nonfarm" employment.

The most important reason that there are as many farm workers in the 1990s as in the 1960s is that so many more fruits and vegetables are produced today. It is sometimes hard to appreciate how the expanded production of labor-intensive crops—reflected in both larger acreages and higher yields—creates additional jobs for farm workers.

Broccoli production provides an example. The average American's consumption of fresh vegetables rose 23 percent to 136 pounds per person during the 1980s, but the increase was sharpest for broccoli: the per capita consumption of fresh broccoli almost tripled from 1.6 to 4.5

pounds during the decade. Broccoli is hand-harvested, and its production in California required an average 52 hours of hired labor per acre in 1990 (Mamer & Wilkie 1990).[1]

Will Americans continue to consume more hand-harvested fruits and vegetables? The U.S. consumption of most farm commodities increases about 1 percent annually due to population growth, but the demand for many FVH commodities increases another 2 or 3 percent annually, or about as much as personal incomes typically go up, because Americans tend to spend about the same percentage more on fresh fruits and vegetables as their incomes rise. For example, if the population increases by 1 percent and personal incomes rise 2 percent, then expenditures on fresh broccoli and strawberries rise by 3 percent.

The Farm Labor Force

Most persons who work on U.S. and California farms for wages are immigrants from Mexico. Farm labor data are notoriously unreliable, and the two major sources of such data paint very different pictures of who farm workers are.

The Current Population Survey (CPS), the source of most data on worker characteristics, reports that most farm workers are non-Hispanic U.S. citizens. The monthly CPS of 60,000 households includes about 1,500 who worked in agriculture during the previous week and, based on CPS-expansion factors, an estimated 2.5 million persons sometime during the year worked on a farm for wages during most years in the 1980s (Oliveira 1989).

These farm workers were 78 percent white, 14 percent Hispanic, and 8 percent black and other races. White workers were the majority or plurality in every region of the U.S., including the Pacific states of California, Oregon, and Washington, where white farm workers outnumbered Hispanics 54 to 44 percent (Ilg 1995).

The U.S. Department of Labor (DOL) National Agricultural Worker Survey (NAWS), by contrast, finds that hired workers on crop farms are recent immigrants from Mexico. The NAWS found that 70 percent of the crop workers employed on U.S. farms in 1993–1994 were born in Mexico or Central America and that most had been in the United States for less than ten years. Many of these immigrant farm workers are so-called Special Agricultural Workers (SAWs)—aliens who were illegally in the United States in the mid-1980s and who were legalized under special provisions of the Immigration Reform and Control Act of 1986.

The NAWS emphasizes that most farm workers are "working poor" adults who are trying to support families with their seasonal farm earnings (Griffith & Kissam 1995); more than 60 percent of the Mexican-born farm workers in 1993–1994 were settled in the United States, and newspaper accounts emphasize that more and more previously-migrant farm workers are settling in the United States (Mydans 1995). However, these immigrant farm workers have relatively low farm earnings—typically $4,000 to $5,000 annually—and they lack the English, skills, and contacts needed to obtain nonfarm jobs that would offer them higher earnings (Huffman 1995).

California farm workers are more likely to be Mexican-born, to be employed by farm labor contractors rather than directly by growers, and to live in nonemployer-provided housing than farm workers in other parts of the United States. The percentage of male and unauthorized farm workers is about the same in California as in the rest of the United States. As with most hired farm workers interviewed in the NAWS, most California farm workers do not speak English (only 11 percent in 1990–1991) and few finished high school (only 13 percent).

Despite the legalization of 1.1 million farm workers in 1987–1988, there is a significant and growing percentage of unauthorized workers in the farm labor force. The estimated percentage of unauthorized workers who harvested fruits and vegetables ranged from 0 percent in Georgia peaches in the early 1990s to 35 percent in Fresno raisins (Commission on Agricultural Workers 1992:74). Most California estimates were that, six years after IRCA, less than 30 percent of the work force was unauthorized and less than 10 percent of the Stockton tomato harvesting work force was unauthorized.

The percentage of unauthorized workers in the farm workforce seems to be climbing. The apparent percentage of unauthorized workers in the NAWS, doubled between 1989–1990 and 1993–1994, about 12 to 25 percent nationwide, and 27 percent in California. One reason for the rising percentage of unauthorized farm workers is that so-called "new-new" migrants—indigenous peoples from southern Mexico and Central America, such as non-Spanish-speaking Mixtec Indians—have begun to enter the U.S. farm work force in significant numbers (Zabin &

Hughes 1995). There were relatively few such workers in the mid-1980s, so they did not get legalized.

The dominance of foreign-born workers affects the structure and functioning of the farm labor market, e.g., non-English-speaking immigrant workers often require intermediary bilingual FLCs or foremen to help them find housing and other social services; they are usually more willing to accept variation in days worked and piece-rate earnings than U.S.-born workers; and immigrants are more likely to pay without question charges for housing, transportation, and eating arrangements in areas with farm jobs. Such behavior makes immigrants preferable to U.S. citizens in the eyes of many farm employers (U.S. DOL 1994; Commission on Agricultural Workers 1992).

Most immigrant farm workers do not remain farm workers for their working lives. Instead, farm workers frequently do farm work for a few weeks or months or even a season and then return to Mexico or find a nonfarm job in the United States. Most farmers do not worry about such worker turnover. As they rely on a foreman or crew boss to bring a crew of workers to their farm, they do not know or care if the same workers return year-after-year. Turnover, or the number of individuals hired to keep a crew of 20 at full strength, sometimes reaches 100 percent or more *monthly*.

One reason why worker turnover is so high is that there are few incentives for workers to remain employed by any one employer. Wages are usually uniform for the task being done, and there are few benefits, such as health insurance or vacation pay, that a worker would forfeit by quitting. Seniority usually does not lead to a preferred place in the crew next year; in most cases, personal ties or favors earn a worker a preferred job, not length of service.

Most of the farm work is done by so-called "professional" farm workers—those who begin doing farm work between the ages of eighteen and 25 do the hardest and highest wage hand-harvest work until age 30 to 35, and then switch from so-called heavy harvesting tasks to such easier tasks as irrigating and pruning. It is these "professional" farm workers who predominate in the NAWS data. A combination of few transferable skills and high unemployment in the early 1990s kept more than 95 percent of them who were doing farm work one year in the farm work force the next year.

The job ladder for professional farm workers involves a trade-off between hours worked and hourly earnings. Young men often aim to earn $100 daily picking grapes, citrus, or melons for piece-rate wages. After ten or more years, many switch to farm tasks that generate lower hourly earnings but provide easier work and, perhaps more hours. A few of these workers are able to earn higher wages if they acquire a skill, such as equipment operation, or become a crew boss who recruits workers.

Few young Americans dream of growing up to be farm workers. In the past, it was often feared that farm worker children would be trapped by the inadequate education they get because of migrancy and be forced into the migrant farm worker stream for lack of skills useful elsewhere. Most of the evidence today indicates that farm worker children may do farm work alongside their parents as teens but, if they go to U.S. schools, they tend to take nonfarm jobs by age eighteen or 20 to avoid being trapped as their parents were. The farm workforce is reproduced abroad; most new entrants to the farm workforce are born in rural Mexico.

The Farm Labor Market

How do 900,000 mostly immigrant farm workers find jobs with the 25,000 California employers who hire them? The farm labor market is like other labor markets in the sense that it matches workers and jobs. However, it handles the three essential functions of a labor market in unique ways.

First, farmers rarely recruit or speak directly with prospective employees. One farmer described his hiring policy: "When we need 30 workers, we call up the FLC, and they supply the workers." This means that recruitment is usually done by bilingual foremen or FLCs in the language of the worker.

Second, agriculture has dealt with the problem of training and motivating diverse workers to work either by paying piece-rate wages—e.g., $10 per bin of oranges picked—so that each worker's pay reflects her productivity, or by paying an hourly wage, but in a manner that permits farmers to control the pace of work, e.g., by, having workers follow a conveyor belt that moves slowly through the field.

Third, many farmers have concluded that it is better to work collectively to maximize the supply of farm workers than to try to identify the best workers and retain them individually.

Contractors or such intermediaries as foremen and crew bosses handle the recruitment of most harvest workers in several ways. In some "farm worker towns," especially those along the U.S.-Mexican border, there is a so-called day-haul labor market. Workers begin to congregate in parking lots at 3:00 or 4:00 A.M., contractors arrive with buses and tell the workers the task and the wage, and the workers then board the bus that seems to offer the best job. Some workers board the same bus every day; others switch from bus to bus.

The most common way in which farm workers are recruited is for the crew boss to tell current workers that more workers are needed and the workers then inform their friends and relatives that jobs are available. Such "network recruiting" is very helpful to employers. There is no need to spend money on "help wanted" ads and workers, who often are grateful for the chance to tell friends and relatives about jobs, tend to bring only "good" workers to join the crew.

Decentralized hiring by contractors and crew bosses means that there are many farm labor markets. These markets may appear to be similar in the sense that many of the jobs involve harvesting, most of the workers are Mexican immigrants, and the piece-rate wages tend to be similar from field to field. Nonetheless, take-home pay can vary significantly from worker to worker.

Once hired, workers must be motivated to work. There are two major wage systems used to pay seasonal farm workers. According to the NAWS, 70 percent of the jobs held by California farm workers in the early 1990s offered hourly wages, and the remaining 30 percent piece-rate wages or a combination of hourly and piece-rate wages (U.S. DOL 1993b:36–7).

According to earnings data collected from employers, the average hourly earnings of farm workers traditionally have been about one-half of nonfarm private sector earnings, both in California and throughout the United States. However, in the mid-1970s and the mid-1980s, the ratio of farm to nonfarm hourly earnings rose above 50 percent. Beginning with the end of the *bracero* program in the mid-1960s, the ratio of farm to nonfarm earnings in California crept steadily upward, reaching 58 percent of nonfarm levels in 1977. The California farm to nonfarm earnings ratio fell to 51 percent in 1983, rose in 1989 after the minimum wage was increased, and then fell sharply in the early 1990s (see Figure 8.3).

In the rest of the United States, by contrast, the farm to nonfarm

Figure 8.3
Ratio of Farm to Nonfarm Hourly Earnings: 1962–1994

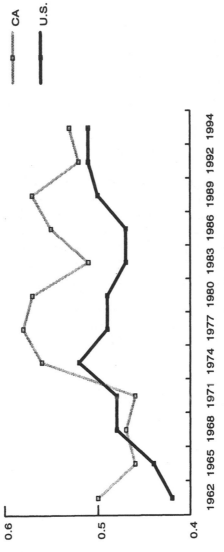

1962 1965 1968 1971 1974 1977 1980 1983 1986 1989 1992 1994

Sources: Economic Report of the President 1996 (Using 1977 = 100).
Employment & Earnings, 1995 (October). USDOL (data for month of July).
Farm Employment & Wage Rates 1910–1990. USDA.
Farm Labor Report. Quarterly. USDA National Agricultural Statistics Service (data for month of July).

earnings ratio behaved differently, remaining below 50 percent throughout much of the 1970s and rising to 50 percent only in 1989, again in response to the 1988 minimum wage increase to $4.25 that affected most farm workers.

Some employers pay more—$4.50 or even $5—in order to be able to select the best workers, but reports that U.S. farm workers' hourly earnings averaged, for example, $6.54 in 1995 and $6.83 in California, can be misleading because these average earnings data are weighted by the hours that the various subgroups of workers work. For example, average hourly earnings of workers on a farm with a tractor driver paid $7 hourly for 70 hours of work weekly, and two $4.25 hourly hoers who each work 35 hours, would be reported by USDA to be $5.62 ($490 + $297.50 divided by a total 140 hours of work), even though neither the tractor driver nor the hoers is earning this average reported wage.

Piece-rate wages seem to be more straightforward, but there are few consistent time-series data on piece rates that vary by commodity, availability of housing, season, etc. Under piece-rate wages, workers are paid, for example, $12 per bin of oranges picked, or $0.16 per each 25 pounds of raisin grapes cut and laid on a paper tray to dry, and guaranteed at least $4.25 hourly.

In addition to wages, many farm workers receive unemployment insurance payments when they are without jobs. In California, virtually all employers are required to cover their workers under the UI system, which in 1994 collected $2.8 billion in employer contributions and paid $3.3 billion in UI benefits to unemployed workers.

The third dimension of the farm labor market is retention—what do farm employers do to identify the best workers, and persuade them to return to the farm? The answer is not much.

Perhaps the easiest way to describe prevailing attitudes toward worker retention is by analogy to irrigation. Water is vital to produce crops in California and there are two major ways to supply water to the crops: "flooding" a field with so much water that at least some trickles to each plant or laying pipes under the soil so that only the water needed by each plant is allowed to "drip" to it.

The choice depends largely on the cost and availability of water. Where water is scarce and expensive, farmers tend to invest in drip irrigation systems; where water is cheap, farmers tend to flood their fields. The choice is either to work collectively so that there is plenty of water for all or to invest farm-by-farm and use water as efficiently as possible.

Farmers acknowledge that securing labor presents the same basic choice: working collectively to maximize the number of workers available or treating labor as scarce and trying to select and retain the fewest workers necessary.

IS THERE A SHORTAGE OF AGRICULTURAL LABOR?

The most recent manifestation of California agriculture's interest in immigration occurred during the debate that preceded the enactment of the Immigration Reform and Control Act of 1986. IRCA imposed sanctions or fines on U.S. employers who knowingly hired unauthorized alien workers and offered legal immigrant status to many illegal aliens who worked in U.S. agriculture.

IRCA's Agricultural Provisions

IRCA included three major agricultural provisions: deferred sanctions enforcement and the requirement that the INS obtain search warrants to check the status of workers in open fields; the SAW legalization program; and the H-2A and Replenishment Agricultural Worker (RAW) foreign worker programs. Each provision had both anticipated and unanticipated consequences.

IRCA made significant changes in agricultural enforcement practices. Before IRCA, immigration enforcement in agriculture usually involved the Border Patrol driving into fields and apprehending aliens who tried to run away. Farmers pointed out that the INS was required to obtain search warrants before inspecting factories for illegal aliens and argued that the INS similarly should be obliged to show evidence that illegal aliens were employed on a farm before raiding it. IRCA extended the requirement that the INS have a search warrant before raiding a workplace for illegal aliens from nonfarm to agricultural workplaces.

IRCA created two legalization programs: a general (I-687) program that granted legal status to illegal aliens if they had continuously resided in the United States since 1982, and the Special Agricultural Worker (I-700) program that granted legal status to illegal aliens who did at least 90 days of farm work in 1985–1986. It was much easier for illegal alien farm workers to satisfy the SAW work requirement than it was for nonfarm aliens to satisfy the I-687 residence requirement. Some 1.3 million SAW applicants came forth, although it is likely that only a portion were legitimate agricultural workers.

All were supposed to be experienced farm workers, and farmers expected a significant movement of now-legal workers to restaurants, hotels, and other employers who could offer year-round and less strenuous work. Employer sanctions, if successful, could have further depleted a source of agricultural labor.[2]

Part of the last-minute farm worker compromise that allowed IRCA to become law were a Replenishment Agricultural Worker program and changes to the nonimmigrant H-2A program that permits farmers with vacant jobs to bring foreigners to fill them if U.S. workers are not available. Both the RAW and the H-2A program permit the admission of legal foreign workers.

RAW program admissions depended on national calculations of farm labor "need" and supply made by the Secretaries of Labor and Agriculture (Martin 1990). However, continuing illegal immigration and the proliferation of "documented illegals" in the farm work force made it unnecessary to admit RAWs during its four-year life from 1989–1993. At no point could an IRCA-related shortage of agricultural labor be detected.

Instead of national calculations triggering RAW admissions, U.S. farm employers facing shortages could individually initiate requests for H-2A workers. This indicator of local labor shortages did not jump to requests for 200,000 alien farm workers per year as expected; instead H-2A admissions dropped from 30,000 in 1989 to about 15,000 in FY 1995.

Most of the reasons the H-2A program did not expand lie in continuing illegal immigration and false documents. Shrinkage of the H-2A program, on the other hand, is partly due to mechanization of the Florida sugarcane harvest.

November 1995 Employer Survey

In November 1995, California's Employment Development Department mailed a two-page survey to a 5 percent sample of reporting units with SIC codes 01 (crop production), 02 (livestock production), or farm-oriented 07 (agricultural services).[3] Some 1,000 surveys were mailed and 197 were returned for a 20 percent response rate.

Agricultural employers were asked about their employment of seasonal workers—persons employed for less than 150 days in 1995. About 55 percent of the responding farms—102 farms—employed 5,100 seasonal workers in 1995, or an average 50 seasonal employees per reporting unit.

The purpose of the survey was to determine if INS's Operation Gatekeeper or other border control efforts affected the supply of seasonal workers in 1995 compared to 1994. For this reason, there were a number of questions asked about the characteristics and availability of seasonal workers.

Virtually all seasonal farm workers hired in 1995 were immigrants who were recruited by fellow workers (36 percent), foremen (31 percent), or labor contractors (11 percent). The "other category" included 22 percent of respondents, and they relied mostly on seasonal workers returning to their farms—about two-thirds of the seasonal workers employed in 1995 were reported by employers to have worked on their farms in 1994. None of the responding employers used the Employment Service or a union hiring hall; just one used the H-2A program to obtain two workers.

Responding farms provided estimates of the number of seasonal workers with various types of work authorization documents. According to employers, about 5 percent of the seasonal workers hired in 1995 were U.S. citizens, 46 percent were legal immigrants, and 9 percent were believed to be falsely documented. Farmers reported that they did not know the legal status of 41 percent of their seasonal workers.

Farmers were asked to estimate how many workers were employed in California agriculture for the first time in 1995, and they reported that about 1 percent were first time U.S. workers.[4]

According to farm employers, about 46 percent of the seasonal workers hired in 1995 presented green cards (INS I-551 forms) to establish their right to work in the U.S., while 45 percent presented social security cards. About 7 percent presented SAW documents, which are no longer valid. To prove their identity, 72 percent of the workers presented drivers' licenses.

The seasonal workers hired in 1995 have characteristics similar to those reported in the NAWS. For example, 68 percent were male, 87 percent were born in Mexico, and 69 percent were under age 40. The most common hourly wage paid to seasonal workers in 1995 was $5.38 per hour, and 45 percent of farm employers reported that this was a higher wage than was paid in 1994.

Few farm employers house seasonal workers on their farms—only 26 percent reported that they provided housing for seasonal workers, but 61 percent reported that their seasonal workers lived "in town." One farmer used the H-2A program to obtain two foreign workers in 1995, and four others investigated the H-2A program, but 92 did not. Among those who commented on the H-2A program, most did not know about the program, and those who did know about it asserted that it was too expensive or bureaucratic to use to get farm workers.

About 35 percent of the responding farms used a farm labor contractor or custom harvester to obtain seasonal workers in 1995 and they got an average 67 workers from such intermediaries. Contractor employees received an average $5.59 per hour, slightly more than workers hired directly, and an average overhead rate of 40 percent was paid to cover the FLC's payroll taxes and costs associated with hiring and providing toilets, etc., for farm workers.

The survey asked how IRCA was affecting farming operations, and most employers asserted that the government needs to develop a better employee verification system and that an agricultural guestworker program is necessary.

Yet, most employers had no trouble finding seasonal workers in 1995—91 percent of employers who hired seasonal workers in 1995 reported that they were able to find enough seasonal workers. The nine employers who reported difficulties finding sufficient seasonal workers cited the general unavailability of workers as well as a unique reason, such as planting additional acreage or bad weather.

County and commodity specific details from the survey emphasize the same points—namely, most used informal recruitment methods to obtain seasonal workers, most paid about $5 per hour, and virtually all employers had enough seasonal workers in 1995.

PROPOSED GUESTWORKER PROGRAMS

There are two major types of guestworkers, nonimmigrants and probationary immigrants, and two major methods to admit them to the United States, through certification or attestation procedures.

Nonimmigrants are foreigners in the United States for a specific time and purpose, and experience in the United States as a lawful nonimmigrant is not supposed to advance a person's priority to enter the United States as an immigrant.[5]

Probationary immigrants, on the other hand, if they are still needed and do a sufficient amount of qualifying work, can "earn" an immigrant status. European guestworkers were probationary immigrants, and RAWs would have been.

There are also two major ways to admit guestworkers. Certification means that the border gate stays shut until a government agency agrees with the employer that there is a shortage of U.S. workers, and then the foreign workers are admitted to fill a specific job vacancy under contracts approved by the government.[6] Attestation, on the other hand, means that employers open the border gates with their petitions asserting that they could not find U.S. workers after attempting to recruit them at prevailing wages, and the border gate stays open until complaints and enforcement prompt the government to shut the door.

California farmers developed a proposal in February 1995 to substitute an attestation procedure for the current certification procedure. Under the growers' proposal, employers would attest that they face labor shortages after attempting to recruit workers at prevailing wages. Associations, farmers, or farm labor contractors would fax applications that include promises to recruit local workers and to pay prevailing wages to the U.S. Department of Labor. DOL could review the request for completeness and accuracy, but not initiate an investigation unless there was a complaint. Unless DOL disapproved the application within seven days, growers would be free to employ foreign workers, either workers in the United States, or those abroad.

Growers would pay for the administrative cost of the program with a fee equivalent to their payroll tax savings for social security and unemployment insurance taxes—perhaps 12 to 15 percent—that would not be paid on behalf of the foreign farm workers. Foreign farm workers admitted under the program could be shifted from farm to farm and could remain in the United States for up to 36 months. Up to 30 percent of each worker's wages would be withheld and sent to the U.S. consulate nearest the workers' hometown for pickup, or forfeited by workers who failed to appear to collect the withheld wages.

RECOMMENDATIONS

The certification procedure used to determine whether to admit H-2A workers is rife with controversy and litigation. Farm employers criticize it for being too bureaucratic, costly, and uncertain. Farm worker advocates criticize it for permitting employers to obtain the foreign workers who, they assert, employers prefer because the H-2A workers must please their employers to remain legally employed in the United States.

The government is not well suited to mediating between these parties. If experience has demonstrated anything, it is that, if the only party that wants to make the H-2A program work is government, the program will not work smoothly.

However, the H-2A program may be a bit like democracy—it's not perfect, but it does look better than the alternatives. To my knowledge, no country admits unskilled foreign workers on the basis of employer attestations of labor shortages. I find it hard to believe that, given the history of controversy surrounding the employment of foreign workers in U.S. agriculture, the United States will in the late 1990s introduce an attestation program for alien farm workers.

All governments make employers who want temporary foreign workers pay for the privilege. However, employers currently pay lobbyists to push for the fewest and lowest hurdles between themselves and the foreign workers they want. This means that employers pay for the privilege of obtaining access to foreign workers up front and then reap the rewards of using foreign workers afterward. This accentuates dependence on foreign workers and means that, once an employer becomes hooked on foreign workers, there is no continuing economic incentive to look seriously at U.S. workers.

If the likely outcome of the debate over certification versus attestation is a change in certification procedures, then I suggest careful consideration of such changes as substituting employer-paid user fees for some of the regulations that now govern admissions.

I suggest that employers who bring H-2A workers into the United States pay a user fee equivalent to 15 to 25 percent of the wages paid to H-2A into an industry-specific trust fund. This fund, administered by employers, labor, and government representatives in a manner similar to current trust funds that promote, inter alia, milk and pork, should be charged with spending the funds collected in a manner that would end the industry's dependence on nonimmigrant workers.

Trust funds would, I believe, have several advantages over the current system. First, they would encourage employers to return to the U.S. labor market to look for workers—experience shows that, once employers master the intricacies of the H-2A program, they rarely return to hiring U.S. workers. Second, trust funds tie the funds available to find alternatives to foreign workers directly to dependence on foreign workers. If there were 200,000 foreign farm workers, each earning $5,000, then a 25 percent user fee would generate $250 million to administer the program and to find alternatives to foreign workers.

Third, tripartite administration of the program permits the parties closest to the problem of insufficient U.S. workers—those who have the most expertise in the causes and solutions for labor shortages—to deal with ending dependence on foreign workers. Tripartite administration may reduce the controversy and litigation that usually surrounds the H-2A program.

NOTES

I am indebted to Patrick Ramsey for research assistance in mailing and tabulating the employer survey.

1. The increased production of broccoli, a commodity worth just 1 percent of the total value of FVH commodities, required 2,000 to 4,000 additional seasonal workers just to handle the 1980s increase in production.

2. No one knew how many illegal aliens were employed in U.S. agriculture in the mid-1980s. Most farmers and farm worker advocates accepted a USDA estimate that 350,000 illegal aliens were employed in U.S. agriculture sometime during a typical year, and this number became the anticipated maximum number of applicants. However, the major surprise was that 1.3 million aliens applied for SAW status, a discrepancy mostly attributable to the ease of fraudulent application, not to a much larger illegal labor force than anticipated. California Unemployment Insurance data, for example, suggest there should have been 200,000 legitimate SAWs, but 700,000 applications were submitted (Martin 1990). Employers argued that independent estimates of SAWs in agricultural employment, which were likewise only one-third the number of applicants, implied that two-thirds of their labor supply had left for better union jobs. Some SAWs did leave agriculture, but the major reason that so few SAWs were "still working" there is that many who legalized had not been farm workers at all.

3. There were 36,200 reporting units in California in 1994 with SIC codes between 01 and 09, agriculture, forestry, and fisheries. They paid total wages of $6.6 billion and, as most workers are low earners, about 56 percent of the wages paid were taxable for UI purposes (California employers pay a tax on the first $7,000 paid to workers to cover the cost of UI benefits). Agricultural employers made $167 million in contributions in 1995, and unemployed workers received about twice as much in UI benefits—$335 million.

4. Surveys done for Employment Services in the mountain states in summer 1995 found higher turnover—in some crops, as few as 15 percent of the seasonal workers were employed the year before (Thilmany 1995).

5. Thus, H-2 workers employed in 1985–1986 were not eligible to apply for the SAW legalization program, which was restricted to persons who were unauthorized workers on U.S. crop farms.

6. Under the H-2A program, growers must ask DOL to certify their need for workers at least 60 days before the shortage is anticipated. DOL does not certify that growers need H-2A workers unless the grower tried to recruit U.S. workers at prevailing wages and with offers of free housing, transportation, and contracts for work.

REFERENCES

Brown, G. K. 1984. Fruit and Vegetable Mechanization. In P. Martin, ed., *Migrant Labor in Agriculture: An International Comparison*, pp. 195–209. Berkeley, CA: Giannini Foundation.

California Assembly Committee on Agriculture. 1969. *The California Farm Workforce: A Profile*. Sacramento (April).

Cargill, B. F., and Rossmiller, G. E. (eds.). 1969. *Fruit and Vegetable Harvest Mechanization* (3 vols.). East Lansing, MI: Rural Manpower Center.

Commission on Agricultural Workers. 1992. *Report of the Commission on Agricultural Workers*. Washington, DC: Available from the Commission on Immigration Reform.

Dean, G. W. et al. 1970. Projections of California Agriculture to 1980 and 2000. *California Agricultural Experiment Station Bulletin 847*.

Fisher, L. 1952. *The Harvest Labor Market in California*. Cambridge, MA: Harvard University Press.

Fuller, V. 1942. The Supply of Agricultural Labor as a Factor in the Evolution of Farm Organization in California. In *Violations of Free Speech and the Rights of Labor Education and Labor Committee* (The LaFollette Committee). 19778–19894. Washington, DC: Senate Education and Labor Committee.

Gabbard, S., Mines, R., and Boccalandro, B. 1994. Migrant Farmworkers: Pursuing Security in an Unstable Labor Market. *ASP Research Report 5* (May). Washington, DC: U.S. Department of Labor.

Griffith, D., and Kissam, E. 1995. *Working Poor: Farmworkers in the United States*. Philadelphia: Temple University Press.

Huffman, W. 1995. Immigration and Agriculture in the 1990s. In P. Martin et al., eds., *Immigration Reform and U.S. Agriculture*. Berkeley, CA: University of California, Division of Agriculture and Natural Resources (publication 3358).

Ilg, R. E. 1995. The Changing Face of Farm Employment. *Monthly Labor Review* 188:4 (April):3–12.

Mamer, J., and Wilke, A. 1990. Seasonal Labor in California Agriculture: Labor Inputs for California Crops. *California Agricultural Studies Report* 90–6. Sacramento, CA: Employment Development Department.

Martin, P. 1990. The Outlook for Agricultural Labor in the 1990s. *UC Davis Law Review* 23:3 (Spring):99–523.

Martin, P. L., and Miller, G. P. 1993. Farmers Increase Hiring Through Labor Contractors. *California Agriculture* 47:4 (July):20–23.

Martin, P., and Olmsted, A. 1985. The Agricultural Mechanization Controversy. *Science* 227:4687 (February 8):601–6.

Martin, P., and Martin, D. 1994. *The Endless Quest: Helping America's Farmworkers*. Boulder, CO: Westview Press.

McWilliams, C. 1949. *California: The Great Exception*. New York: Current Books.

Mines, R., and Kearney, M. 1982. The Health of Tulare County Farmworkers. Mimeo (April).

Mines, R., and Martin, P. 1986. A Profile of California Farmworkers. *Information Series 86–2*. Berkeley, CA: Giannini Foundation.

Mydans, S. 1995. A New Wave of Immigrants on Lowest Rung in Farming. *New York Times* (August 24):A-1.

Oliveira, V. 1989. Trends in the Hired Farm Work Force, 1945–87. *Agricultural Information Bulletin* 561. Washington, DC: U.S. Department of Agriculture, Economic Research Service.

Rosenberg, H. et al. 1995. Hiring and Managing Labor for Farms in California. Mimeo.

Thilmany, D. 1995. *An Analysis of Contract Relationships between Farm Labor Contractors and Farmers in California Agriculture*. Berkeley, CA: Agricultural Personnel Management Program (March).

Thomas, R. 1985. *Citizenship, Gender, and Work: Social Organization of Industrial Agriculture*. New York: Cambridge University Press.

Thompson, O., and Schering, A. 1978. *From Lug Boxes to Electronics: A Study of California Tomato Growers and Sorting Crews*. Davis, CA: mimeo (December).

U.S. Department of Labor. 1991a. *Findings from the National Agricultural Workers Survey (NAWS) 1989: A Demographic and Employment Profile of Perishable Crop Farm Workers.* Washington, DC: Office of the Assistant Secretary for Policy, Office of Program Economics (November).

————. 1991b. *Findings from the National Agricultural Workers Survey (NAWS) 1990: A Demographic and Employment Profile of Perishable Crop Farm Workers.* Washington, DC: Office of the Assistant Secretary for Policy, Office of Program Economics (July).

————. 1993a. *U.S. Farm Workers in the Post-IRCA Period.* Washington, DC: Office of the Assistant Secretary for Policy, Office of Program Economics (March).

————. 1993b. *California Findings from the National Agricultural Workers Survey.* Washington, DC: Office of the Assistant Secretary for Policy, Office of Program Economics.

————. 1994. *Migrant Farm Workers: Pursuing Security in an Unstable Labor Market.* Washington, DC: Office of the Assistant Secretary for Policy, Office of Program Economics (May).

Zabin, C., and Hughes, S. 1995. Economic Integration and Labor Flows: Stage Migration in Farm Labor Markets in Mexico and the United States. *International Migration Review* 24:2 (Summer):397–422.

Part III

Students

Chapter 9

Policy Analysis of Foreign Student Visas

BARRY R. CHISWICK

"Foreign students" are foreign nationals who are in the United States on temporary visas for the expressed purpose of attending a U.S. college or university or a related training program. They are a familiar presence on American campuses and they play an integral part in the intellectual life of these campuses, both as students and as scholars, often serving in academic apprenticeship roles. Unlike other foreign nationals in the United States, such as illegal aliens, refugees, and permanent resident aliens, who have been extensively studied and discussed, there has, unfortunately, been remarkably little research on, or public policy discussion of, foreign students. Foreign students play an important role in one major sector of the economy (the higher education sector) and many enter the broader labor market, some in an illegal status (e.g., violating the work restrictions on their student visas) and others on temporary work visas or as permanent resident aliens. Public policy regarding foreign students needs to be made, not in a vacuum, but with an understanding and weighing of both the positive and negative aspects of their presence. The positive aspects need to be encouraged, while the negative aspects need to be curtailed.

THE UNITED STATES AS A MAGNET

The United States is a magnet for foreign nationals seeking university level and advanced (graduate) level training. This is particularly true in the fields of science (biological and nonbiological), engineering,

Table 9.1
Students and Family Members Admitted to the United States:
Selected Years, FY 1981 to FY 1993

Year	Students	Spouses and Children of Students
1981	240,805	31,056
1985	257,069	28,427
1989	334,402	26,369
1990	326,264	28,943
1991	282,077	32,315
1992	241,093	33,431
1993	257,430	33,379

Source: U.S. Department of Justice (1995), table 40.

computer science, mathematics, certain social sciences (e.g., econom-ics) and, more recently, business and management. Hereafter these fields are referred to collectively as ''science.''

Tables 9.1 and 9.2 present data on the admission of foreign students into the United States over time and by country of origin. Although there have been ebbs and flows, there is little trend in the number of foreign students admitted annually—241,000 in 1981 and 257,000 in 1993 (including 4,383 in the vocational training program). With the growth in college and university enrollment over this period (from 12.4 million to 14.4 million students) there also has been little change in the number of admissions of foreign students per hundred students enrolled in U.S. colleges and universities, a small decline from 1.9 per hundred in 1981 to 1.8 per hundred in 1993. By country of origin (Table 9.2), foreign student admissions now come primarily from Asia (61 percent), with Japan (16 percent), China, Taiwan and Hong Kong (14 percent), Korea (9 percent), and India (5 percent) the primary sources. Other important source countries outside of Asia are Canada, Mexico, the United Kingdom, Germany, and Spain.

There has, however, been an increase in the stock of the foreign student population in the United States, from about 300,000 in 1981 to just more than 450,000 in 1995.[1] Relative to the total enrollment in colleges and universities, foreign students have increased from 2.5 percent of the student population to just more than 3 percent.

The growth in the foreign student population relative to annual admissions reflects a lengthening in the average stay in student visa status. This has been due, in part, to the increase in the proportion of foreign students in graduate-level education, which generally involves a longer stay in a U.S. educational institution than does enrollment, often for just one semester or one year, in an undergraduate program.

Foreign students now comprise about 1 percent of enrollment in associate degree (two-year college) programs, 2.5 percent in bachelor's (four-year college) programs, and just more than 9 percent in graduate level programs. Or, expressed as a proportion of foreign students, 13 percent are in associate degree programs, 41 percent in bachelor's programs, and nearly one-half (46 percent) are in graduate level programs. By field of study, nearly 30 percent are in the physical and life sciences, engineering, mathematics, and computer sciences, 20 percent are in business and management disciplines. In contrast, less than 4 percent are in the humanities.

There are two fundamental reasons, not necessarily mutually exclusive, why foreign nationals seek a student visa: (1) to obtain high quality education in the United States that may not be available at all or in the same form in the home country; (2) the student visa may be the easiest or least costly mechanism for entering and remaining for some time in the United States.

In spite of the many shortfalls and failings in its system of higher education, the United States is recognized internationally for having the highest quality and most flexible college and university system in the world. This is even more so for graduate-level education than for undergraduate education, although it is true at the undergraduate level as well.

The students feeding into this system come from two primary sources—U.S.-trained (grades kindergarten through four years of high school) students and foreign students. The U.S.-trained students often come from middle schools and high schools that are not up to the quality standard expected at the university level. In particular, while U.S. schools emphasize original thinking rather than rote learning, compared with some schools in some other countries they are not as de-

Table 9.2
Students Admitted to the United States by Country of Citizenship, FY 1993

Country		Number of Students	Percent of Total
Europe			
	France	45,677	17.7
	Germany	4,688	1.8
	Spain	5,942	2.3
	UK	5,422	2.1
		6,205	2.4
Asia			
	China & Taiwan	157,355	61.1
	Hong Kong	29,860	11.6
	India	5,842	2.3
	Indonesia	12,826	5.0
	Japan	6,679	2.6
	Korea	40,492	15.7
		22,286	8.7

Malaysia	6,263	2.4
Thailand	6,732	2.6
Africa	**7,067**	**2.7**
Oceania	**2,177**	**0.8**
North America	**30,469**	**11.8**
Canada	11,659	4.5
Mexico	8,975	3.4
South America	**12,999**	**5.0**
Stateless and Unknown	**1,686**	**0.7**
TOTAL	**257,430**	**100.0**

Note: Only countries providing at least 4,000 foreign student admissions are identified separately.
Source: U.S. Department of Justice (1995), table 39.

215

manding of their students in terms of classroom hours and homework, and they do not provide high quality learning in mathematics or science.

Moreover, many foreign students, particularly at the graduate level, are drawn from among the best and the brightest from around the world and often have had outstanding training in secondary schools and institutes in their countries of origin. The foreign students can compete very successfully with U.S.-trained students for college and university admission, particularly at the graduate level. Indeed, in spite of a preference on the part of colleges and universities for U.S.-trained students, they admit foreign students on the basis of their outstanding records.

It is not by coincidence that foreign students are disproportionately in science-oriented fields rather than uniformly distributed across all fields. The United States has a particular comparative advantage in training in the science-based fields in contrast to the humanities; the United States is at the forefront of scientific research in many fields. Moreover, science involves internationally transferable skills in contrast to the tendency for the humanities to be much more country specific. Medicine, for example, involves the human body and, although environmental factors may differ, the human body and the biological processes it involves are not country specific. In contrast, the legal system and the institutional environment in which the legal system operates is very much country specific. As a result, a ''disproportionate'' number of high-quality foreign students apply for U.S. science, rather than humanities, programs. The result is a larger proportion of foreign students in science and a larger proportion of native-born students, who have more of the U.S.-specific skills, in the humanities. These differing relative proportions do not imply discrimination nor do they imply an ''imbalance'' that needs to be corrected. Rather they imply a rational allocation by students across disciplines based on their relative skills.

Another reason the United States draws such a large number of international science students is that the language of instruction (English) has become the international language, or the lingua franca, of science. Although lesser fluency in English is generally required in U.S. science programs than in U.S. humanities programs, the experience of studying in a U.S. science program improves English speaking, reading, and writing skills that now are required of scientists who wish to operate on an international level, if only by reading international journals. Indeed, even science journals published in non-English-speaking countries increasingly are published in English.

There are, however, less laudable reasons for foreign nationals to seek a foreign student visa. A foreign student visa can be the easiest long-term visa that many foreign nationals can obtain. It has a longer duration than a tourist visa, puts one at less risk and provides greater freedom of movement than being in an illegal status, and does not require demonstrating a "well-founded fear of persecution" if one returns to one's home country (refugee visa). Moreover, a foreign student visa does not involve having one's name placed on a waiting list or backlog, as is often required for a permanent resident alien visa. Indeed, most potential immigrants cannot claim refugee status, do not have close relatives in the United States, and either cannot quality for or, especially if living outside the United States, cannot find an employer willing to petition for the labor certification that is needed for an occupational preference visa. As a result, most potential immigrants have little prospect for obtaining an immigrant visa.

At least some applicants for a foreign student visa are motivated by the desire to obtain a "cheap" visa to enter the United States rather than by a genuine interest in studying in a U.S. institution and then returning to their country of origin. While in the United States they may "search" for ways of obtaining a resident alien visa, such as marrying a U.S. citizen or finding an employer who will petition on their behalf for a labor certification. Both mechanisms for obtaining a visa are easier if one is inside the United States in a legal status than if one is in an illegal status or outside the United States.

ADVANTAGES TO THE UNITED STATES

The foregoing outlined reasons why foreign nationals have a "demand" for foreign student visas. The crucial question is: Why does the United States "supply" or make student visas available?

Foreign students, especially graduate students in science, are important in fulfilling the two key roles of a university: the transmission and generation of knowledge. With a relative "shortage" of native-born students seeking advanced study in science there is a relative shortage in these fields of teaching assistants (TAs), research assistants (RAs), and postdoctoral fellows. Yet, the current economic situation in higher education in the United States has made graduate students essential in the functioning of most colleges and universities, particularly the large research universities.

The economics of teaching undergraduates requires a large number of teaching assistants, graduate students who grade homework and examinations, tutor students, lead discussion sessions, supervise laboratory experiments, and teach small independent sections of basic courses. Without the graduate student teaching assistant services the cost of higher education would increase significantly.

Moreover, there is much validity to the often-made argument that part of the training of graduate students involves their learning how to teach and that the best way to do that is through supervised hands-on experience or on-the-job training. Supervised teaching experience sharpens an individual's own basic skills in science and provides the necessary training for the teaching many graduate students will be doing upon completion of their advanced degree program.

Similarly, science-based research projects at the major universities depend on research assistants and postdoctoral fellows, many of whom are foreign nationals. This research, generally funded by the federal government and private foundations, now often requires the input of research teams, and an important component of these teams are the RAs and postdoctoral fellows. A decline in foreign graduate students would raise the cost of research to the funding agencies and decrease the amount of research funded and performed. Yet, this university-based research is vital to maintaining the frontline position of the United States in science and technology.

The comparative advantage of the United States in international trade is in products (goods and services) that are intensive in "human capital." To maintain this comparative advantage requires a labor force well-educated in science and a scientific community that is advancing the frontier of knowledge. Foreign students, whether in teaching or in research, help maintain the competitive edge of the United States.

There are also potential benefits to the U.S. when the foreign students graduate from their science-based programs of study. If they return to their country of origin or to a third country, they carry with them links to the United States that can be invaluable in enhancing both trading opportunities and international collaborative research. A negative aspect, however, may be a technological "leak"—with foreign countries learning U.S. technological secrets. One partial protection is security clearances for those working on highly sensitive projects involving national security. But in another sense, it is very difficult for any democratic country to maintain nonclassified technological secrets developed in universities, regardless of whether or not there are foreign students. These ideas get disseminated rapidly in international conferences, working papers, technical journals, and most recently, electronic publications.

Among the foreign students in science who remain in the United States, most eventually enter a career that makes at least some use of their training. Their training in the United States as graduate students serves as an apprenticeship program in U.S.-specific, as well as international, skills. They develop credentials that are easier for U.S. employers to interpret than the purely foreign credentials of job applicants from outside the United States.

There is no question that the U.S. economy has been kept at the leading edge of science and technology over the past century in part through the influx of foreign-born scientists. Yet, one objection to occupational-based visas and to foreign student visas is that foreign nationals are "crowding out" U.S.-born scientists by depressing their wage and employment opportunities. It should be noted, however, that for about the past fifteen years there has been a widening of skill differentials in the United States and in the other Organization for Economic Cooperation and Development (OECD) countries—that is, the earnings of highly skilled workers (including those in science-based professions) have increased relative to lesser-skilled workers.

Several reasons have been offered for this phenomenon. One is the internationalization (globalization) of the world economy that has put lower-skilled U.S. manufacturing workers in more direct competition with lower-income workers in emerging third world economies. Another is the rapid pace of technological advance due to the computer revolution that has given more highly skilled workers an advantage in the labor market, perhaps because they have adapted more readily to the new technological changes (which would have only a short-term effect on relative wages) or because the new technology is "biased" in favor of highly skilled and professional workers (which would have long-term effects).

The widening of skill differentials in earnings in the United States has been responsible for an increase in income inequality and a higher rate of return to science-based training. The increase in income inequality has negative social consequences. The higher rate of return to science-based occupations has not attracted enough native-born Americans to college and university training to either fill the available slots or to prevent the widening of skill differentials.

POLICY CONSIDERATIONS

Thus, in general, foreign students are not "crowding out" U.S. nationals either in colleges and universities or in the labor market. Fewer foreign-origin scientists would undoubtedly increase the earnings of U.S. scientists, but the price to the American economy would be a slower rate of technological advance and further widening in income inequality. There may be particular subsectors that, at particular times, appear to experience a larger adverse impact from foreign students than others. It is difficult, however, to identify these subsectors in advance and even more difficult to develop ameliorative policies; and, because of rapid responses in enrollments and the labor market to economic incentives, most such policies would come into play only after market forces already have mitigated the impacts.

There are, however, potential abuses in the foreign student visa program that can be mitigated through some changes in policy.

It is important to enforce rigorously requirements that students be in good standing with the university. Students on academic probation should not be considered to be in good standing for the purpose of a foreign student visa. For students enrolled in courses or at the thesis or dissertation (independent research) stage a document should be required, signed by the relevant person in the student's department (e.g., advisor or department chair), certifying that satisfactory progress is being made toward completing the degree requirements or research project.

A condition of entry for a foreign student should be a prepaid return airline ticket from the airport nearest to the university to the country of origin. This ticket should be nonrefundable unless the INS certifies that the student has left the United States, become a permanent resident alien, or is deceased. This is important to prevent the lack of a return airline ticket from discouraging a return to the home country and encouraging remaining in the United States in an illegal status.

To reduce even further abuse of a student visa as an instrument for providing legal cover while seeking another visa, two changes in immigration law would be beneficial. The current labor certification requirements for the labor market (occupational) preference visas give a substantial advantage to aliens already living in the United States compared to potential applicants living abroad. A skill-based points system, along the lines used in Canada and Australia, would be an excellent substitute. Even if the skill-based point system included a small number of points for "prearranged employment" in the United States, it would provide less of an incentive than currently exists to abuse the foreign student visa program.

Under current law there is a three-year waiting period to demonstrate that a marriage to a U.S. citizen is bona fide before it qualifies an alien for a permanent resident alien visa. It would be desirable to raise this to a five-year waiting period to reduce even further the incentive to use a foreign student visa as a mechanism for being in the United States while searching for a U.S. citizen spouse.

Another deterrent would be a permanent bar to obtaining a resident alien visa or a temporary visa for those found to have violated a significant provision of their foreign student visa, including by being employed in violation of the visa or by submitting a visa application based on a fraudulent marriage.

Regulations currently require that a foreign student visa applicant be able to demonstrate a level of financial support from legally authorized sources sufficient to cover tuition, fees, room, board, and other living expenses. This support level can serve as a policy instrument to increase or decrease the number of foreign students by lowering or raising the required minimum level of financial support or by extending its duration beyond the first year in a foreign student visa status.

There are some things that should *not* be done. It has been suggested by some that a quota be set on the number of foreign student visas. Establishing this quota would be difficult: How would the number be determined? How would the limited number of visas be allocated by country of origin, academic discipline, and university? A rationing mechanism would be needed. The visa backlog, now a prominent feature of the resident alien visa system, would make no sense for a student visa program. It would be unreasonable to ask a graduate student or a university to wait, say five years, before the visa could be approved. Administrative procedures could be used to develop a rationing allocation formula or visas could be auctioned off to universities, although either would be likely to be even more hotly contested than the mechanism for rationing immigration visas.

A more fundamental question, however, is why one would want to place a limit on bona fide foreign student visas. With the adoption of the administrative procedures discussed above, abuse and fraud in the foreign student visa program would be reduced. It is not obvious that having done so there would be "too many" foreign students in the United States. These visas have served the national interests of the United States and could be expected to continue doing so in the future.

NOTE

1. The data in this paragraph and the next two paragraphs are from the Institute of International Education (1995).

REFERENCES

Institute of International Education. 1995. *Fast Facts: Open Doors 1994/95*. New York.

U.S. Department of Justice. 1995. *1993 Statistical Yearbook of the Immigration and Naturalization Service*. Washington, DC.

heapest and best producer of products, then the education of the bot-
om half of the labor force is more critical to effective and efficient
roduction because if they cannot learn new, high-technology, highly
roductive processes, those processes cannot be employed (Thurow
992:227).

Thurow points out that in a low-wage industrial policy, the societal
ducation resource priority is on the upper 25 percent of the educational
stribution. Thus, America has some of the greatest research univer-
ties—and many of the worst elementary and secondary schools—in
e world. Our private sector and federal government research support
 a relatively small number of universities has permitted these selected
d elite institutions to become a world-recognized asset. Unfortu-
tely, our world-renowned research universities have not served our
frican American population well, a situation (almost as bad for other
merican minorities) that continues because we do not hold our re-
arch universities accountable for how well they serve our African
merican population. In the past, when industrial and manufacturing
bs were more plentiful, this lack of accountability may not have made
ıch difference. Now, and in the immediate future, as our economy
comes more and more dependent upon knowledge-based skills, we
 longer can ignore the consequences of gross underrepresentation in
cess to the higher-order academic training increasingly vital for ec-
omic development.

Even so, Thurow aptly observes that we now know that the past
toric explanation for American's economic success was inadequate;
torians traditionally overstated the impact of cheap, plentiful, well-
ated raw materials and farmland in explaining American economic
ccess. America did not become rich because a small population lived
 a rich resource environment or because Americans worked harder or
ed more than their neighbors. The real reason was that America's
urce advantages were combined with the first compulsory public
12 and mass higher educational systems in the world. Both these
antages, plus some others, gave America its great economic edge,
ecially after World War II. Americans did not work harder, but they
ked smarter and they were better skilled. Once rich, it was easier
America to stay rich (Thurow 1992:40).

he benefits most Americans receive come from the differential ac-
 of their ancestors, parents—or even themselves—to natural re-
ces that they could exploit without paying either replacement or

Chapter 10

Denial of Doctoral Opportu[nities]
for African Americans

FRANK L. MORRIS, SR.

As the U.S. moves to a de facto low-wage industrial [...]
ized by high immigration, a low-wage-influenced re[...]
agreement, and a societal value on graduate more t[...]
education, American education's current practices wi[...]
majority of African Americans are relegated to second [...]
in the next, as in the past, century. The extreme unde[...]
African Americans (and other minorities) among t[...]
doctorates from U.S. universities will be a major fa[...]
living standard and quality of life for African Ameri[...]

The disproportionate use of federal research fundin[...]
access to higher education to non-American citizer[...]
minorities, especially in the sciences, is a tragic and [...]
example of actions against our collective American [...]

African Americans have paid and continue to pa[...]
costs because most Americans are *not* aware that [...]
order skilled people, not low wages, are the only s[...]
ative economic advantage. American public inve[...]
race-and class-equitable investments in human cap[...]
often are discredited and receive low public policy p[...]
row, Dean of MIT's Sloan Business School, puts i[...]
economic success was determined by who was abl[...]
new products, then it would make sense to concent[...]
resources on the top 25 percent of our labor force—[...]
currently does. If, however, the key to economic [...]

environmental degradation costs, and from government subsidies, ranging from free or low-cost land, education, help in research, development, and promotion, and, especially, extensive tax subsidies. Our common future heritage depends on effectively utilizing and developing *all* of our human resources—especially our poor and minorities. Current policies and practices in doctoral education are counterproductive to this goal.

THE NEED FOR MORE AFRICAN AMERICAN DOCTORATES

Many current practices place all American graduate students at a disadvantage vis-à-vis international students. Many American research universities abuse the concept of merit in responding to the needs of our African American population. There are numerous reasons for comparing African American and international doctoral recipients:

- Non-American doctoral recipients benefit *most* from the *best* graduate financial assistance, while African American doctoral recipients benefit *least*.

- This best university support—in the form of research assistantships—is financed primarily through federal research grants funded from taxes taken from all Americans—including American minorities.

- Research universities have less incentive either to care about or to help produce more American minority scholars if they can find all the students they need—and more—overseas.

- The lack of public accountability, financial incentives, or penalties does not create adequate motivation for American research universities to produce more American minority Ph.D.'s.

Only in America is it necessary to make the argument that it is in our national interest to develop our underutilized human resources (who disproportionately happen to be American minorities). It is already clear that future quality of life, as well as economic development, requires greater utilization of knowledge-based communication and information skills. American Ph.D.'s are more likely to stimulate our economy, more likely to pay taxes, and more likely to be creditable role models for future faculty and students. The converse is also true. If current American research university patterns of benign neglect of African

American doctoral students in the sciences is allowed to continue, we are mortgaging our future.

THE PROBLEM

African American citizens constituted more than 13 percent of the U.S. population but received less than 3 percent of the doctorates from U.S. universities in 1990; non-American citizens received 28 percent of all doctorates from U.S. universities that year (Thurgood & Weinman 1991:10, 84).

Although African American doctorates have increased from 1975 to 1991, the total is still 16 percent less than the peak year of 1977. This loss is in spite of a 27 percent increase in Ph.D.'s to African American women since 1977. African American males are the only underrepresented American minority group that suffered a loss of more than 44 percent in the receipt of Ph.D.'s from American universities since 1975–1977 (NRC 1992:64). The number of Ph.D.'s going to all other underrepresented American minority groups increased considerably (Figure 10.1); the number of Ph.D.s from American universities going to non-American citizens increased more than 70 percent during that time.[1]

African American males constitute 6 percent of the U.S. population, 47 percent of the U.S. prison population (Hacker 1992:197), 5 percent of the private sector top corporate positions, but less than 3 percent of those with access to postsecondary education and less than 1 percent of those who received doctorates from American universities in 1990. In comparison, non-American citizen males received 21 percent of all doctorates from American universities in that same year.[2]

The 1990 Doctoral Project of the National Research Council (NRC) of the National Academy of Sciences documented that American research universities provided better support to the international students who received doctorates compared to African Americans who received doctorates. This greater support for non-American citizens over African Americans held for every doctoral and professional field, including the humanities, education, and the social sciences. (Thurgood & Weinman 1991:24, 47).

The result was that in 1990, of the more numerous 9,500 international students, 70 percent received doctorates without incurring any debt. In contrast, almost 70 percent of the much smaller number of

Figure 10.1
Doctorates Awarded by U.S. Universities to U.S. Citizens

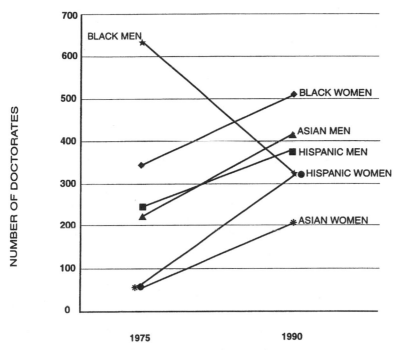

Source: Thurgood & Weinman (1991). Copyright © 1999 by the National Academy of Sciences. Courtesy of the National Academy Press, Washington, DC.

African Americans (820) and Hispanic doctoral recipients incurred debt. For 25 percent of the African American recipients and 33 percent of the Hispanic recipients doctoral education debt was more than $10,000 (Thurgood & Weinman 1991:26, 34). The 1991 data is even more discouraging. The greater the amount of debt that doctoral students owe, the greater the gap between America minority students and international noncitizen recipients of doctorates from U.S. universities (NRC 1992: Table 17).

Direct federal grant funding for doctoral support has declined in favor of more loan funding (for American citizens) with the result that almost 70 percent of all funding for graduate doctoral education is in the form of federally-subsidized research assistantships that research university faculty are much more likely to give to international students than to American minorities.[3]

American universities produced non-American citizen doctorates in fields where they did not produce a single African American doctorate in 1990—in some cases, for more than this one year. Over the last decade this trend is even more devastating. Figure 10.2 shows the future critical scientific fields where American universities averaged less than one and, in some cases, less than two African American Ph.D.'s per year for the entire decade. Remember, 13 percent more Ph.D.'s were awarded to international students in 1991 than in 1990.

DOCTORAL FINANCING: RACIAL BIAS WITHOUT ACCOUNTABILITY

In its excellent annual report on minorities in higher education, the American Council on Education (1993) reported that even though more African Americans have been attending college in recent years, the number of African American faculty members has remained stagnant for a decade. In 1980, African Americans represented 4.3 percent of college professors; in 1990 they accounted for 4.5 percent of college professors, only a marginal improvement, and more than half of these teach at historically black colleges and universities.

American universities contend that they cannot find African American faculty because of an alleged "pipeline" problem. Yet, only 55.8 percent of the African Americans who received doctorates from American universities in 1990 were hired by American universities, compared with 68 percent in 1975. The percentage of the much larger number of international doctorate recipients hired by American universities increased from 52 percent in 1975 to 56 percent in 1990. Thus American universities hired a slightly higher percentage of a much larger number of non-American-citizen doctoral recipients from American universities than African American doctoral recipients (Thurgood & Weinman 1991:22, 50).

Statistics clearly demonstrate that doctorate degrees for African American males declined more than half once the federal government began to cut back on direct assistance. As African American doctoral students had to depend upon American universities as the prime source for financing their studies, they became much worse off because American universities allocated more of their resources to fields where they admit and support foreign students. *Ironically, as much of this university-administered support for international students is in the form of research assistantships, universities use federal funds directly or indirectly to disproportionately fund international, rather than American minority, students.*

If there were no readily available pool of foreign students, American universities would have greater incentives to help develop and increase the supply of American students—possibly even American minority students—in many science fields. Instead, American universities and the major organizations that primarily speak for American education, unanimously supported changes in the immigration law of 1990 that accelerates the recruitment of international scientists and scholars, thus insuring that American minorities continue to be shut out of these academic openings. These are serious charges; let us examine some of the evidence.

Although American university departments do not attribute the dearth of African American doctoral students to the lack of financial aid, data suggests otherwise. In his excellent study commissioned by the Graduate Record Examination Board, Michael Nettles concludes that the reduction in (federal) financial assistance since the 1960s has had a negative effect on prospective African American graduate students at both the master and doctoral levels. That reduction also may explain why more than 60 percent of African American and Hispanic graduate students attend graduate school part-time. In 1970, twice the number of students received fellowships, scholarships, and traineeships as in 1981; the federal budget for these forms of assistance declined by more than 50 percent from 1970 to 1981. While these federal grants decreased, federal loans increased from $717 million in 1976 to nearly $3.5 billion in 1984 (Nettles 1987:1.5). Nettles notes that as federal direct student funding declined, students became more dependent upon universities for assistance, a shift, he asserts, that profoundly affected the ability of African American students to afford graduate school. As universities became the prime determining financing factor for doctoral degrees, African American males fared far worse than any other—especially international—students.

The annual National Research Council 1990 data that traces the financing of those who were successful in achieving the doctorates is informative. For international students, American universities were the primary source of doctoral support for 68.8 percent, while for African

Figure 10.2
Fields Where the Average Number of African American Ph.D.'s from All U.S. Universities Is Less Than One or Two Per Year: 1982–1991

Less than 1	Less than 2	Less than 1	Less than 2
MATH		**EARTH, ATMOSPHERIC & MARINE SCIENCES**	
Applied Math (86)	Probability & Statistics (87)	Atmospheric Physics & Chemistry (8)	
Algebra (15)	Topology (16)	Meteorology (6)	
Analysis/Functional Analysis (45)		Atmospheric & Metrology Science (10)	
Geometry (23)		Geology (21)	
Logic (6)		Geophysics & Seismology (29)	
Number Theory (11)		General Geological Sciences (7)	
Computing Theory & Practice (3)		Environmental Sciences (7)	
Operations Research (16)		Hydrology & Water Resources (4)	
General Math (91)		Oceanography (33)	
Other Math (14)			
		ENGINEERING	
COMPUTER SCIENCE		Aerospace, Aeronautical & Astro (86)	Civil (258)
Information Systems (23)	Computer Science (240)	Agricultural (42)	
		Bioengineering & Biomedical (41)	
PHYSICS & ASTRONOMY		Computer (62)	
Astronomy (12)	Elementary Particles (63)	Engineering Mechanics (60)	
Astrophysics (17)	General Physics (128)	Engineering Physics (7)	
Acoustics (8)		Engineering Science (13)	
Atomic & Molecular Physics (25)		Environmental Health Engineering (19)	
Nuclear (24)		Industrial (77)	
Optics (28)		Materials Science (146)	
Plasma (13)		Metallurgical (42)	
		Mining & Mineral (19)	
CHEMISTRY		Nuclear (3)	
Agricultural & Food	Inorganic (48)	Operations Research (10)	
Nuclear (4)		Petroleum (22)	
Pharmaceutical (15)		Polymer (24)	
Polymer (30)		Systems (21)	
		General Engineering (24)	

BIOCHEMISTRY

Biophysics (37)
Plant Genetics (8)
Plant Pathology (11)
Plant Physiology (9)
Botany (25)
Ecology (19)
Developmental Bio/Embryology
Endocrinology (2)
Entomology (1)
Microbiology & Bacteriology
Parasitology (5)
Human & Animal Genetics (17
Genetics (2)

Biometrics & Biostatistics
Immunology (21)
Neurosciences (27)
General Biological
Sciences (67)

HEALTH SCIENCES

Environmental Health (11)
Public Health/Epidemiology (22)
Rehabilitation/Therapeutic Services
Veterinary Medicine (24)
General Chemistry (167)

Pharmacy (48)

AGRICULTURAL SCIENCES

Animal Breeding & Genetics (6)   Agricultural Economics (61)
Animal Nutrition (11)
Animal Sciences (36)
Agronomy (54)
Plant Breeding & Genetics (27)
Plant Pathology (23)
Plant Sciences (8)
Food Sciences (69)
Soil Sciences (36)
Horticultural Science (30)
Fisheries Science (9)
Fish & Wildlife (21)
Forestry Science (21)
Renewable Natural Resources (11)

Sources: Unpublished data from the Doctoral Research Project (NRC 1992).

Note: Parentheses show number of non-American citizen doctorates from U.S. universities in 1990.

Table 10.1
Sources of Support for 1990 Doctoral Recipients (percentages)

	Personal	University	Federal	Other
All U.S. Citizens	48.0	41.8	6.6	3.7
African Americans	62.8	24.8	6.3	6.3
Foreign Students/ Temporary Residents	13.8	68.8	1.3	16.3

Totals do not add up to 100 percent due to rounding.
Source: Thurgood & Weinman (1991). Copyright © 1999 by the National Academy of
Sciences. Courtesy of the National Academy Press, Washington, DC.

Americans, universities were the primary source of support for less than
25 percent (Thurgood & Weinman 1991:24, 47). For more than 60
percent of African Americans (and Native Americans) the primary
source of support for their doctoral education was their own personal
funds, such as loans; only 13.8 percent of international students primarily depended on personal funds (Table 10.1).

American universities attempt to explain these trends by contending
that minorities are in fields where less university and federal support
is available. The different fields misnomer is apparent if we compare
the fields where a much higher proportion of American minority students than international students are found. Of African Americans who
received their degree in education in 1990, 81 percent listed personal
resources as the prime source of financing for their doctoral studies;
only 12 percent were primarily funded by American universities. In
contrast, only 41 percent of international students who received doctorates in education that year listed personal resources as their primary
source of funding; more than 28 percent were primarily funded by
American universities. Keep in mind that the absolute number of international students is many times greater than African Americans—or
all American minorities combined. This large positive funding percentage in favor of international students translates into almost geo-
metric differences in actual dollars.

Thus, if we just look in the doctoral field where about 50 percent of
all African Americans achieve their doctorates, the proportion of African Americans who had to finance their doctoral studies personally

was twice that of non-American citizens. *Equally important, American universities were more than twice as likely to provide funds to international students in education than to African Americans* (Thurgood & Weinman 1991:24, 47).

We find similar patterns in fields such as the social sciences and the humanities. In the social sciences, 48.5 percent of 1990 African American Ph.D.'s financed their education by personal funds, while only 22.5 percent of international students had to pay for their education with personal funds. American universities were the prime source of financing for 37 percent of African American Ph.D.'s but for 56 percent of international student Ph.D.'s (Thurgood & Weinman 1991:24, 470).

It is difficult to understand why American universities should favor non-American citizens in the humanities, but they do. Only 28 percent of international doctoral students in the humanities primarily used personal funds to finance their doctoral studies, compared to 50 percent of African American doctoral students. Universities were the primary source of support for almost 57 percent of international students in 1990 compared to only 50 percent of African American doctoral students. Remember these figures are for those who successfully completed their doctorates!

While American universities were giving preferential doctoral financing to international doctoral students over American doctoral students in education, African American and Hispanic doctoral awardees in education were accumulating significant graduate debt to go with high undergraduate debt. One-third of all Hispanic doctoral awardees and more than one-quarter of the African American awardees reported debt of more than $10,000 (Thurgood & Weinman 1991:24, 47). These high debts are often in fields where salaries are lower than in the sciences.

Other indicators show the preference or bias of American university graduate departments toward international students over American minorities—especially African Americans and Native Americans. In both real and total time to complete the degree, international students appear to have the advantage over African Americans and Hispanics. In education, for example, the median total time for noncitizen international students was 12.8 years, compared to 19.6 for African Americans and 16.4 for Hispanics. The real time median differentials were 6.1 for international students in education compared to 8.5 years for both African American and Hispanic doctoral degree recipients (Thurgood & Weinman 1991:15, 46). Part of this difference could be related to the university preference for support for international students in the form of research assistantships that also encourage interaction with faculty and promote the possibility of both mentoring and provision of a basis for a dissertation.

Yet, American universities contend that factors other than their differential allocation of financial aid account for the dearth of minorities in graduate programs. This is despite the indication from Nettles and others that the much lower median family income and extreme difference in black and white family wealth in the United States require that minority students, especially African Americans, non-Cuban Hispanics, and Native Americans, assume much greater undergraduate debt burdens than white American graduate students. Nettles strongly suggests (1987:4) that this differential debt burden affects minority and majority students differently when they make education and career decisions. It is an entirely rational decision not to go on to a doctoral degree program when you see that the majority of your peers who do are not favored in comparison with international students and that students of your race are forced to take longer to complete their degrees.

American universities' contention that a ''pipeline'' problem keeps them from finding ''qualified'' African American graduate students has less merit after an examination of the American university funding preference for international students (see above). The NRC report notes that such ''qualified,'' potentially successful African American graduate students are disproportionately located on the campuses of historically black colleges and universities. Although such colleges and universities enrolled only about 16 percent of all African American students in American higher education, they were the baccalaureate-granting schools for almost 60 percent of the African Americans who received Ph.D.'s in 1975 and almost 40 percent who received Ph.D.'s in 1990 (Thurgood & Weinman 1991:32). This author proudly taught and worked on one such campus that, according to recent figures, produces more African American Ph.D.'s than any other public American university. Yet American universities do not try actively to recruit extensively or to offer support to all of our African American science graduates who have the capability to succeed in doctoral programs. So much for the alleged pipeline problem.

Keep in mind that in 1990 international students received more than twice as many doctorates from American universities as all American minorities combined, a trend that clearly seems to freeze out American minorities, especially African American males, from future faculty positions. African Americans resentment is even greater when we see American universities recruit international scholars of color and then label them as "minority," rather than the more accurate "international," faculty.

Three countries provided 44 percent of all non-American-citizen doctorates in 1990: Korea and the two Chinas (Thurgood & Weinman 1991:11). Why is there this overwhelming preference in American graduate university departments for international students, especially international Asian students in the sciences?

The lobbying of major educational associations/organizations that represent American universities in support of the 1990 immigration law changes to make it much easier for foreign professors and students to get both access to and permanent status in the United States clearly worked to the detriment of U.S. minorities. This trend is likely to accelerate as David Simcox, former executive director of the Center for Immigration Studies, noted in a paper presented at the Northeast Association of Graduate Schools meeting (1991:3–4):

There are several factors that will make these trends worse in the future, the greatest of which is the rapid population growth among the young, highly mobile working-age population in the third world. Almost all third-world countries are falling further and further behind in the race to create jobs for the expanding populations. For example, in the next few years Mexico's labor force will grow at the rate of over 1 million persons per year, but Mexico's economy, even with the most optimistic assumptions about a free trade agreement, will create less than half that number of new jobs per year. The International Labor Organization anticipates that the third-world labor force will grow by 50 million per year with less than half that number able to find jobs. Many of these economies have been overproducing college graduates for many years. Some, such as India, Pakistan, Korea, and the Philippines, seem to be deliberately overtraining some of their surplus skilled workers with the expectation that they will find advanced training, and possibly employment, in countries such as the United States. Most of this oversupply will be science graduates and students because those disciplines are viewed as more culturally neutral, because American universities are still considered as the best in science and technology, and last, but not least, the transition to permanent residence in the United States is easiest for those with science skills.

This is consistent with the historical preference pattern of American research university faculty for international faculty and students over

American minorities, especially African American males. This situation will not change unless major funding and funding incentives for American universities change.

RECOMMENDATIONS

African American and other legislators concerned about American long-term interests must take steps to insure that the resources committed to American minority students in doctoral training by American universities are at least equal to the commitment of taxpayer research support subsidies to international students in all fields. Academic administrators, such as college presidents, provosts, and deans, should make academic department discretionary funding conditional until these departments provide all American minorities doctoral opportunities that are at least equal to their commitment to non-American citizens.

Legislation that will guarantee research assistant-type support for all qualified American doctoral students should be supported. We should not require American students, especially American minority students from families with less wealth and income, to go into debt to finance their education while we subsidize noncitizen guests to the extent that the overwhelming majority of them get their doctorates debt-free.

Whenever American universities use federal (or state) funds for graduate student research support, and whenever that support covers more than one student, then for every international student that American faculty members chose to support with these government monies, they should also support an underrepresented American minority student.

It is clear that major American research universities are not now going to provide research opportunities for American minority students comparable to those they provide international students. These major heavily-federally-subsidized American research universities *never* have provided opportunities for American minorities of color comparable to those provided by the historically black colleges and universities. The underfunded black institutions, however, have been given neither the resources nor the state authority to provide comparable comprehensive graduate research opportunities. Now it is time to address this issue by providing major research commitments to historically black colleges and universities that have successfully demonstrated their ability to graduate quality undergraduates, especially in the sciences. It is likely that only these institutions will provide the quality research environment that will develop the minority talent currently being lost to this nation.

There should be an *American incentive computation* in every federal (or state) research contract that supports doctoral students. Universities where the underrepresented minority percentage of Ph.D. graduates in the state equals the proportion of underrepresented minorities in their state population should receive a ten-point bonus in every federal or state competitive research contract. Conversely, universities that use federal funds to support more non-American citizens than underrepresented American minorities in research should have ten points deducted from their score. Such a system would finally create the financial incentives necessary for research universities to develop and recruit underrepresented American Ph.D.'s in a manner more comparable to the way they willingly recruit underrepresented minorities from all kinds of limited academic backgrounds for revenue-generating athletics.

NOTES

1. There were 684 African American male doctorates in 1977 and 385 in 1991 (NRC 1992:71). There were at least 9,398 non-American-citizen doctorates in 1990 compared to approximately 5,338 in 1975 (Thurgood & Weinman 1991:84).

2. The 6 percent black male population figure is a conservative estimate without the benefit of adjustments to reflect a significant black male U.S. census undercount (Thurgood & Weinman 1991:10, 84–85).

3. In the tables in the NRC study, "university" funding is primarily federally-sponsored research dispensed as research assistantships (NRC 1992).

REFERENCES

American Council on Education. 1993. *Twelfth Annual Report on Minorities in Higher Education.* Washington, DC: American Council on Education.

Carter, D. J., and Wilson, R. 1993. *Annual Status Report: Minorities in Higher Education.* Washington, DC: American Council on Education.

Hacker, A. 1992. *Two Nations: Black and White, Separate, Hostile, Unequal.* New York: Scribner.

National Research Council (NRC). 1992. Affirmative Action Table: Ph.D.'s Awarded to U.S. Citizens by Race, Gender, Fine Field of Study, and

Year, 1975–1991. Data provided to this author by the Doctoral Research
Project, Office of Scientific and Engineering Personnel.

Nettles, M. 1987. *Financial Aid and Minority Participation in Graduate Education: A Research Report of the Minority Graduate Education Project*. Princeton, NJ: Educational Testing Service.

Simcox, D. 1991. Immigration in the 90s and Graduate Education. Paper presented at annual meeting of the Northeast Association of Graduate Schools, Newport RI, April 12.

Thurgood, D. H., and Weinman, J. M. 1991. Summary Report 1990: Doctorate Recipients from United States Universities. Washington, DC: National Academy Press.

Thurow, L. 1992. *Head to Head: The Coming Economic Battle Among Japan, Europe and America*. New York: Morrow.

Chapter 11

Foreign Students in Science and Engineering Ph.D. Programs: An Alien Invasion or Brain Gain?

JAGDISH BHAGWATI AND MILIND RAO

THE PREPONDERANCE OF FOREIGN STUDENTS IN SCIENCE AND ENGINEERING (S&E) PROGRAMS: THE PHENOMENON

Were the Nobel Laureate Paul Samuelson to walk into a graduate economics class at MIT today, he would be struck by a dramatic difference in the composition of students since he first taught the class. In the 1940s, the class was predominantly American; today, however, more than one-third of the students in the class are foreign students.

This phenomenon is not confined either to MIT or to economics.[1] Thus in 1990, more than one-half of the engineering Ph.D.'s in the United States were awarded to foreign students. The figures are almost as high in mathematics, physics, chemistry, and computer science (see Figure 11.1 for S&E and the components Science and Engineering and Figure 11.2 for major sciences).

But the phenomenon of foreign student dominance in the U.S. is ill-understood and ill-explained. Its public policy implications are, therefore, couched in alarmist terms, turning the phenomenon into a problem that must be contained when it is, as we argue in this paper, a cause for celebration that calls for a policy of tolerance, even encouragement.

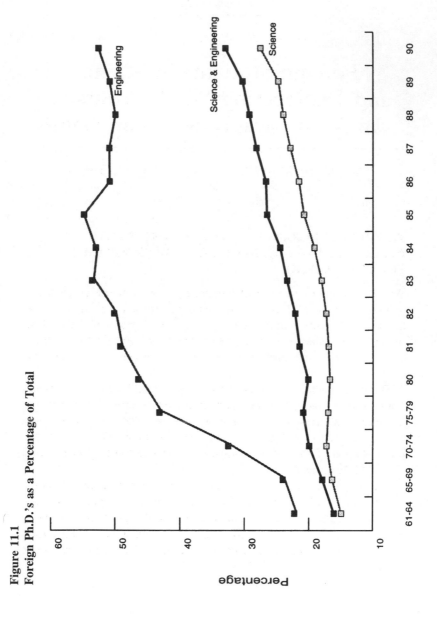

Figure 11.1
Foreign Ph.D.'s as a Percentage of Total

Figure 11.2
Foreign Ph.D.'s as a Percentage of Total

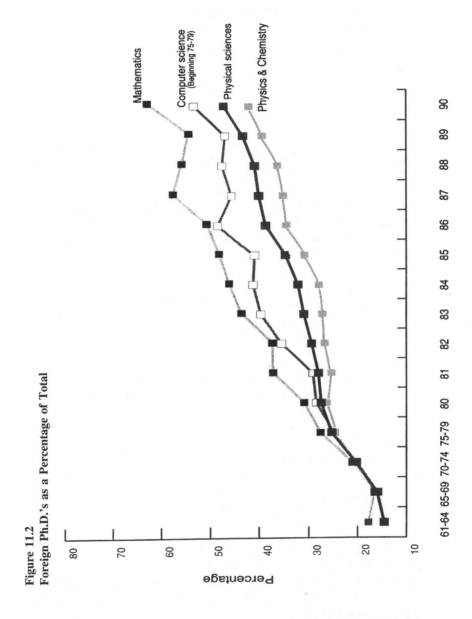

CURRENT EXPLANATIONS AND POLICY SUGGESTIONS

The conventional explanation of the phenomenon seems to proceed as follows:

• The United States has a comparative advantage in promoting graduate education. Foreign students, therefore, come to get it.

• The preponderance of foreign students get into technical and scientific programs because they (chiefly Asians) happen to be "good at" mathematics and far less so at "verbal" skills.[2]

• Finally, Derek Bok (1993) argues that the earnings of doctors, lawyers, and top corporate executives have grown substantially relative to those of professors, drawing talented Americans to these professions and away from teaching. Presumably, this argument extends to technical and science Ph.D. programs as well.

The net result then is to increase foreign student—and reduce native enrollment—in S&E Ph.D. programs. The consequences that are expected to ensue from this phenomenon are fearful.

• Since Ph.D.'s plough back into teaching, Bowen and Sosa (1989), in a book featured on the front page of the *New York Times*, predicted a major shortage of academic faculty in the United States by the mid-1990s, due in no small measure to the presence of foreign students who presumably would return to their native lands.

• The preponderance of foreign students in S&E Ph.D. programs also is alleged by many critics to endanger our leadership in research and development.

• Finally, a number of black critics attribute the failure of blacks to get an increasing number of Ph.D.'s in S&E programs to the increased dominance of foreign graduate students (e.g., Morris 1993).

The policy prescriptions that naturally follow from these diagnoses center around the notion that "reliance" on foreign graduates is a mistake the United States cannot afford. Proposals to restrict the influx of foreign students through visa denial and reduced financial aid have, therefore, been advanced.

OUR RIVAL EXPLANATION

Our view, however, is that the conventional explanation—and the prejudicial implications following from it—are flawed. Our rival explanation of the phenomenon leads, instead, to more sanguine implications and to policy conclusions altogether opposed to currently proposed restrictionist ones.

Alarmist predictions that there would be a shortage of S&E Ph.D's for the academe (Bowen & Sosa 1989) already have proven false. A recent study by Massy and Goldman of Stanford and RAND, widely reported in the media (Greenberg 1995; Browne 1995), concludes that "doctoral production in S&E averages about 25 percent above employment opportunities." Our rival explanation also is better able to suggest why such a large "surplus" could have developed and is likely to persist even though the labor market normally adjusts to correct imbalances because students confidently can be expected to walk away from education that yields low and diminishing returns.

The Theory

At the outset, we must note that the U.S. graduate programs generally admit students on merit. There is no discrimination against foreign students (though in recent years there may have been affirmative action to assist native minorities, which then are marginally favored in relation to *both* foreign and native nonminority students).[3]

This being so, as the applicant pool shifts in favor of foreign students relative to native students, assuming quality to be unchanged, so would the admissions and hence, all else equal, the Ph.D.'s awarded.[4]

The explanation of the rising share of foreign students in S&E Ph.D. programs must then be found in the relative shift in favor of foreign students in the application pool. Indeed, it can.

The Explanation

Our explanation proceeds by citing the many factors that have dramatically increased the applicant pool for foreign students.

Immigration economists know that rivulets of immigrants build up into streams as information networking goes to work. Casual empiricism underlines how talented students follow others who ventured into specific graduate programs as pioneers and then spread the word.

In turn, the success of the foreign students from specific institutions abroad serves to supply the necessary "certification" for the admissions committees that new applicants from these institutions are, indeed, likely to be as good as they appear, thus turning them into effective and potentially successful applicants. Thus, new applicants from Seoul National University are treated more seriously in competition than the former ones on whom universitites took a chance and who went on to do well in the programs.

But, for some of the successful "sending" countries, the most significant factor is that they steadily have been building up their technical education to levels comparable to some of our best institutions—often with these institutions' help! Entry into these foreign elite schools (such as the prestigious Indian Institutes of Technology [IIT]) often is based on nationally administered entrance examinations with the programs subsidized by the government, permitting the most gifted students to attend. A favorable evaluation of the graduates of these institutions when they apply for admission to S&E Ph.D. programs is therefore inevitable; these students often are superbly trained and greatly gifted.

Indeed, all these factors are seen to work in the case of the four Asian countries that provide currently more than one-half of the S&E Ph.D.'s: China; India; South Korea; and Taiwan (see Figure 11.3 for S&E totals and components and Figure 11.4 for major sciences).

Thus, while each of these top "source" countries today has numerous colleges/universities offering undergraduate S&E programs and degrees, most of the Asian students in American Ph.D. programs are graduates of a very small group of schools that increasingly have come to be regarded as having exceptionally high and improved standards of instruction.

India, for instance, produces about 25,000 engineers (at the bachelor's level) every year; only 2,000 (or about 8 percent) of these graduate from the elite Indian Institutes of Technology. However, 78 percent of recent U.S. engineering Ph.D's awarded to Indians went to graduates of the IIT. Almost one-half (48 percent) of all Taiwanese students who received Ph.D.'s in the United States attended either National Taiwan University or Cheng Kung University. Even more telling, 65 percent of the Korean students who received S&E Ph.D.'s in the United States are graduates of one university—Seoul National University! The fig-

Figure 11.3
Top Four Asian Countries with American Doctorates

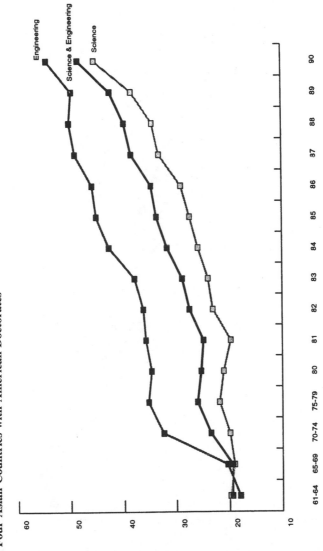

Figure 11.4
Top Four Asian Countries with American Doctorates

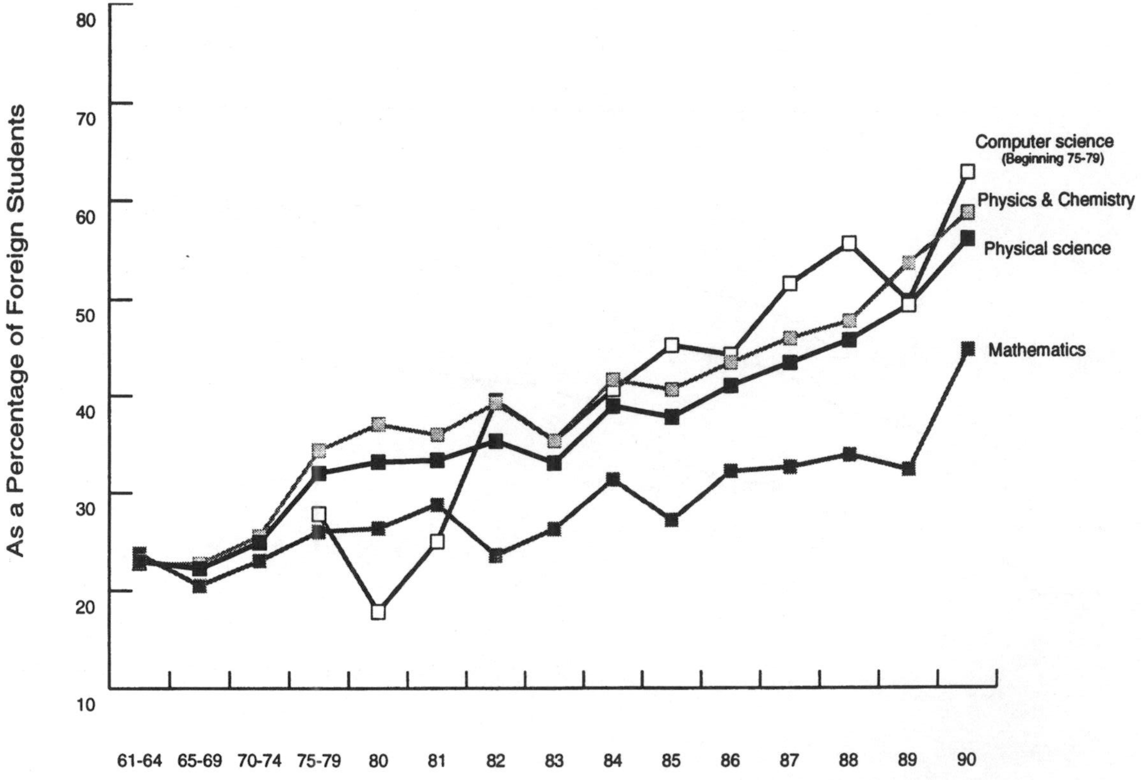

ures are almost as high for the elite schools of China—Peking University and Tsinghua University.[5]

From these countries' perspective, the flow to the United States from these elite institutions has increased significantly. At least, 70 percent of their graduates now leave for the United States. For the IIT, the figures are about 85 percent. About 30 percent of all IIT graduates, since its founding in 1954, currently are in the United States (Ananth, Babu, & Natarajan 1989; Bhagwati & Rao 1996b).

It also is worth noting that the *quality* of students turned out by these elite foreign institutions has increased over time, in turn increasing these students' ability to compete against native students. In 1964, there were 18,000 applications for the 2,000 places at the IIT in India. By the end of the 1980s, applications for these places had increased to 100,000 (Bhagwati & Rao 1996b)!

Moreover, this phenomenon of a rising and high share of foreign students in our graduate programs has surfaced differentially in the S&E (also in the mathematics and economics) programs. Why has it not arisen equally in the "professional" schools of law and business?

Part of the reason lies, of course, in the fact that the "source" countries themselves have not allocated equal energies and financing to attract their most talented students into these professions, as against the S&E, programs.[6]

But the principal reason is that the qualified and talented students from these source countries face a major liquidity constraint. Tuition at the graduate schools in the United States is generally beyond their financial capabilities.[7] Besides they do not qualify for U.S. governmental and bank loans.

As it happens, graduate programs in the United States have different financial aid possibilities. Professional schools (law, business, and medicine) offer very little financial aid; only 1 percent of the entering class receives primary support from the university. Only somewhat better are the Ph.D. programs in the humanities and education: 20 percent of the students in non-S&E programs receive financial assistance from the university. A striking contrast is offered by S&E Ph.D. programs; more than 70 percent of the students (and 80 percent of the foreign students) in S&E Ph.D. programs list the university as the primary source of financial assistance (Ries & Thurgood 1993). This picture is reinforced when we look at Figure 11.5 that shows alternatively the source-composition of support in different fields for doctoral students. Uni-

Figure 11.5
Support Sources for Doctorates Different Fields, 1991: Total Students

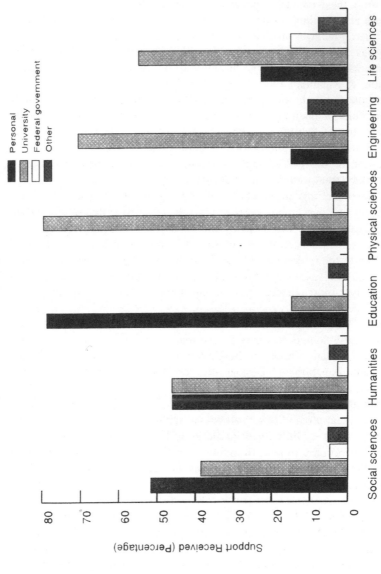

Source: Ries & Thurgood (1993). Copyright © 1999 by the National Academy of Sciences. Courtesy of the National Academy Press, Washington, DC.

versity support, reflecting lab work and other research assistance, clearly is a much more important source of support in Engineering, Physical Sciences, and Life Sciences than in the Social Sciences, Humanities, and Education.

To explain the increased share of foreign students in S&E Ph.D. programs, the foregoing analysis of the factors augmenting the supply of qualified foreign applicants into these programs is not entirely sufficient. Of course, the explanation does not require but would be strengthened if we also could argue that the supply of *native* applicants into these programs has shrunk. But we do need to dismiss the possibility that the native supply of comparably qualified and talented applicants also has not increased simultaneously.

This seems wholly reasonable to assert. There is no counterpart in American education, prior to graduate school, to the factors augmenting the supply of foreign student applications in S&E graduate programs. At the same time, the common complaint is that the starting salaries and possibly even the rates of return to "professional" education— MBAs, medical and law degrees—have attracted growing proportions of the best graduating native students.

POLICY IMPLICATIONS

Our explanation of the rising share and predominance of foreign students in the S&E graduate programs then shows that it reflects "supply" factors that are critically tied into the meritocratic and nondiscriminatory approach underlying U.S. graduate school admissions. The implications below then follow.

The meritocratic approach to admissions to graduate programs results in their attracting the best talent and the best trained candidates from around the world. While itself a reflection of the scientific and academic strength of these programs, it reinforces that strength in turn. The increased influx of talented foreign students into S&E, mathematics, and economics Ph.D. programs is a sign of strength, not of weakness.

The general notion that the share of foreign students is rising because native students are "no longer interested in" S&E Ph.D.'s and careers lacks force. At minimum, it omits the prince from *Hamlet*. The rising share of foreign students reflects the dramatically increased supply of competitive foreign students. The decline in the supply of competitive native students, even if true, is at best a minor part of the story. As admissions are not wholly inelastic, it is worth noting that the overall graduate S&E admissions of natives have not fallen as the admissions of foreign students have risen.

The increased supply of the foreign students as a source of the phenomenon of their rising and risen share in S&E Ph.D.'s also implies that the responsiveness of such graduate production to a fall in the rate of return to such education is likely to be very low. Hence, one could predict sharp falls in these rates of return and "surplus" production without the normal corrective mechanism provided by the fact that the students will simply walk away from enrolling in these programs and, thus, reduce the output of Ph.D.'s to levels at which better and competitive rates of return are restored.

This is because foreign students will compare their rates of return from S&E Ph.D.'s in the United States to the much inferior rates of return to staying or returning home. The earlier-cited RAND-Stanford study of the "excess demand for Ph.D.'s in many science fields" (Browne 1995) argues that currently a science doctorate yields a one-in-four chance of not getting suitable employment: ". . . universities in the United States are producing about 25 percent more doctorates in science and engineering fields than the United States economy can afford." But a rate of return here that is diminished by one-fourth will still exceed the alternative rates of return at home. This also is partly because the direct cost of graduate schooling in the United States is substantially taken care of by financial support (usually linked to labs and projects).

Thus, the prospect of quick reversal of "surpluses," such as the one described in the RAND-Stanford study, is diminished. But why should we worry? The effect of such a "surplus" is certain to force one-in-four (if that estimate is properly arrived at and argued plausibly to endure) eventually to work their way downstream to jobs below their expectations. But, as these Ph.D.'s cannot find jobs at such places as Stanford, MIT, Caltech, and Bell Labs and, therefore, go downstream to smaller colleges and lesser institutions, they upgrade the quality of instruction and research at these institutions.[8] Surely, that is a reason for us to rejoice rather than lament.

Nor do we need to worry that we are becoming "too dependent" on foreign students. They typically stay on, are even called "stay ons" in the immigration literature! Even when Ph.D.'s go back to their home countries, they often return. Professional markets are heavily globalized now and one often gets either "yo-yo" immigrants or migrants who, having returned home or gone elsewhere, eventually come back here to the magnet country they chose in the first place for their graduation into a Ph.D.[9]

As is well-established in immigration studies, few nations can match the facilities for professional research and advancement that the United States offers. Nor can other nations match the opportunities that are open to second-generation children in the United States. Just imagine bringing up your children in Tokyo instead of New York or in Kobe instead of Austin. It's no contest.

Foreign students typically see their U.S. education as a stepping stone to immigration into the United States.[10] Since the 1965 Immigration Act, which opened up a number of "preferences" for admissions of Professional, Technical, and Kindred (PTK) immigrants, this incentive for foreign students to acquire first-rate U.S. degrees and to improve their ability to stay in the United States thereafter has been a powerful one.[11]

The fear that foreign students will disappear from the United States, leaving us with inadequate scientific personnel, often is expressed or lies behind exhortations to encourage natives to go for S&E Ph.D.'s. But, if these students stay on, for the most part, the fear is misplaced.

The United States is uniquely a country of immigrants. There is enormous ethnic diversity in the country. Naturalization is the easiest in the world. The distinction between "us" and "them," directed against foreign students, is wholly incongruous with the country's history and culture. It also flies in the face of the culture of excellence and nondiscrimination that has characterized and enriched the American educational scene.

In light of these considerations, we disagree with the reported view of Dr. Phillip Griffith, director of the Institute for Advanced Study at Princeton and chairman of a recent study conducted by the National Academy of Science, that "since foreign students account for a large proportion of graduate enrollments, he and his colleagues [would] urge better science education so that even more Americans will be drawn to Ph.D. training" (Greenberg 1995).[12] Getting young Americans to appreciate science is a laudable objective; but surely it is not to be urged because we have foreign students in S&E Ph.D. programs.

Our analysis suggests, contrary to the agitation about the current "surpluses" of S&E Ph.D.'s and about the preponderance of foreign students in these programs, that the foreign students phenomenon is not a problem. Rather, it benefits the country. Other nations' "brain drain" is our "brain gain."

Instead of curtailing the inflow of these talented foreign students or trying to reduce their share in S&E Ph.D. programs, we ought to make their immigration easier, so that we reap the benefits to us from their settling here.[13] Towards this end, we propose that the immigration of S&E Ph.D. students from several designated high-performance institutions should be practically automatic, their abundant *human* capital justifying their immigration, just as immigration law permits those bringing substantial *financial* capital to immigrate readily. That could reverse the balance in favor of importing the talented, rather than the rich, bringing us closer to the ideas that built this nation.

Finally, we must turn to a question that bothers many black leaders: Is the entry of foreign students harming the entry of blacks into our S&E Ph.D. programs? Some in the black community express the view that blacks are being "crowded out" by foreign students (e.g., Morris 1993). Our view is that this argument is incorrect (see also Bhagwati & Rao 1996b).

The facts on black students are of course alarming (National Science Foundation 1991b:310; 1994a:318). Of the 36,027 Ph.D.'s in all subjects awarded in 1990, only 320—less than 1 percent—were awarded to black men; and 508, or just more than 1 percent, were given to black women. Even more ominous is the trend: the number of blacks getting Ph.D.'s in all subjects has dropped since 1977. This contrasts strikingly with the experience regarding foreign students highlighted above. But the inference that foreign students come at the expense of blacks is unwarranted.

To begin with, we must reject the notion that there are a fixed number of places in graduate programs and, therefore, that an increase in the numbers of foreign students must be at the expense of natives— black or otherwise. The facts show that the supply of places in graduate S&E programs, which attract the greatest concern, is not rigorously fixed. Over the past two decades, the number of natives in these Ph.D. programs has remained constant (at about 13,000). The Ph.D. programs have, thus, expanded in size as foreign students have increased (National Science Foundation 1991b:310). Thus, there is no prima facie presumption that the increase in the numbers of foreign students in these Ph.D. programs has been at the expense of natives.

of Labor must, on the basis of an American employer's sponsorship, certify that "no American can do or is available for this job." The Department of Labor regulations provide, in addition, for special handling of labor certification applications for college or university teachers; an employer can select the best qualified candidate, regardless of citizenship, for the position. Hence, for those without U.S. citizen family members, the only feasible route to immigrate legally to the United States is to secure employment certification from an American employer. And this route is much more readily traveled when one has a U.S. graduate degree.

12. We should stress that Dr. Griffith's views (conveyed in personal communication) concerning the desirability of foreign students in S&E programs are thoroughly consonant with ours.

13. These benefits accrue to us in numerous ways, for instance, through the spillover effect of their ideas and research (Bhagwati & Rao 1994a; 1996a; 1996b).

REFERENCES

Ananth, M. S., Babu, K. G., and Natarajan, R. 1989. *Data Base for Brain Drain: Institution Based Study*. Madras: Indian Institute of Technology.

Bhagwati, J., and Rao, M. 1994a. Foreign Students Spur U.S. Brain Gain. *Wall Street Journal* (August 31).

———. 1994b. Immigration, Education and U.S. Brain Gain. *Economic Times* [India] (November 28).

———. 1996a. "Too Many" Ph.D.'s: A False Alarm. *American Enterprise* (January/February).

———. 1996b. U.S. Brain Gain: Consequences for Efficiency and Distribution. *Challenge* (March/April).

Bhagwati, J., Schatz, K-W., and Wong, K. 1984. The West German *Gastarbeiter* System of Immigration. *European Economic Review* 26(3): 277–94. Reprinted in D. Irwin, ed., *Political Economy and International Economics*, Chapter 21. Cambridge, MA: MIT Press, 1991.

Bhagwati, J., and Srinivasan, T. N. 1975. Education in a Job-Ladder Model and the Fairness-in-Hiring Rule. *Journal of Public Economics* 7:1–2. Reprinted in R. Feenstra, ed., *Essays in International Economic Theory*, vol. 2, Chapter 49. Cambridge, MA: MIT Press, 1983.

Bok, D. 1993. *The Cost of Talent: How Executives and Professionals Are Paid and How It Affects America*. New York: Macmillan, Free Press.

Bowen, H. R., and Schuster, J. 1986. *American Professors: A National Resource Imperiled*. New York: Oxford University Press.

Bowen, W., and Rudenstine, N. 1992. *In Pursuit of the Ph.D.* Princeton, NJ: Princeton University Press.

Could we then argue instead that the black students are crowded out in a financial sense, that the limited financial support available in the universities for their Ph.D. programs is competed away by better-trained foreign students and would otherwise be available to the black students (e.g., DePalma 1992)? We do not think so.

At first glance, of course, the "crowding out" thesis appears plausible as, unlike most foreign students, most black graduates do not receive extensive financial assistance from the universities. In 1990, 69 percent of all foreign graduate students were supported by the universities, whereas only 25 percent of all black graduate students received grants and assistantships (National Science Foundation 1994b:301).

But this contrast is mostly explained by the fields of study of the two groups (National Science Foundation 1991b:310; 1994a:318). Thus, 81 percent of foreign graduate students are in S&E Ph.D. programs; only 14 percent of black graduate students are in these programs. Most black graduate students are in humanities and especially in education Ph.D. programs; more than 50 percent of black graduate students are in education graduate programs. As it happens, graduate programs in the U.S. have different financial aid policies (National Science Foundation 1994a:318; 1994b: 301). S&E graduate students are overwhelmingly supported by their universities; more than 70 percent of the students in S&E Ph.D. programs list the university as a primary source of financial assistance. In contrast, only 25 percent of the students in Ph.D. programs in the humanities and a mere 13 percent of the students in education Ph.D. programs receive financial assistance from their university.

Hold the field of study constant, and the disparities in financial assistance awarded by the universities greatly diminish, indeed virtually disappear. Black American students in S&E Ph.D. programs do receive primary financial support from the university; for instance, more than 70 percent of black graduate students in the physical sciences receive primary support from the university (Thurgood & Weinman 1991).

Besides, much (about 40 percent) of the financial support in S&E comes in shape of research assistance in federally supported projects; the S&E share is more than 75 percent of such support (National Science Foundation 1994b:301). These projects are funded by the Department of Defense, Department of Energy, NASA, and the National Science Foundation. These awards generally go to those who are best prepared to undertake the research, including, of course, black students.

On the other hand, federal "affirmative action"–based funding, for which foreign students are ineligible, is based on different criteria and awarded and administered by different government agencies—the U.S. Department of Education, in particular—as well as the Higher Education Opportunity Program (HEOP) funded by the states. The budget for this type of aid is distinct from, and not in the least affected by, the federal "projects-oriented" grants. The latter, where the foreign students predominate, does not cut into the former, where the black students do.

Most telling, the numbers of black Americans securing S&E Ph.D.'s—precisely the fields to which foreign graduate students flock—actually have increased over the past two decades (National Science Foundation 1991b:310). Hence, while the total number of Ph.D.'s awarded to blacks did, indeed, fall from 999 in 1975 to 828 in 1990, in engineering they increased from 11 in 1975 to 28 in 1990, in life sciences from 56 in 1975 to 63 in 1990, and in social sciences from 153 in 1975 to 172 in 1990.

The real problem appears to be that the pool of black students that the Ph.D. programs draw upon is small and, worse, getting smaller (National Science Board 1991:1). The number of blacks securing baccalaureate degrees in S&E actually fell slightly, from 18,700 in 1975 to 18,400 in 1990 (so that the fraction of black S&E baccalaureates who secured Ph.D.'s actually *increased*). And, this occurred during a period when the total number of baccalaureate degrees in S&E awarded in the United States *increased*; so the proportion of blacks in these areas decreased significantly. Evidently, the problem for the black community arises at levels *below* the graduate S&E programs; its solution, therefore, will not lie in restrictions on the number of foreign students or on their access to financial support at the graduate level.

NOTES

1. Thanks are due to Daniel Greenberg, Phillip Griffith, Brendan O'Flaherty, Duncan Foley, and Andre Burgstaller for helpful conversations. The ideas developed in this chapter and the statistics to support them owe greatly to Rao's research.

Indeed, several recent studies of academic labor supply (Bowen & Rudenstine 1992; Ehrenberg 1991; Ehrenberg 1992) note the preponderance of foreign students in Ph.D. programs.

2. An element of this "cultural" argument may be detected in the recent Report of the Committee on Graduate Economics Education (Krueger, et al. 1991), which attributes the increasing mathematization of economics partly to the presence of technically-skilled, but verbally-unskilled, Asian students from the Far East, chiefly Japan, South Korea, Taiwan, and China.

3. This complication is of trivial importance, however, as the S&E graduate applicant pool has itself shrunk (Bhagwati & Rao 1996b).

4. The pooling model explains well why, when the 1965 Immigration Act introduced PTK (Professional, Technical, and Kindred) preferences for which there was *worldwide* competition, and the national quotas generally were not applicable to this competition, the composition of such immigration shifted to such third-world countries as India and the Philippines; there were more applicants from these countries in the pool. The model also has been successfully applied econometrically to explain the source-composition of the guestworker (*gastarbeiter*) immigration programs in West Germany (Bhagwati, Schatz, & Wong 1984).

5. Figures provided by the National Research Council (Ries & Thurgood 1993; Thurgood & Weinnman 1991).

6. Such exceptions as the two Indian Institutes of Management and the famous All-Indian Institute of Medical Sciences in New Delhi must be mentioned.

7. According to a *Wall Street Journal* (Lee 1995) story on applications at top business schools, the price of an MBA rises to as high as $60,000 for two years at private schools.

8. The downstreaming model is at the heart of the analysis of education in the context of an alternative paradigm to the "human capital" and other theories of education (Bhagwati & Srinivasan 1975). It has been utilized in the context of the theoretical analysis of international migration of professionals (Hamada & Bhagwati 1976).

9. While we stress here the advantages to us of foreign students "staying on" in the United States, there also are many indirect advantages to us when and if they return home.

10. See Hamada & Bhagwati (1976) where educational enrollment by foreign students in the United States was first described as an instrument for immigration, rather than as a method of human capital formation. Numerous instances exist of students from first-rate foreign institutions coming to third-rate U.S. universities, the only motive being to acquire the qualifications that makes immigration less difficult.

11. Broadly speaking, a nonrefugee foreigner can immigrate legally to the United States under one of two principal categories: family-based or employment-based. The former requires "sponsorship" by a U.S. citizen family member. The latter requires sponsorship by an American employer. The Depar

Bowen, W., and Sosa, J. 1989. *Prospects for Faculty in the Arts and Sciences.* Princeton, NJ: Princeton University Press.

Browne, M. W. 1995. Supply Exceeds Demand for Ph.D.'s in Many Science Fields. *New York Times* (July 4).

Consortium on Financing Higher Education (COFHE). 1982. *Graduate Admission Trends in Selected Departments of COFHE Graduate Research Project Institutions, 1970–1980.* Cambridge, MA.

————. 1985. *The Highest Achievers: Post Baccalaureate Enrollment of Four Classes between 1956 and 1981.* Cambridge, MA.

DePalma, A. 1992. As Black Ph.D.'s Taper Off, Aid for Foreigners is Assailed. *New York Times* (April 2).

Dumont, R. 1969. *False Start in Africa.* New York: Praeger.

Ehrenberg, R. G. 1991. Academy Labor Supply. In C. Clotfelter, R. Ehrenberg, M. Gertz, and J. Siegfried, eds., *Economic Challenges in Higher Education, Part II.* Chicago: University of Chicago Press.

————. 1992. The Flow of New Doctorates. *Journal of Economic Literature* 30:830–75.

Greenberg, D. 1995. So Many Ph.D.'s. *The Washington Post Weekly Edition* (July 10–15):29.

Hamada, K., and Bhagwati, J. 1976. Domestic Distortions, Imperfect Information and the Brain Drain. In J. Bhagwati, ed., *The Brain Drain and Taxation, Vol. II: Theory and Empirical Analysis* Amsterdam: North-Holland. Reprinted in R. Feenstra, ed., *Essays in International Economic Theory*, vol. 2, Chapter 48. Cambridge, MA: MIT Press, 1983.

Immigration and Naturalization Act. 1992. Washington, DC: U.S. Government Printing Office.

Krueger, A. et al. 1991. Report of the Commission on Graduate Education in Economics. *Journal of Economic Literature* 29:1035–53.

Lee, M. 1995. Applications Rise at Top Business Schools. *Wall Street Journal* (August 15):B1.

Morris, F. 1993. Doctoral Opportunities in the U.S.: Denial of Equal Treatment for African American Students. *Urban League Review* 16:1 (Winter).

National Science Board. 1991. *Science and Engineering Indicators—1991.* Washington, DC.

National Science Foundation. 1987. *Foreign Citizens in U.S. Science and Engineering: History, Status, and Outlook.* Washington, DC.

————. 1990. *Selected Data on Science and Engineering Doctorate Awards.* Washington, DC.

————. 1991a. *International Science and Technology Data Update.* Washington, DC.

————. 1991b. *Science and Engineering Doctorates: 1960–90.* Washington, DC.

————. 1993. *Human Resources for Science and Technology: The Asian Region*. Washington, DC.

————. 1994a. *Selected Data on Graduate Students and Post Doctorates in Science and Engineering*. Arlington, VA.

————. 1994b. *Selected Data on Science and Engineering Doctorate Awards: 1993 Special Survey of Race and Ethnicity*. Washington, DC.

Ries, P., and Thurgood, D. H. 1993. *Summary Report 1991: Doctorate Recipients from United States Universities*. Washington, DC: National Academy Press.

Sukhatme, S. P., and Mahadevan, I. 1989. *Pilot Study on the Magnitude and Nature of the Brain Drain of Graduates of the Indian Institute of Technology, Bombay*. Bombay: Indian Institute of Technology.

Thurgood, D. H., and Weinman, J. M. 1991. *Summary Report 1990: Doctorate Recipients from United States Universities*. Washington, DC: National Academy Press.

Chapter 12

Limited Duration Admissions

SUSAN MARTIN

This chapter presents the final recommendations of the U.S. Commission on Immigration Reform (a bipartisan commission mandated by Congress) that build upon the work in this volume and the Commission's extensive investigations. Individuals who are statutorily referred to as "nonimmigrants" are referred to here as "limited duration admissions (LDAs)," a term that better captures the nature of their admission. When the original admission expires, the alien must either leave the country or meet the criteria for a new LDA or permanent residence. The term "nonimmigrants" is misleading as some LDAs entering the United States are really in transition to permanent residence; other LDAs enter for temporary stays and become permanent residents based on marriage or skills.[1]

The benefits of a well-regulated system of LDAs are palpable. LDAs represent a considerable boon to the U.S. economy. The tourism and travel industry (domestic and international) is the second largest employer in the United States and generates 6 percent of the nation's gross domestic product (GDP). International tourism provides a net trade surplus (dollars international visitors spend here minus dollars U.S. visitors spend outside the United States) of $18 billion. Worldwide, the United States earned the most from international visitors—more than $64 billion.

Foreign students and workers often enrich the cultural, social, and scientific life of the United States. Our universities gain access to many talented students worldwide, thus maintaining the global competitiveness of the U.S. system of higher education. Foreign students give U.S. students the opportunity to learn about foreign societies and cultures and, on returning home—often to positions of leadership—share their exposure to our democratic values, constitutional principles, and economic system. Foreign workers give employers timely access to a global labor market when they cannot identify or quickly train U.S. workers with knowledge and expertise required for a specific job. These worker programs also help companies conducting business both in the United States and internationally to reassign personnel as needed to maintain their competitiveness. As economies become increasingly integrated, companies are attracting more and more U.S. workers abroad as well.

Yet, LDAs pose problems for U.S. society under two principal circumstances: when the aliens fail to depart at the end of their legal stay, and when they present unfair competition to U.S. workers. The first problem is an enforcement one. Although overstayers represent a minute portion of the LDAs admitted each year, they are a significant part of the illegal immigration problem. The Immigration and Naturalization Service (INS) estimates that as many as 40 percent of the illegal aliens currently in the country originally entered with LDAs, many as short-term visitors. An equally pressing problem is the current inability to track the continued presence and whereabouts of many longer-term LDAs, particularly foreign students, after their arrival in the United States. This lack of capacity to monitor their presence exacerbates the problems of overstay and other violations of their legal status.

The second issue arising in limited duration admissions relates to the criteria for admission of foreign workers and the procedures used to determine their impact on U.S. workers. A proper balance must be struck in the LDA system between enhancing the productivity and global competitiveness of the U.S. economy through access to foreign workers and protecting U.S. workers against unfair competition.

The availability of foreign workers may create a dependency on them. It has been well documented that reliance on foreign workers in low-wage, low-skill occupations, such as farm work, creates disincentives for employers to improve pay and working conditions for American workers. When employers fail to recruit domestically or to pay wages that meet industrywide standards, the resulting dependence—even on professionals—may adversely affect both U.S. workers in that occupation and U.S. companies that adhere to appropriate labor standards. For many of the foreign workers, even wages and working conditions that are very poor by U.S. standards are much better than those available at home. In a few egregious cases, businesses have hired temporary foreign workers after laying off their own domestic work force.

The Immigration Act of 1990 imposed numerical limits on two employment categories where such dependence was feared: H-1B (specialty workers) is capped at 65,000 per year, and H-2B (unskilled workers) is capped at 66,000 per year. While the H-2B category is far from its numerical limits, the statutory cap on annual H-1B admissions was reached for the first time in FY 1997. INS announced in August 1997 the formation of a waiting list because approved workers would be ineligible to enter until the start of the next fiscal year. If the trend in applications continues, the cap is likely to be reached even earlier in FY 1998. Hence, employers petitioning late in the year would be required to wait for the admission of approved workers.

The current business users of the H-1B tend to fall into two distinct categories. One group of employers is clearly unlikely to become dependent on foreign workers but potentially is adversely affected by the numerical limits. These employers tend to hire relatively few foreign workers (for example, measured as a proportion of their overall work force). Generally, they have identified specific foreign workers whose specialized skills are needed. Often, the company has done extensive recruitment in the United States and has been unable to find qualified workers with the specific skills they seek. Because foreign workers represent a relatively small proportion of their work force, there is little risk that foreign hires will cause either job displacement or wage depression for U.S. workers.

A second group of employers includes companies that make extensive use of H-1B professionals (again, as measured by proportion of their workforce). Sometimes, they seek approval in the same application for a large number of foreign workers who share minimal professional qualifications. But even within this more dependent group, there is variation in the risk posed to U.S. workers by the importation of foreign workers. Some employers recruit domestically or take other steps to employ U.S. workers, but they are unable to find sufficient professionals to fill their needs. Other employers recruit exclusively overseas and make no effort to employ qualified U.S. workers. They may utilize the H-1B workers in their own operations or contract the foreign workers to other employers.

Under current law, the numerical limits, and now required waiting time, pertain equally to the employer who has few foreign workers and the employer who has only foreign workers. Similarly, the same provisions apply to the employer who has recruited extensively within the United States and been unable to find a worker with the needed specialized skills and to the employer who does no domestic recruitment.

The recommendations presented here seek to maximize the potential benefits for the U.S. economy and society resulting from the admission of LDAs while minimizing the potential negative effects. The overarching goal is to maintain the advantages that accrue to American society from entry of LDAs while protecting the legitimate interests of American workers and businesses from unfair competition.

PRINCIPLES FOR A PROPERLY-REGULATED SYSTEM

LDA policy should rest on the following principles:

Clear goals and priorities. LDA policy should clearly differentiate the goals of each set of visa categories, with procedures that reflect the requirements of each type of visa and subsequent admission. With more than 40 different LDA visas provided for under current law, as discussed below, it is often difficult to identify how the goals of one category differ from those of others.

Systematic and comprehensible organization of LDA categories. The statutory definitions, criteria, and procedures for visas and admission have developed in an ad hoc fashion. There is now accumulation of more than 40 different LDA visas (subsumed under nineteen alphabetical headings), including overlapping categories for students, workers, and other visitors, as well as additional visas added to address the concerns of specific interest groups. Simplification of the system would enable businesses, educators, persons with LDAs, government officials, and the general public to understand more clearly the requirements for visa application and admission and the responsibilities of the persons with LDAs and their sponsors. Administration of the LDA system could be simplified, with attendant reduction in cost and confusion.

Timeliness, efficiency, and flexibility in implementation. LDA policy should be implemented in a timely and efficient way with sufficient flexibility in law and regulations to respond to such domestic considerations as changes in the economy and our educational systems. Because of the time-limited nature of the stay, it is imperative that the system allow admissions decisions to be made expeditiously, while retaining a capacity to identify unqualified or fraudulent applications. Similarly, the provisions to protect U.S. workers must allow for timely and efficient mechanisms to investigate complaints and impose appropriate sanctions. Although a good part of the LDA system now functions in a timely way, the diffusion of responsibility in foreign worker categories reduces the potential efficiency of that part of the system.

Compliance with conditions for entry and exit and effective mechanisms to monitor and enforce this compliance. The LDA system should be designed to allow for greater compliance, monitoring, and enforcement. Policies should specify clearly the conditions of entry and the penalties for noncompliance. It is the responsibility of the government, with the cooperation of the private sector where appropriate, to record, track, and report on those entering for limited duration stays. Americans expect that aliens will respect and observe the conditions of their temporary admission, including departure at the end of their lawful stay, and that they will be subject to government enforcement if they fail to comply with the conditions of their admission or if they overstay. Their sponsors (generally, businesses and schools) also bear responsibility for complying with all relevant requirements. Penalties for noncompliance must be commensurate with the offense. The current system does not yet have exit controls in place. In sum, the LDA system should meet a "truth-in-advertising" test.

Credible and realistic policies regarding transition from LDA to permanent immigrant status. Realistic policies should continue to differentiate between LDAs who will remain only temporarily and those who become permanent. For example, LDAs should continue to be able to transition to immigrant status as expeditiously as possible if they enter bona fide marriages with U.S. citizens or meet the justifiably high education, skill standards, and prescribed labor market tests of the permanent skill-based immigration categories.

Protection of U.S. workers from unfair competition and of foreign workers from exploitation and abuse. LDA worker categories present special challenges in ensuring that U.S. workers are protected from unfair competition while legitimate foreign workers are protected from exploitation. Any system of LDA admissions must include protections for both U.S. and foreign workers, protections that are commensurate with the risk of unfair competition or abuse that the specific category presents. For example, lesser-skilled workers (whether American or foreign) who are newly entering the work force and whose skills are easily replaced are generally more vulnerable—both to displacement and exploitation—than are more highly skilled, specialized workers. Businesses that contract out their foreign workers to other businesses pose a greater risk for labor market violations because of the greater diffusion of employer responsibility. Also, employees of firms whose work forces consist primarily of temporary foreign workers, particularly from low-wage countries, are more vulnerable to exploitation; these foreign workers may be used to displace American workers because of their fear that any complaint about wages and working conditions might lead to deportation.

Appropriate attention to limited duration admission policies in trade negotiations. Important policy decisions on admission of temporary workers occurred during negotiations on the North American Free Trade Agreement (NAFTA) and the General Agreement on Trade in Services (GATS). Some are concerned that these treaty obligations restrict the capacity to reform our LDA policies by locking current immigration law into place or establishing minimum requirements to which changes in immigration law must adhere. In the future, both the administration, in negotiating trade agreements, and the Congress, in passing enabling legislation, should assess more carefully the long-term ramifications of trade negotiations for immigration policy. The aim should be to ensure that options for future immigration reform are not unknowingly foreclosed.

The following recommendations aim at maximizing the potential benefits accruing from admission of LDAs while minimizing the potential harmful effects.

FRAMEWORK

Visa categories for limited duration stays in the United States should be reorganized to make them more coherent and understandable. The current proliferation of visa categories should be restructured into five broad groups: official representatives, short-term visitors, foreign workers, students, and transitional family members. Subcategories of these groups may be appropriate in some cases. This reorganization reflects such shared characteristics of different visa categories as entry for like reasons, similarity in testing for eligibility, and similar duration of stay in the United States.

The definitions and objectives of the five limited duration admission groups would be:[2]

Official representatives are diplomats, representatives of or to international organizations, representatives of NATO or NATO forces, and their accompanying family members. The objective of this category is to permit the United States to admit temporarily individuals who represent their governments or international organizations. The presence of official representatives in the United States is based on reciprocity; the United States expects similar treatment for its own persons in similar capacities abroad. Under current law, these individuals are admitted under the A and G visas. For the most part, members of these groups are admitted to the United States for the duration of their status as official representatives.

Short-term visitors come to the United States for commercial or personal purposes. In 1995 alone, an estimated 43.5 million inbound visitors from other countries spent $76 billion on travel to and in the United States (on U.S. flag carriers, lodging, food, gifts, and entertainment).[3] This supports the U.S. national interest in encouraging tourism and business exchange. The majority of short-term visitors enter the United States under the visa waiver program, which is available for nationals of countries demonstrating little visa abuse. (For these nationalities, visas are required for all other purposes). ''Nonwaiver'' nationalities must possess a B visa for tourism or business, or a C visa for transit. Some short-term visitors also enter with the J visa if they are sponsored by the U.S. Information Agency (USIA) or other U.S. government agency. Short-term visitors generally have little or no effect on the U.S. labor market as they are severely limited in what they can do in the United States. Under current law, waiver visitors are admitted for 90 days, with no option for extension; visitors admitted with B visas are normally authorized a six-month stay, with flexibility to apply for another six months. Those in transit with C visas are given up to 29 days' stay. The majority of visitors by their own volition stay for very short periods. This category also includes informants/witnesses (current S classification) whose temporary entry is in the U.S. national interest because their knowledge is needed for criminal prosecutions.

Foreign workers are those who are coming to perform necessary services for prescribed periods of time, at the expiration of which they must either return to their home countries or, if an employer or family member petitions successfully, adjust to permanent residence. This category would serve the labor needs demonstrated by U.S. businesses with appropriate provisions to protect U.S. workers from unfair competition. Under current law, numerous types of foreign workers are admissible under the D visa for crewmembers, E visa for treaty traders and investors, H visa for "specialty workers" and other temporary workers, I visa for foreign journalists, L visa for intracompany transferees, O visa for aliens of extraordinary ability, P visa for performers and entertainers, Q visa for participants in cultural exchange programs, and R visa for religious workers. In addition, certain other workers enter under the TN provisions created by NAFTA. There is a second, parallel system under which other workers enter with J visas because they are sponsored by an institution approved by USIA to engage in cultural exchange. Some of these J workers are paid by their own governments or home institutions, whereas others receive compensation from the U.S. institutions and businesses employing them. Also included as foreign workers are trainees—that is, individuals receiving on-the-job training by working in U.S. institutions. The present multiplicity of LDA work categories could be rationalized and made to parallel similar immigrant visa categories. (See below for specific recommendations regarding foreign workers.)

Students are persons who are in the United States for the purpose of acquiring either academic or practical knowledge of a subject matter. This category has four major goals: to provide foreign nationals with opportunities to obtain knowledge they can take back to their home countries; to give U.S. schools access to a global pool of talented students; to permit the sharing of U.S. values and institutions with individuals from other countries; and to enhance the education of U.S. students by exposing them to foreign students and cultures. Students now enter under at least three visa categories: F visa for academic students; J visa, also for academic students (but generally including those whose education is paid by their own government or the U.S. government rather than themselves); and M visas for vocational students.

Transitional family members include fiancé(e)s of U.S. citizens. These individuals differ from other LDAs because they are processed for immigrant status, although they do not receive such status until they marry in the United States and adjust. Another category of transitional family members should be added: spouses of U.S. citizens whose weddings occur overseas but who subsequently come to the United States to reside. At present, a U.S. citizen cannot petition for the admission of a spouse until after the marriage. Months often pass before the foreign spouse can come to the United States. Under this additional category, the newlywed would be permitted to enter the United States under a transitional family visa and then complete the paperwork for legal permanent resident status.

SHORT-TERM VISITORS

The current visa waiver pilot program for short-term business and tourist visits should be made permanent upon the implementation of an entry-exit control system capable of measuring overstays. A permanent visa waiver system requires appropriate provisions to expand the number of participating countries and clear and timely means for removing those countries that fail to meet the high standards reserved for this privilege. Congress should extend the pilot three years while the control system is implemented.

Most observers recognize that the waiver has been a positive factor in increased tourism and trade and in less processing time for many travelers at ports of entry. More than one-half of the short-term visitors from waivered nationalities come to the United States under the waiver, and INS reports little overstay or other immigration violations from these visitors. The Department of State (DOS) has been able to reallocate its relatively high-cost overseas resources to areas that need greater attention, such as increased antifraud efforts, coping with the Diversity Visa workload, and staffing new posts in the former Soviet Union. A key factor in the success of the waiver program is the electronic sharing of ''watch list'' data of persons ineligible for visas between DOS and INS on an almost immediate basis. Being able to screen visitors arriving without visas at ports of entry serves the fundamental purpose of ensuring that statutorily ineligible aliens are not admitted to the United States.

FOREIGN WORKER CATEGORIES

Each year, more foreign workers enter the United States as LDAs for temporary work than enter as skill-based immigrants. In FY 1996, the Department of State issued almost 278,000 limited duration worker visas, including those for spouses and children. (Other LDA workers who changed status within the United States are not reflected in these statistics. Also not considered are LDA foreign students working in the United States during their course of study or as part of their practical training or researchers entering under J visa programs.) By contrast, only 117,000 immigrant visa issuances and domestic adjustments of status in worker categories were recorded in FY 1996, far less than the legislated limit of 140,000.

The limited duration admission classification for foreign workers should include three principal categories: those who, for significant and specific policy reasons, should be exempt by law from labor market protection standards; those whose admission is governed by treaty obligations; and those whose admission must adhere to specified labor market protection standards. LDA worker categories thus would be organized around the same principles that guide permanent worker categories. LDA workers would be subject to rigorous tests of their impact on the labor market unless they are exempt from these tests because their admission will generate substantial economic growth and/or significantly enhance U.S. intellectual and cultural strength and pose little potential for undermining the employment prospects and remuneration of U.S. workers.

Within the labor market protection standards group, criteria for admission are consistent with the potential adverse effect of given categories of workers. Adverse impact is broadly related to educational and skill level of the affected workers. Although there sometimes is an adverse effect from even the most highly skilled and experienced foreign workers, the benefits of such workers are usually large to American society as a whole. They are likely to enhance the U.S. national interest through the generation of economic activity, including the creation of jobs. In general, the higher the levels of education and skill required in a given occupation, the more likely U.S. workers will be able to compete successfully with workers from abroad. Even at the very highest levels of skill and education, however, this generalization fits some high-skill occupations, but not others.

Entry-level professionals and lesser-skilled workers pose somewhat greater risk of displacing U.S. workers because their work can more likely substitute for that of U.S. workers. If they accept lower wages and benefits or poorer working conditions, they present unfair competition to U.S. workers and their employers may gain an unfair advantage over other U.S. employers. Similarly, unskilled foreign workers present the greatest potential for adverse impact because they are competing with some of the most vulnerable of American workers. There should be different subcategories with labor market protection standards commensurate with the risks posed by the workers:

Those exempt by law from labor market protection standards because their admission will generate substantial economic growth and/or significantly enhance U.S. intellectual and cultural strength and pose little potential for undermining the employment prospects and remuneration of U.S. workers. These include:

Individuals of extraordinary ability in the sciences, arts, education, business, or athletics, demonstrated through sustained national or international acclaim and recognized for extraordinary achievements in their field of expertise. These individuals now enter under the O visa. This category is comparable to the first priority in our permanent resident system. The U.S. national interest is well served by entry of individuals at the very top of their chosen fields who can contribute during their temporary stay to U.S. economic growth and intellectual and cultural strength.

Managers and executives of international businesses (current L visa), also comparable to the first priority in the legal permanent resident system. The global competitiveness of U.S. businesses is enhanced by the capacity of multinational corporations to move their senior staff around the world as needed. Often, there is only temporary need for a transfer, although permanent relocation may later be required. Under current law, the person with a LDA visa must have been employed by the firm, corporation, affiliate or subsidiary continuously for one year within the three years preceding the application for admission. Greater safeguards must be in place to ensure that only bona fide international businesses benefit from this policy.

Professors, researchers and scholars whose salary or other compensation is paid by their home government, home institution, or the U.S. government in a special program for foreign professors, researchers, and scholars. Each year, professors, researchers, and scholars enter the United States on sabbatical from their own universities or research institutes, often with a J visa. Also in this category are foreign members of research teams cofunded by the United States and other countries. These individuals present substantial benefits to the United States in the expertise and resources they bring, and they pose no threat of displacement of U.S. researchers as their salaries are from foreign sources or they enter under a U.S. government-funded program, such as the Fulbright Program, whose resources are earmarked through an appropriation process for foreign researchers and scholars.

Religious workers, including ministers of religion, professionals, and other workers employed by religious nonprofit organizations in the United States to perform religious vocations and religious occupations. Under current law, religious workers must have had at least two years' prior membership in the religious organization (current R visa).

Members of the foreign media admitted under reciprocal agreements (current I visa). The United States benefits from the presence of members of the foreign media who help people in their countries understand events in the United States. Just as we would not want our media to be overly regulated by labor policies of foreign governments, the United States extends the same courtesy to foreign journalists working in the United States.

Foreign workers whose admission is subject to treaty obligations. This includes treaty traders, treaty investors, and other workers entering under specific treaties between the United States and the foreign nation of which the alien is a citizen or national. Under the provisions of NAFTA, for example, Canadian professionals are not subject to numerical limits or labor market testing; Mexican professionals continue to be subject to labor market tests, but will be exempt from numerical limits in 2003.

Foreign workers subject by law to labor market protection standards. These are principally:

Professionals and other workers who are sought by employers because of their highly-specialized skills or knowledge and/or extensive experience. Included in this category are employees of international businesses who have specialized knowledge (now admitted under the L visa) and professionals (now covered by the H-1B visa). A diverse range of individuals may be admitted in this category, including, but not limited to, university faculty and researchers with advanced degrees, accountants and lawyers with specialized knowledge of the tax and legal codes of other countries, and electrical engineers and software systems engineers with specialized knowledge needed for systems design. This category would also cover highly skilled workers without professional degrees if they have substantial experience in their occupation. This category also includes aliens now admitted under the H-1B visa who have a bachelor's degree but little specialized expertise or experience.

Trainees admitted to the United States for practical, on-the-job training in a variety of occupations. They now enter through the H-3 visa, practical training arrangements under the F visa, and the J visa provisions pertaining to physicians seeking graduate medical education and to some researchers with J visas engaged in postdoctoral studies. All of these groups have in common work in U.S. institutions as part of a training program. They are paid U.S. wages and, in many cases, are not readily distinguished from U.S. residents in the same type of on-the-job training activities.

Institutions petitioning for foreign workers as trainees would be required to demonstrate that the principal purpose of the program is training by showing a significant educational component to the work experience. Trainees would be paid the actual wages provided to U.S. trainees in similar programs. The trainees would be admitted for the specified duration of the training program. For example, a foreign physician admitted for graduate medical education would be admitted for the period of the specific residency program.

Artists, musicians, entertainers, athletes, fashion models, and participants in international cultural groups that share the history, culture, and traditions of their country. This category includes aliens now admitted under the P visa and Q visa, as well as fashion models admitted under H-1B visa, and athletes, musicians, and other performers admitted under the H-2B visa.

Lesser-skilled and unskilled workers coming for seasonal or other short-term employment. Such worker programs warrant strict review, as described below. This category includes aliens now admitted with H-2A and H-2B visas. Requests for admission of unskilled and lesser-skilled workers should be met with heightened scrutiny. Temporary worker programs for lesser-skilled agricultural workers exert particularly harmful effects on the United States. There should not be a large-scale program for temporary admission of lesser-skilled and unskilled workers along the lines of the *bracero* program. A new guestworker program would be a grievous mistake.

Historically, guestworker programs have depressed the wages and working conditions of U.S. workers. Of particular concern is competition with unskilled American workers, including recent immigrants who may have originally entered to perform the needed labor but who can be displaced by newly entering guestworkers. Foreign guestworkers often are more exploitable than lawful U.S. workers, particularly when an employer threatens deportation if the workers complain about wages or working conditions. The presence of large numbers of guestworkers in particular localities—such as rural counties with agricultural interests—presents substantial costs for housing, health care, social services, schooling, and basic infrastructure that are borne by the broader community and even by the federal government rather than by the employers who benefit from the inexpensive labor.

Despite the claims of their supporters, guestworker programs also fail to reduce unauthorized migration. To the contrary, research consistently shows that they tend to encourage and exacerbate illegal movements by setting up labor recruitment and family networks that persist long after the guestworker programs end. Moreover, guestworkers themselves often remain permanently and illegally in the country in violation of the conditions of their admission.

If new initiatives to reduce illegal migration were at some point to create real labor shortages in agriculture or other low-skill occupations, employers could request foreign workers through the proposed LDA provisions for the admission of unskilled workers.

LABOR MARKET TESTS

The labor market tests used in admitting temporary workers in this category should be commensurate with the skill level and experience of the worker.

The admission of temporary workers with highly specialized skills or extensive experience should be contingent on an attestation that:

The employer will pay the greater of actual or prevailing wage and fringe benefits paid by the employer to other employees with similar experience and qualifications for the specific employment in question. Actual wage rates should be defined in a simple and straightforward manner. This does not mean a complicated, bureaucratically defined wage analysis. Rather, businesses should be able to use their own compensation systems to determine appropriate wages and benefits for the individual foreign worker hired. The entry of a small number of highly skilled foreign workers should have minimal effect on these wage scales, which will be determined by the majority of U.S. workers employed by the business. In the absence of a companywide system that ensures equitable compensation for similarly situated workers, the employer would be required to attest to paying prevailing wages for that job category, wages that are typical of the enterprise or nonprofit company. (See below for recommendations for at-risk employers with a significant proportion of foreign workers.)

The employer has posted notice of the hire, informed co-workers at the principal place of business at which the LDA worker is employed, and provided a copy of the attestation to the LDA worker employed.

The employer has paid a reasonable user fee that will be dedicated to facilitating the processing of applications and the costs of auditing compliance with all requirements. Currently no fees are collected by the Department of Labor (DOL) for either processing or monitoring purposes. In effect, this requires taxpayers to subsidize these programs. To ensure that the employer, and not the foreign worker, pays the user fee, penalties should be imposed upon violators.

There is no strike or lockout in the course of a labor dispute involving the occupational classification at the place of employment.

The employer has not dismissed, except for cause, or otherwise displaced workers in the specific job for which the alien is hired during the previous six months. Further, the employer will not displace or lay off, except for cause, U.S. workers in the specific job during the 90-day period following the filing of an application or the 90-day periods preceding or following the filing of any visa petition supported by the application.

The employer will provide working conditions for such temporary workers that are comparable to those provided to similarly situated U.S. workers.

The admission of lesser-skilled workers should be contingent on employers meeting a stricter labor market protection test. Such employers should continue to be required to demonstrate that they have sought, but were unable to find, sufficient American workers prepared to work under favorable wages, benefits, and working conditions. They also should be required to specify the steps they are taking to recruit and retain U.S. workers, as well as their plans to reduce dependence on foreign labor through hiring of U.S. workers or other means. (For example, sugar cane growers in southern Florida who had petitioned for foreign workers had success in reducing their dependence on H-2A workers through mechanization.) Employers should continue to be required to pay the highest of prevailing, minimum, or adverse wage rates, provide return transportation, and offer decent housing, health care, and other benefits appropriate for seasonal employees.

Certain businesses pose greater risk than others of displacing U.S. workers and/or exploiting foreign workers. The risk factors that should be considered in determining whether stricter protection standards must apply include:

The employer's extensive use of temporary foreign workers. Extensive use can be defined by the percentage of the employer's work force that is comprised of LDA workers. It also can be measured by the duration and frequency of the employer's use of temporary foreign workers.

The employer's history of employing temporary foreign workers. Those employers with a history of serious violations of regular labor market protection standards or specific labor standards related to the employment of LDA workers should be considered as at risk for future violations.

The employer's status as a job contracting or employment agency providing temporary foreign labor to other employers. Risk of labor violations increases as responsibility is divided between a primary and secondary employer.

At-risk employers, even of skilled workers, should be required to attest to having taken significant steps—for example, recruitment or training—to employ U.S. workers in the jobs for which they are recruiting foreign workers. Some companies now petitioning for H-1B workers recruit exclusively in foreign countries. U.S. recruitment or hiring efforts will help ensure that qualified U.S. citizens and permanent residents have access to these jobs. However, current labor certification processes should not be used to document significant efforts to recruit. These procedures are costly, time consuming, and ultimately ineffective in protecting highly skilled U.S. workers.

Under the now expired H-1A visa program for the admission of LDA registered nurses, several alternative steps were described as meeting the requirement of timely and significant steps to employ U.S. workers. These alternatives include: operating a training program for such workers at the facility (or providing participation in a training program elsewhere); providing career development programs and other methods of facilitating workers to become qualified; paying qualified workers at a rate higher than currently paid to other similarly employed workers in the geographic area; and providing reasonable opportunities for meaningful salary advancement. Examples of other steps that might qualify as meeting the timely and significant requirement include monetary incentives, special perquisites, work schedule options, and other training options.

AT-RISK EMPLOYERS

At-risk employers should also be required to obtain regular independently-conducted audits of their compliance with the attestations made about labor market protection standards, with the results of such audit being submitted for Department of Labor review. The independent audits should be done by recognized accounting firms that have the demonstrated capacity to determine, for example, that wages and fringe benefits were provided as promised in the attestation and conformed to the actual or prevailing wages and fringe benefits provided to similarly situated U.S. workers.

MONITORING OF ENFORCEMENT

Enhanced monitoring of and enforcement against fraudulent applications and postadmission violations of labor market protection standards are needed. To function effectively, both the exempt and nonexempt temporary worker programs must provide expeditious access to needed labor. To ensure adequate safeguards for U.S. workers, the government agencies responsible for processing applications and enforcing the law must have adequate capacity to identify and act quickly against fraudulent applicants and to monitor postapproval violations of the terms under which foreign workers enter. More specifically, there should be:

Allocation of increased staff and resources to the agencies responsible for adjudicating applications for admission and monitoring and taking appropriate enforcement action against fraudulent applicants and violators of labor market protection standards. These agencies require additional resources to investigate potential fraud among applicants for temporary worker visas as well as violations of the labor market protection standards. Enhancing this capability has significant resource implications, especially if such antifraud investigations are undertaken in a manner that does not delay visa adjudication and issuance.

Increased costs required for more efficient adjudication of applications can be covered by applicant fees. However, additional costs incurred for more effective investigations of compliance with labor market standards will require appropriated funds.

Sufficient funds should be appropriated to provide the additional resources needed for adequate enforcement by the Department of Labor. These resources should be targeted at employers and contractors at special risk of violating labor market protection standards. Targeting these employers makes the most sense both in terms of economical use of resources and in protection of workers.

The Department of State also must have the capacity to make a proper investigation of cases in which fraud is suspected. This capacity is particularly needed in applications for admission of LDAs in exempt categories to ensure that use of these categories does not become a means of evading labor market protection standards. For example, the visa for intracompany transfers has been abused by persons setting up sham corporations. To comply with appropriate requirements for timely decisions, the government must have the resources to investigate suspected fraud.

A bar to the use of LDA workers by any employer who has been found to have committed willful and serious labor standards violations with respect to the employment of LDA workers. Further, upon the recommendation of any federal, state, or local tax agency, a bar to the use of LDA workers by any employer who has been found to have committed willful and serious payroll tax violations with respect to LDA workers. The law currently provides for such debarment for failure to meet labor condition attestation provisions or misrepresentation of material facts on the application. Implementation of this recommendation would enable penalties to be assessed for serious labor standards violations that are not also violations of the attestations. This would address the knowing misclassification of some LDA workers as independent contractors, with subsequent failure to pay payroll taxes or other legally required deductions to the appropriate governmental agency.

Development of an enforcement strategy to reduce evasion of the LDA labor market protection standards through use of contractors. U.S. businesses' growth in contracting out functions has raised questions of employment relationships and ultimate liability for employment-related violations, including those related to temporary foreign workers. A uniform policy for dealing with these situations is desirable for the enforcement agencies involved, as well as for employers, contractors, and workers.

CONCLUSION

Limited duration admissions are an important part of immigration policy because they are linked closely to the admission of legal permanent immigrants and to our policies for deterring unlawful migration. The opportunities presented by the admission of limited duration admissions are significant. With the type of regulation recommended here, the United States will be able to continue to benefit from these admissions while mitigating potential harmful effects, particularly on vulnerable U.S. populations.

NOTES

1. Certain LDA categories, such as those for fiancé(e)s, intracompany transferees, and specialty workers provide explicit bridges to permanent immigration.

2. The current system includes the J visa for cultural exchange, which is used for a variety of purposes, ranging from short-term visits to study and work. The workers include scholars researchers, camp counselors, au pairs, and various others. Some work activities under the J visa demonstrate a clear cultural or education exchange; other work activities appear only tangentially related to the program's original purposes. Protection of U.S. workers by labor market tests and standards should apply to the latter group in the same manner as similarly situated temporary workers in other LDA categories. The Department of State should assess how better to fulfill the purpose of the Mutual Educational and Cultural Exchange Act of 1961 (Fulbright-Hays Act). Such an analysis is particularly timely in light of the merger now being implemented between the Department of State and the United States Information Agency, which is responsible for administering the J visa.

3. The 43.5 million visitors include the admission entries of individuals from countries where a visa or visa waiver is required as well as those from Canada (no visa, visa waiver, or border crossing card required) and Mexico (border crossing card required).

Index

About the Contributors

JAGDISH BHAGWATI is the Arthur Lehman Professor of Economics and Professor of Political Science at Columbia University. He is a Director of the National Bureau of Economic Research. He conducted some of the initial research on the subject of the "brain-drain" from developing to industrial countries and has followed foreign students for nearly three decades. Dr. Bhagwati is an internationally recognized expert on economic development and trade, and was an Advisor to the Secretary-General of the GATT (General Agreement on Tariffs and Trade). His many publications include the following recent books: *Protectionism, The World Trading System at Risk, India in Transition: Freeing the Economy,* and *Stream of Windows: Unsettling Reflections on Trade, Immigration, and Democracy.*

BARRY R. CHISWICK is Chair of the Department of Economics of the University of Illinois at Chicago. He has held visiting appointments at several universities, including Princeton and the University of Chicago; numerous professional positions on editorial boards and as chairman of the Midwest Economics Association; and he has consulted with the World Bank and the U.S. government, including being a former Senior Staff Economist on the President's Council of Economic Advisors. He is widely known for his research in labor economics, human resources, and the economics of U.S. minorities and immigrants. He has published eleven books and monographs and over 120 journal articles, book chapters, and technical reports. Recently he has edited *The*

Economics of Immigration Skill and Adjustment and *Immigration, Language and Ethnicity*, and co-authored *Post-Immigration Qualifications in Australia.*

GREGORY DeFREITAS is Professor of Economics at Hofstra University and Director of the Center for the Study of Labor and Democracy. He has published extensively on immigrants in the U.S. labor force, analyzing both economic impacts and assimilation. Dr. DeFreitas is especially well known for his research on Hispanics; his last book was *Inequality at Work: Hispanics in the U.S. Labor Force.* His forthcoming book is *Futures at Risk: Youth in the Urban Economy.*

JACQUELINE HAGAN is Associate Professor of Sociology and Co-Director of the Center for Immigration Research at the University of Houston. Her research interests include immigration, social policy, community organization and human rights. She has been involved in field research for a number of years and is the author of *Deciding to Be Legal: A Maya Community in Houston.* She is currently conducting a multi-site study on the effects of the1996 immigration and welfare reform initiatives on border communities in Texas and Mexico with Nestor Rodriguez of the Center for Immigration Research.

CHARLES B. KEELY holds the Donald G. Herzberg Chair in International Migration in the Department of Demography and is a member of the Core Faculty of the School of Foreign Service at Georgetown University in Washington, DC. His study of U.S. immigration policy and its labor market effects began with the Immigration Act of 1965 and continues today with the study of temporary visas for high-level workers. More recently, he has written on international refugee policy and a monograph on European diplomacy to harmonize asylum policies will be published shortly. He served on the National Academy of Sciences' Committee on Population and the National Institute of Medicine–National Academy of Sciences' Committee on Contraceptive Development, as well as a number of panels on immigration. He has written or edited seven books and over 50 articles about international migration.

B. LINDSAY LOWELL is the Director of Research for the Institute for the Study of International Migration at Georgetown University. He was previously Director of Policy Research for the congressionally appointed, bipartisan U.S. Commission on Immigration Reform; Assistant National Coordinator of the Mexico–U.S. Binational Study on Migration; and a Research Analyst at the U.S. Department of Labor. His research interests are in the comparative causes of migration, the economic and social impacts of immigration, and policy-relevant program evaluation. He has co-authored and published some four dozen edited volumes, book chapters, and articles in journals such as the *International Migration Review*, *Demography*, and the *Journal of Labor Economics*.

PHILIP MARTIN is Professor of Agricultural and Resource Economics at the University of California–Davis and chair of the University of California's 60-member Comparative Immigration and Integration Program. He co-chairs Migration Dialogue, a not-for-profit organization for nonpartisan migration analysis which publishes *Migration News* and *Rural Migration News*. An acknowledged authority, he was a member of the Congressionally mandated U.S. Commission on Agricultural Workers, and his 1996 book on collective bargaining in California agriculture won the Richard Lester award as the "Outstanding Book in Labor Economics and Industrial Relations." Internationally, his expertise has been called upon by the UN Development Program, the World Bank, and the International Monetary Fund, and he was a member of the Mexico–U.S. Binational Study of Migration.

SUSAN MARTIN is Director of the newly founded Institute for the Study of International Migration in the School of Foreign Service at Georgetown University. She also serves as Co-Chair of the Trans-Atlantic Learning Community Workgroup on Immigration and Integration. Previously, she served as the Executive Director of the congressionally mandated U.S. Commission on Immigration Reform, which made recommendations to reform immigration policy, to institute immigrant policies to help newcomers and the communities in which they settle, to reinvigorate U.S. leadership in refugee policy, and to restructure the federal agencies responsible for implementing immigration policy. Her past and current emphasis is on the study of international migration, including various bilateral, regional, and multilateral approaches to both migration and refugee policy. She is the author of *Refugee Women* and numerous monographs and articles on immigration and refugee policy.

SUSANA McCOLLOM is a Research Associate at Drug Strategies, a non-profit policy group in Washington, DC. Prior to joining Drug Strategies, she was the Project Manager of an immigration study funded by the Pew Global Stewardship Initiative in Washington, DC. She has extensive experience in field interviewing and running focus groups, and she has published in Z magazine.

FRANK L. MORRIS, SR., now twice retired, is Visiting Professor in the School of Social Sciences at the University of Texas at Dallas, and a principal representative of the European-based Focus Consulting Group. Previously he held the positions of Dean of Graduate Studies and Research at Morgan State University in Baltimore, Associate Dean of the Graduate School of Public Affairs at the University of Maryland, and President of the Council of Historically Black Graduate Schools. He is on the boards of the Center for Immigration Studies and the Carrying Capacity Network, and has held leadership positions on various boards, committees, and special summits. His areas of expertise include international management, immigration policy, and public policy on African Americans.

DAVID S. NORTH is Public Affairs Specialist of the Office of Insular Affairs at the U.S. Department of Interior. He has worked on a range of migrant worker issues since 1960, when he was assigned H-2 farmworker concerns while on the staff of the New Jersey State Employment Service. Later he was Assistant to the U.S. Secretary of Labor for Farm Labor during the dismantling of the Mexico–U.S. agricultural "Bracero" workers program. His numerous published studies reflect his concern that research be relevant to policy on refugees, immigrants, and nonimmigrants (manual and professional) in the United States and its territories, and has been commissioned by various governmental and non-governmental bodies. He has authored pathbreaking studies of permanent and temporary migrants since the 1970s and, most recently, *Soothing the Establishment: The Impact of Foreign-Born Scientists and Engineers on America.*

DEMETRIOS G. PAPADEMETRIOU is Director of the International Migration Policy Program at the Carnegie Endowment for International Peace. He is Co-Chair of Metropolis, a cooperative research effort involving researchers from 18 countries. Previously he was the Director for Immigration Policy and Research at the U.S. Department of Labor, Chair of the Migration Committee of the Paris-based Organization for Economic Cooperation and Development, and editor of *International Migration Review*. Currently he focuses on the policies and practices of advanced industrial nations and the role of multilateral institutions in coordinating responses to voluntary and involuntary population movements. His has written over 120 articles, reports, book chapters, and books, including *Converging Paths to Restriction: French, Italian and British Responses to Immigration* (with Kimberly Hamilton) and *Balancing Interests: Rethinking the U.S. Selection of Skilled Immigrants* (with Steven Yale-Loehr).

MILIND RAO is visiting the Graduate School of Business at Columbia University and is Associate Professor in the Department of Economics at Colgate University in New York. He has been a Research Fellow at the Jerome Levy Economics Institute and he taught at Columbia University. His research interests are economic theory, monetary growth theory, and international migration. He has published articles in several academic journals, as well as in the *Wall Street Journal, Economic Times, American Enterprise*, and *Challenge* magazine.

MICHAEL P. SMITH is Professor of Community Studies and Development at the University of California–Davis. Previously he taught at Boston University and Dartmouth, and was a visiting scholar at Cambridge and Essex and at Berkeley. His interests include the development of transnational social movements and immigrant networks and the social, cultural, and political consequences of networks. He has published several books and monographs, most recently co-editing *Transnationalism from Below*. His work on transnationalism has appeared in such journals as *Theory and Society*, the *International Journal of Urban and Regional Research, Social Text*, and in numerous collected works.